William Henry Bishop

The house of a merchant prince

A novel of New York

William Henry Bishop

The house of a merchant prince
A novel of New York

ISBN/EAN: 9783337043339

Printed in Europe, USA, Canada, Australia, Japan

Cover: Foto ©ninafisch / pixelio.de

More available books at **www.hansebooks.com**

THE

HOUSE OF A MERCHANT PRINCE

A Novel of New York

BY

WILLIAM HENRY BISHOP
AUTHOR OF "DETMOLD"

BOSTON AND NEW YORK
HOUGHTON, MIFFLIN AND COMPANY
The Riverside Press, Cambridge
1899

Copyright, 1882,
BY HOUGHTON, MIFFLIN & CO. AND W. H. BISHOP.

All rights reserved.

The Riverside Press, Cambridge:
Electrotyped and Printed by H. O. Houghton & Co.

CONTENTS.

		PAGE
I.	AN AWKWARD MEETING	1
II.	THE ASPIRATIONS OF A MERCHANT PRINCE	21
III.	AT MUSICAL MRS. CLEF'S	37
IV.	A SUNDAY ON THE AVENUE	47
V.	A MAN OF FASHION DRIVES OUT A FRIEND	57
VI.	SOME PERVERSE OPINIONS OF MR. BAINBRIDGE	69
VII.	PROSPECTS FROM HARVEY'S TERRACE	82
VIII.	A FLAW IN A CORNER-STONE	101
IX.	"TO MEET THE PRESIDENT OF THE UNITED STATES"	110
X.	IN MAGOON BUILDING OFFICES	129
XI.	EMBITTERED RECOLLECTIONS OF OLD SLAVE DAYS	140
XII.	OTTILIE HARVEY'S ROUTINE	153
XIII.	SHOWING THE PERFECT FEASIBILITY OF PLATONIC FRIENDSHIPS	172
XIV.	CROSS PURPOSES AT A NEWPORT VILLA	188
XV.	IN TOWN FOR THE WINTER	212
XVI.	THE MERCHANT PRINCE DINES A POLITICAL ECONOMIST	226
XVII.	THE PAST OF KINGBOLT OF KINGBOLTSVILLE	247
XVIII.	AT THE EMPIRE CLUB AND AROUND TOWN	261
XIX.	A GARDEN PARTY ON THE HUDSON, AND ITS SEQUEL	279
XX.	"LALAGE, SWEETLY SMILING, SWEETLY SPEAKING"	300
XXI.	BY FAR LESS FAVORABLE TO THE PLATONIC THEORY	336
XXII.	AN EVENING IN LITERARY SOCIETY	342
XXIII.	A PLEA BY AN INGENIOUS ATTORNEY, BUT THE COURT RESERVES ITS DECISION	374
XXIV.	"THE TOILS ARE LAID AND THE STAKES ARE SET"	383
XXV.	OTTILIE HARVEY CLEARS UP A PAINFUL SITUATION	407

THE HOUSE OF A MERCHANT PRINCE.

I.

AN AWKWARD MEETING.

It was about four o'clock of a February afternoon. A young girl sat in an open hackney coach amid the most extreme bustle and uproar of New York.

She was looking out with interest at the front of one of the great wholesale dry-goods stores situated on that part of Broadway near Canal Street. Some modest traveling trunks were strapped behind the hackney coach.

The simple inscription on two zinc tablets attached to iron columns of the front, was "Rodman Harvey & Co."

The plate-glass windows presented to the street only the cold shoulders, as it were, of some bolts of the variety of textile fabrics contained within. At this dignified height in trade a petty display is unnecessary. Whoever knew anything of the circumstances knew that Rodman Harvey & Co. was one of the oldest and strongest concerns in the metropolis. They knew that its head and founder was prominent in every notable enterprise; that he had rendered patriotic services to the government during the war, and that he was stanch in the opinions of the political majority, by which the government has been chiefly administered ever since; all of which items had their effect in securing custom. The head of the firm was, in fact, the firm itself, his partners being men with but minor interests, brought in from time to time to assist him, and seldom heard of by name. He was rarely mentioned in the public press other than as a "merchant prince;" "one of our leading merchant princes." The house of Rodman Harvey & Co. offered, in its advertisements, "Special Inducements to Cash and Short-Time Buyers," and it sent out a swarm of ingenious commercial travelers to represent its interests through the length and breadth of the land.

A companion for whom the young girl waited had gone into the store. He now presently emerged, having its chief proprietor with him. The two lingered in conversation, at first on a step, later at the curbstone.

There came out at the same time, a tallish, gentlemanly-looking young man, with a light beard. He had a packet of papers in his hand, and seemed attending upon the merchant. He made as if to go away, but was detained by the latter, as if for some further conference.

This young man, having apparently nothing better to do while waiting, fixed his gaze upon the occupant of the carriage with a certain intentness.

"A rather tall, slender girl," he mused. "She has nice brown hair with burnished strands in it. It is 'banged' over the forehead, and gathered into a semi-matronly knot behind. Her skin is of a smooth whiteness. Her eyes are dark gray, without trace of blue. The eye-brows are rather heavier than common, which gives a slight aspect of severity. Is she severe, I wonder? — not that I take a wild interest in knowing." "Dress 'half mourning,'" he continued, — "a bereavement, not too recent. Age, say eighteen, — not twenty-one, at any rate. Whom has the sagacious Klauser with him now? — Klauser, the confidential, who goes over the road twice a year to look after the security of the credits the over-sanguine commercial travelers are inclined to extend. Hardly his daughter? She must be yet in Germany, pursuing her musical studies."

The young woman had given a slight start of annoyance at the appearance of the merchant prince at his own door-way. She had, in fact, reasons, why she did not wish that he should recognize her, in case he were likely to do so. In order to withdraw herself somewhat from observation, she turned away a shapely head, assumed an unconscious air, and began to study the doings in the street.

As in the margins of actual streams each foot of the way presents its local eddies, so here, at every portal, was a separate stir of life.

There was a rise in the ground to the southward. The sidewalks were black with hurrying humanity. A concourse of loaded drays, trucks, vans, and white omnibuses, these last shutting in their parcels of humanity, like a curious sort of freight also, filled all the central space. It was rather a moving glacier than a stream. The boxes and bales piled high upon the wagons, with the swaying bodies, heads, and whips of the drivers, were exalted impressively against the sky. Behind them vanished an interminable perspective of becolumned façades, cupolas, steeples, a dome, many-storied mansards fretted with dormers, the whole made yet more fantastic with flaunting banners and carved and gilded emblems of trade. Into some such aspect the Yellowstone might fashion the walls of the canyon into which it cuts its bed deeper and deeper from the light.

The fresh young observer of the scene, her thoughts involuntarily drawn away in the fascination of its onward movement, had well-nigh forgotten her anxious preoccupation when she was suddenly aroused to herself by a voice close at her ear. Its tones conveyed decision and authority, and it was asking, —

"And whom have you there, Klauser?"

"Your niece, Miss Ottilie Harvey, of Lone Tree, Illinois. I have had the pleasure of taking charge of her on her return to school. She was just setting out when I came to Lone Tree on my rounds, and we made it convenient to travel together."

Turning round, embarrassed and overawed, Miss Ottilie Harvey found herself in the immediate presence and under the sharp scrutiny of a relative whom she had particularly desired not to see. He was a relative who played an important part in the imaginations and speech of the home circle she had left behind her at Lone Tree. He was the arrogant prosperous kinsman in the family, a brother of her father, who had had much poorer luck in the world. Between the two brothers, thus diversely situated, there existed, perhaps owing to fault on both sides, a chronic feud, and this was just now at its most exacerbated pass.

Rodman Harvey may have seen this niece before as a child; he probably had. He regarded her now in a meditative way, shook hands with her, asked after the family, and said she had the Harvey looks. Then he insisted that she should alight, and come into the store with him and Klauser, for whom he discovered that he had some further need. She dared not refuse, but did as requested. The young man with the packet of papers, whose affair, whatever it was, was not yet dispatched, remained of the party.

The roar of the street entered with them through the open door of the dry-goods warehouse like the section of an actual solid.

"It was too bad of you to bring me here, Mr. Klauser," said the girl, finding a moment to complain to him privately. "You know I was merely to have a glimpse of my uncle's store, just as you were to show me, on our way to the depot, the grand new house he is building up town; but I was not to see him. You heard my father expressly interdict my doing so when you dined with us. You said that you but wished to stop at the store for an instant, and that it was wholly improbable that my uncle would be here at this time of the day."

"Well, but your mother; you know,"—began Klauser, a square-built, middle-aged man with a slightly German accent.

"Yes, my mother;—she is weaker, or more politic, perhaps, and given to suggesting that we should throw ourselves in his way, and make advances; but my father does not wish it. He may be a little unreasonable and violent sometimes. When he says that my uncle has never done anything at all for us, that is not quite correct, for I myself remember some substantial favors. But it was my duty to obey him, and you ought to have helped me."

"Well, but you know in the afternoon,"—said Klauser, casting about for excuses.

"And there was another reason why I did not wish to see him," interrupted the young complainant impetuously. "I do not at all like his treatment of the Hasbrouck girls."

The Hasbrouck girls were schoolmates of hers, and it seemed that she had thought good to espouse a cause of theirs which made a private and local motive of resentment, in addition to the rest.

But now the merchant prince, as if having reflected, turned to her in his impressive way, and said,

"Going back to school; what school?"

"Vassar," replied Ottilie, hesitatingly. "I have been there about a year. I am to graduate in the coming summer."

"Your father must be doing very well to pay for such schools as that, and thousand mile journeys back and forth. Let me see; there were five of you, were there not?"

"There were five, but one is dead." The speaker glanced involuntarily at her dark dress. She had thrown back the fronts of a cheviot ulster, which, with collar standing, enveloped her in half-military fashion. It could be seen that her dark dress had a neat furbelow or two, and was trimly fitted to a slender waist and corsage, as yet but little filled out.

"I think my father is not doing better than usual," she said. "It has been my wish to do something for my own support, in order to lighten, in time, his burdens. He has not yet consented, but I trust that he will. I thought that with the diploma of a school of high rank I should be able to command a — a more profitable position as teacher. I have been at home because my brother was going to the Sandwich Islands, where he has got a place, and we did not know when we should see him again; and as I did not go at Christmas "—

She endeavored to disclaim in her manner any appearance of appealing to sympathy. She was angry at having to make these explanations, but they seemed necessary to refute his distorted way of putting things. Oppressed by her idea of his importance, she was not quite mistress of herself.

"So you have been here for some years," said Rodman Harvey, exaggerating the case in a carping way, "and have not thought it worth while to come near us?"

"I have usually passed through New York very quickly. And I knew that the family were a good deal in Europe — and then,"— stammered Ottilie, at a loss to account more favorably for conduct which he was pleased to represent in so heinous a light.

"Your father is a fool!" burst forth the merchant prince, as if under the stimulus of an irritating memory. "You are not to blame for it, of course, but he is a man who would try the temper of saints. I always meant well by him. A person who made so complete a wreck of his own prospects should be at least amenable to counsel. But no; he throws it back in your teeth. It was the same thing when he was in partnership with me. He is the same to-day, and the same he always will be. I started him in business at the West, after he had gone to pieces here, and still he must quarrel with me. As soon as he gets his head a trifle above water he must withdraw his custom, forsooth, from the old house of Rodman Harvey & Co. As though his wretched little custom could make the smallest difference in the world!"

Ottilie, though understanding tolerably well some of her father's imperfections, would have liked now to say many reproachful things in his defense. But she was much more in danger of bursting into tears.

The veteran employee, Klauser, a politic person, with traits of benevolence of his own, wore an uneasy and deploring air at the turn events had taken. He was one who could listen, on his rounds, to the tirades of the less fortunate brother, without relaxing, on that account, his vigilance in the service of the other. He had taken a fancy to Ottilie as he had seen her at her home. She had pleased him still more on the journey, both by her looks and the exhibition of many amiable and vivacious traits. He argued a favorable effect upon Rodman Harvey as well, from the sight of her. The more she won him, along the road, the more he racked his ingenuity for a means of bringing about a meeting in some natural way. Nothing better offered itself finally, than the device of stopping briefly at the store, as for an errand, with the slender chances this presented. This plan had succeeded admirably at first, but its unlooked-for developments caused its inventor to doubt his fancied wisdom, and to dread the coming reproaches for treachery which his conduct now well merited.

The merchant prince, however, having vented sufficiently complaints which were, perhaps, intended to justify to himself a long neglect of his brother's family, and not desiring to increase further the distressed look on his niece's face, now took a more lively and cheerful tone. "I am not saying it is your fault," he said. "I am only laying before you facts that you ought to know. Your father should have sent you to my care when you came here to school, and then we would have done all we could for you."

Having to take Klauser away to consult with Mr. Minn, the head of the white goods department upstairs, and designing, as it seemed, to leave her entertained in the mean time, he introduced, with a certain flourish, the young man with the papers, which were of a legal-looking sort. This individual had been driven, before the discussion we have noted, into the private office of the merchant prince, where all parties had been now for some little time ensconced. The office was partitioned off from a side of the store, near the front. The young man politely affected not to hear what was said. He busied himself over a map on the wall, stirred the fire, and moved an office chair nearer one of the desks. Rodman Harvey appeared abstractedly to have lost sight of his presence. But Ottilie knew very well that he had heard, and she visited upon him a share of her mental resentment. She took him to be, perhaps, a private secretary, before whom his employer was in the habit of speaking with freedom.

"But that makes it none the more endurable," she said, "that he should be a witness of my embarrassment and disgrace."

She chose to imagine in him an odiously conceited and patronizing manner.

"This is Mr. Bainbridge, my lawyer. He is a famous fellow for collecting, and drawing up documents," said Rodman Harvey. "I always need to have him up from Chippendale, Bond & Saxby's. You must bear it in mind if you have anything of that kind to be done."

And to Bainbridge he said: "This is my niece, Miss

Ottilie Harvey. You see they raise girls, as well as pork and cereals, in the great West. If they were all like this one we should n't complain, eh?"

All this was quite an unusual display of facetiousness on the part of the merchant prince, who was not a person of the humorous sort.

Mr. Bainbridge made talk of a facile, courteous sort, but his auditor was cold and unresponsive. She was very uncomfortable. She did not wish to be there at all. Why did not Klauser return and take her away? A small, well-fitting boot tapped the floor nervously below the hem of her garment. The light was becoming to her, as she sat in one of the office chairs. It burnished yet more some strands of her hair, and cast softly-modulated shadows upon her white skin from under the projecting brim of her hat.

But the young lawyer, with a perfect understanding, perhaps, of the state of the case, persevered in efforts which were at length not without a measure of success. He spread before her a variety of ideas without demanding a response. He said,— this, of course, for her peculiar benefit,— that Rodman Harvey was a very upright person and of substantial well-meaningness, though his temper might be uncertain at times, through his many responsibilities.

He even ventured upon a little banter. He would have liked to relax the perverse gravity of those so strongly-marked brows. Perhaps she would have smiled, if they had let her. He seemed so cheerfully indifferent to her reserve that there was a slight absurdity on her side in keeping it up. She surmised that as a school-girl, and owing to the lack of ceremony with which he had seen her treated, he might take her to be younger than she was. This was, in fact, the case. She was twenty, instead of the eighteen years at which he had set her down; and, though she knew little, as yet, of New York, she prided herself upon opportunities for seeing the world she had had not at Lone Tree only, but at Cincinnati and St. Louis, in visits she had made to those places.

"New York is a city of processions," said Bainbridge, among other things. "They go up and down a few grooves in its long, narrow space, till it is a wonder they don't wear it down to the backbone. When I walk up town for exercise sometimes, from my office in the Magoon Building, I seem to be going with a regular military column, — horse, foot, artillery and camp equipage, complete. The noise of the wheels on the Belgian pavement is like the rattle and boom of drums."

"I was thinking that as I sat in the carriage," said Ottilie.

"Procession of small shop-keepers and mechanics in the Bowery," Mr. Bainbridge went on; "procession of thrifty housewives driving bargains on Sixth Avenue; procession of everybody and everything on Broadway. All this down town is the laborious drill for the procession of fashion and splendor on Fifth Avenue, its dress parade."

"New York does not seem as large to me as it ought to. Chicago is in some respects more impressive," said Ottilie.

"In what respects?"

"I can hardly say. I have not analyzed them."

"But you must see more of it. We are really a place of three millions of people, only kept apart by a few nominal barriers. You must go down to the water's edge, and see how all the surrounding coasts are one bristling mass of cities as far as the eye can reach. The sun heats up the business portion of the island daily with a definite magnetic attraction, as it were, so that a vast population from these, and from the country fifty miles round about, is drawn to it like mad. At night it cools off, and back they go again to whence they came. How does that strike you as a figure?"

"I am not very partial to figures. Many Western people," said Ottilie, "judge of importance by the scale of proportions on the maps. They do not all look upon New York, or, perhaps, the Eastern seaboard generally, with the supreme reverence it may think its due."

Whether this were mere perversity, or real conviction, she was certainly found very patriotic to her section.

"I have noticed that Westerners are rather banded together," said Bainbridge, taking the offensive, "so that you seldom get much information from them. But now I will give you my conception of Lone Tree, as I form it, — from the name alone, I assure you, never having been there, — and you shall tell me how far I am right."

"Very well," assented Ottilie Harvey.

"There is a green, or common, surrounded by block houses. The lone tree itself is in the centre. I am not quite sure whether it is a tall, blasted pine, or an umbrageous oak, last of its kind, which has retreated to the Rocky Mountains. At evening the people assemble and compare notes on their escapes from Pottawotamies and rattlesnakes during the day. Sometimes they take hands in rites of mystic worship or rejoicing around the tree."

"Easterners, on the other hand, are joined together to be as wildly egotistical and absurd as possible," responded the partner to this dialogue, flushing a little. "Lone Tree is a place of twenty thousand people, with a park, gardens, water-works, a public library, and one of the best high schools in the country, which sends graduates every year to Yale and Harvard. It has three railroads centring in its midst, and there is talk of heating it by steam. It is so strange," she continued, impatiently, "that intelligent people will make the same mistakes about us that are made by Europeans, who fancy there are buffaloes in New York city. The West has all the newest improvements, the latest and best patterns in everything. Indeed, it could hardly have any others if it wished. It is only in the older communities that you find inconvenient and lumbering things about. You should see our railway cars. The West is very ambitious, and imitative of what is good. It has the young blood."

"The Pottawotamies prefer that kind, do they?"

This sally was rewarded by the smile of which he had been in search. It was worth the waiting for. It showed even, white teeth, and illumined her face quite enchantingly. A miracle had been wrought with her pensiveness and severity, but the fatigued expression soon returned.

"She has peculiar eyes," reflected the famous attorney for drawing documents, continuing, mentally, the analysis of her traits. "They incline to hazel; at least, they have little yellow points in them, amid the gray, like a sprinkling of gold-dust. One might like them better afterwards than at first. They grow on you."

The manner of her advent interested him. He was a person whose fancy responded most readily, let us say, to something a little removed from the common. There was, too, as it happened, a mention of her in the document he had last drawn. This was nothing less than a codification of the merchant prince's will, which had been his work of that afternoon. She was down in that document, though she knew it not, with her several brothers and sisters, children of Alfred S. Harvey, of Lone Tree, Illinois, each for the munificent sum of one thousand dollars. Furthermore, he conjured up — yes, he would admit it, — a faint memory of Madeline Scarrett. Madeline Scarrett was married to that elderly widower and capitalist, Elphinstone Swan, who had daughters older than herself. She was one he had known in days gone by, when he had put much more faith in woman, and in the world generally for that matter, than at the present time. He had, in fact, if we may step so far into his confidence at once, been engaged to her and then betrayed by her, as he believed, on mercenary grounds alone. But Madeline Scarrett was a memory over which he had ceased even to sigh. If Ottilie resembled her it was but a point of slightly scientific interest. He was a deeply experienced person. He was a philosopher; and he was not susceptible. He could make, with entire safety, such observations on feminine nature or any other in the passing interest of the moment, as he might choose. Just now he had merely devoted himself to the task of rescuing a deserving young person from a sense of embarrassment natural in the circumstances. She was not a personage of extreme importance, and the labor was purely benevolent.

"Perhaps it might please you to step out for a look at the store," he suggested.

They stood near the office thereupon and contemplated a while an animated view corresponding in its way to that of the great thoroughfare without. Ottilie conceived with difficulty such a value in goods and such a cohort of employees within the ownership and under the direction of one man. She recalled that her father had told her that the controlling spirit of all this had once been on the verge of bankruptcy. Heaps of goods, with buyers and salesmen half buried in the midst, were scattered in chaos over the wide area of the floor between iron posts. It was another Antwerp Fury, or sack by beneficent Visigoths of trade. The tiers of calicoes and flannels piled upon their packing boxes, made favorable nooks here and there to shelter some knots of employees who could withdraw for a few moments' gossip from the general activity.

Such a little knot observed the advent of Ottilie and Bainbridge. They gave their attention, as was natural, chiefly to the latter, since feminine visitations were rare. The proprietor's daughter Angelica, a dazzling belle, tripped in at rare intervals, perhaps on matters connected with her allowance, and always made a sensation. They knew that this was not Angelica.

"The fellow with her," said McKinley, a man with a moustache which rolled over like a brown cascade, after they had finished with Ottilie, "is the one they call Bainbridge. He served the dispossess warrants for Harvey the time there was so much trouble about getting the shanty tenants off the old Muffett property, now 'Harvey's Terrace.' It's about three years since the old man built those blocks of houses up there. He's given this party odd jobs ever since."

"He *does* look like a go-ahead, plucky kind of customer," said one Widgery.

"Why I see him walkin' round among 'em as cool as you please," assented McKinley. "I was up there the first part of it. I would n't ha' done it myself for no money. It was a perfect fortress of a place upon them rocks, and the squatters they had laid in cart-rungs and bricks for a regular scrimmage. It took a military company finally as well as the police, to put 'em out. I recollect the rocks was painted over with big advertisements of one of these here complexion restorers. I says to myself, '*He*'ll need his complexion renovated pretty bad before he gets through with it,' I says. I recollect thinkin' that. He did n't though; he came out all right."

With this the subject dropped, and the group returned to their former talk. One spoke of fashions, another of the price of board and lodging, another of a recent theatrical performance. "An actor when he first comes on the boards, for me," said this last. "Compare Buskin now and ten years ago. I went to see him the other night. Great Scott! I wanted to get my money back."

McKinley dangled one leg over a box, and paring his nails with a penknife complained that Solomons had taken away a customer of his. "He has always inquired for me when he came to the store before," he said, "and if he did n't this time it's damned strange."

Cutler, a dashing clerk in his shirt sleeves, thus displaying to view a pair of crimson braces and elaborate cuff-buttons, took up a favorite topic of the duty of marrying a rich girl. "A fellow puts in his time and trouble, and managing ability, and all that," said Mr. Cutler, "and the girl, she supplies the money; see? It's a regular partnership. You want to find out first whether she really has the money though. Do you understand what I mean? You can't go by appearances nowadays. It isn't much good that her father has it either, if he won't come down with it. He may fail a dozen times over before he dies; and then where are you?"

"I hear you are going it pretty strong on that good-looking school-teacher, up at Mrs. Proudfoot's," said Mr. Widgery, opening a flank fire. "Is that what you call carrying out your views? You had better go for the plain one, Miss Finley, if that is what you are up to. She has money in the savings bank."

"Never you mind my views! Mrs. Proudfoot's is the champion boarding-place, and Harvey's Terrace can't be beat. Ask Whittemore! Nothing could induce me to go back to Eighth Street now, after having tried it."

"Oh, Whittemore, of course. It's homesickness in his case. He wants to be near Bridgehaven. See?"

"It takes but half an hour in the horse-cars," said Whittemore, "and when you get there you have something worth while: good air, view of the river, quiet, everything fine. Ask Klauser, rather; he knows. He has boarded at Harvey's Terrace ever since Harvey put up houses there. Come up to dinner, and for once in your life you'll say you've had a square meal."

The anxious college graduate, Jobson, who was

learning the business from the bottom up, at three dollars a week, paused in his labor of wheeling a truck about the floor to admire the careless ease of manners in this favored upper stratum.

Ottilie and Bainbridge meantime had happened upon that boon of conversation, a new acquaintance.

" As you are at Vassar," said Bainbridge, " I dare say you may know the Hasbrouck girls ? "

" Oh, yes, indeed ; they are great friends of mine," replied Ottilie, brightening.

" The family were friends of mine, too, formerly. I knew them in Florida, where I planted oranges a year or two, after the war. They were my neighbors. Mrs. Hasbrouck was particularly civil to me at one time, when I had run an orange thorn into my foot. I dare say you never met with that kind of accident ? "

" Not to the best of my recollection."

" Well, it is rather painful, and slow in healing. I was living in an uncomfortable, bachelor way, and she drove over and looked me up. The girls were mere children then. I saw them afterwards in Baltimore, though, when they had grown up. Lulu and Amy — they were of the real Southern type. It was a pleasure to hear them pronounce the English language."

" Oh, yes, they are real Southerners. I had never known any before, and perhaps that drew me to them. I confess to a slight fondness for curiosities." Bainbridge made a mental note of this as a taste not greatly differing from his own. " They are such frank and generous girls. And they tell you about everything that has ever happened to them in such an amusing way. They mention all of their friends and acquaintances by name, and generally the first names. I am perfectly acquainted with a multitude of people in this way. There are Bobs, Johns, and Dicks, who have been their 'sweethearts.' There are 'Judge Bibb,' and 'Major Cooper,' and the Wheeler family, who had plantations near theirs,— Scott Wheeler, and William Henry Wheeler, and 'Brick-House' Wheeler, and I don't know how many more."

She had begun to attend a little more, as she talked, to the looks of her companion. He had one of those heads not too round, but high, clear-cut, and symmetrical, which oftener excel in wisdom of the acute and ingenious, than of the ponderous sort. His features were strong and good. There was the trace of an upright furrow between his brows, and a noticeable small spot of gold sparkled in the front of his otherwise excellent teeth. He might have been twenty-eight. He was no doubt a person of consideration, used, among other things, to the best company, but he was hardly of an age to be her uncle's leading lawyer.

"It was one of the Wheeler places that I occupied as a tenant," said Bainbridge.

"Was it, really? You see, I know them very, very well."

"The Hasbroucks are not in as good circumstances as at one time, I believe?"

"No, indeed; the girls will probably be obliged to teach. We sympathize and lay our plans together. It is harder for them, of course, because they had once such very different expectations. They were defrauded of a part of their property by an agent, one of their own people; and it seems that my uncle," hesitatingly, " has tied up most of the remainder with a lawsuit, which gives them little use of it. He claims it on an old debt, from before the war, and, with his great resources, he will probably win."

" It does not act as an impediment to your friendship, it seems."

" It did at first. When the girls knew that I was Rodman Harvey's niece they thought I would, of course, side with him; but when I came to understand the true state of the case, I soon let them know that I was of their way of thinking, and sympathized with no such oppression. Since then they have not considered me at all to blame."

A certain naiveté in this statement was the result of its earnestness. The speaker suddenly realized, when it was uttered, who it was that she addressed. She had been imprudent enough to betray her adhesion to an obnoxious cause to a stranger, and a confidential agent of the enemy. Would he make mention of it to his principal at an early opportunity?

The merchant prince was seen coming back, and this constituted the most valid of interruptions.

II.

THE ASPIRATIONS OF A MERCHANT PRINCE.

THE merchant prince came back down the length of his store, stopping for a word or two with this person and that, and attended by a halo of respect wherever he moved.

He was a small, spare man of sixty, with bushy gray hair, which curled in a roll behind his ears. He had a yellowish skin, tufts of gray side whisker, and a mouth which, by long habit of compression, was but a straight incision across his face. He had something of a stoop. His dress was black broadcloth, neat, but free from any air of excessive newness. He carried one hand to his ear, in a way very imposing to inferiors, to catch what you had said. In moments of excitement his hearing was perfectly good without this device.

He brought back with him his eldest son, Selkirk Harvey.

"Selkirk," he said, "is in the white goods department, under Mr. Minn. We are making a business man of him. I wish him to be trained in accurate business habits, for the responsibilities which are to fall upon him hereafter."

Selkirk took a slightly deprecating air at this description of himself. He had rather mopish manners, and a dull but not disagreeable expression. His teeth projected upon his under lip in the way which seems to be always pronouncing the letter "v." He was more student than merchant. He had not, if the truth may be told, developed business talent of a high order, nor a keen scent for gain. With all parental fondness, his father could not yet estimate him in these respects as of a calibre equal to his own. But there was time yet, and the family looked for Selkirk to improve.

When presented to his cousin, he shook hands with her in an elaborate manner, and afterwards stood about, regarding her in silence, — whether with favor or the opposite it would not be easy to say.

Rodman Harvey took Bainbridge aside for a moment. The matter for which he had detained him required no great delay. When it had been disposed of, he said further, "Oh, by the way; just write into the copy for the amended draft of the will, that this niece is to have the share also of the one who is dead. It seems that one of them is dead. Do you understand? And bring me the whole in proper shape to-morrow."

"Very well, sir," answered Bainbridge, "it shall be done."

Rodman Harvey was now ready to take his departure. His man, Joseph, was waiting without in a buggy, behind a pair of fast-traveling horses. Turning to Ottilie, in an affable mood, the merchant pressed her hospitably to get in and go up town with him.

"We are at the Bayswater Hotel as yet," he said. "Our new house is not yet completed. They turned us out of Union Square, you know. They wanted the place for business. Our accommodations are naturally but limited, but we can keep you a few days as well as not. Your aunt will be very glad to see you. You will also meet my daughter. She is home from Europe now. She will tell you all about her travels."

"Thank you, so much," returned Ottilie, nervously, with a secret dread lest her resistance might somehow be overborne in spite of herself; "but I have only a short leave of absence, which has expired. Every day is important. I really think I must — return at once."

"Well, another time, then; another time. I shall speak to your aunt about you, and she will bear you in mind. You must write to her. She will make an arrangement for some of your vacations. Since you wish to teach, perhaps you could take hold of our youngest, Calista, and brighten her up a bit. She makes very hard work of everything. Or you might call it a secretaryship to Mrs. Harvey, or something of that kind."

Ottilie, still dissimulating, murmured thanks for these embarrassing offers. She made her farewells in a timidly smiling manner, and took her seat once more beside Klauser in the hackney coach.

She renewed her reproaches to that faithless individual, as they rolled up town to the railway station. Klauser defended himself in but a jumbled way. He could plead only the comparative astoundingness of the fact that Rodman Harvey should have been found at his place of business at that hour.

"He thinks of withdrawing from trade," he said, "and now generally gives his afternoons to multiplying outside affairs. He will set up a new firm, of which he wishes Selkirk to be the head. He will go into politics again. I should not wonder if we saw him a member of the next Congress. He lost the nomination the last time, you know, — or perhaps you don't know, — through the manœuvres of his rival, General Burlington. He could attend to his other interests, his railways and the like, just as well in political life, — perhaps better. I have also heard him complain sometimes of attacks of vertigo. Trade is too confining for him. He " — Klauser was fast departing from the subject at issue.

"Still," said Ottilie, "you should not have done it."

They had got on so well together, however, during their long journey, that she had not the heart for an enduring resentment. The young girl had practiced her German with him, and had become interested in his daughter. This latter was named Wilhelmina. She was now at the musical conservatory of Leipsic. Ottilie had asked him how long he had been in our country, and fancied, perhaps, that he might have been a child of the revolutions, with some romantic story. To this he replied that he was, indeed, an exile for political reasons, but he had come in '42, instead of '48, and it was due to an extra tax, which made it bad for the business in which he had been engaged.

"You see that I, too, have a German name," Ottilie had told him. "It comes down in the family. My mother's father came from Hesse Darmstadt, and settled at Cincinnati."

Klauser was expecting his daughter back in no long time. "I hope you will do me the favor to come and see what you think of her," he said, " if you visit your uncle in the spring."

"But I shall *not* visit my uncle," she replied

sharply, wondering at his obtuse lack of comprehension.

The tide of life which had eddied deep and strong in the purlieus of the lower city all day long, had set upward on its return. It moved at a uniform pace, and surged impatiently around all obstacles that came in its way. Well-dressed young men from the business offices marched with breasts thrown out and swinging arms. They made the miles in sturdy pedestrian fashion, not forgetting to ogle, on the way, the pretty shop-girls hurrying to the ferries. The brokers drove, leaning sedately back in their coupés. The wild-eyed and distraught of the morning, who had strained to be on time, to be competent for desperate exactions, sinking, perhaps, under the frown of taskmasters and dread of failure, came back more languidly, respited for the day.

Strangers clustered in the porches and low windows of the hotels. The formal waiters at the luxurious restaurants began to stand with folded arms beside their small tables, set with glass and silver and snowy damask. Half a million cooks were giving the last anxious thought to half a million dinners. Half a million housewives were expecting the advent of their liege lords and masters. If the click of all the latch-keys which now began to turn could have been heard in succession, it would have been a genuine fusilade.

As our acquaintance, Bainbridge, went onward in the procession with the rest, his thoughts recurred, from time to time, to the arrival of Ottilie, her amusing pique at himself, and the slender legacy which had befallen her.

"I am glad her visit availed her even so much," he

said. "She will get little more, should he take never so great a fancy to her. Besides, she is not likely to give him much opportunity."

He deemed himself justified in this view with much positiveness. His general knowledge of the merchant's character, and a glimpse of certain specific aims for the distribution of his property which he had obtained, both enforced the conviction. Rodman Harvey had desired to have his last will and testament, which, by successive alterations, had grown a trifle cumbrous, re-cast into simpler form, and had engaged the young man for this service. It was to be couched in such clear and explicit terms as to leave no room for impeachment by legal quibbles.

The expressed purpose of this document was to found a family. The bulk of the testator's possessions were to go to his eldest son, chiefly in trust. By him they were to be passed on, through a limited species of entail, to the farthest generation possible; and it was hoped that this system would be continued.

Further than this, Bainbridge knew his patron's ingrained habit of disparagement of all who had shown a less virile mastery of fortune than himself. Their failure was too apt to be ascribed to voluntary lack of effort. The merchant prince, perhaps, exempted his own children from the rule, as somehow of a finer clay; but for all others what was needed was unaided exertion, that their full powers might be developed under the goad of necessity.

"Whom did I ever have to extend a helping hand to me?" he asked. "And where should I have been if I had waited for it? Have I not shown, by my own career, that nothing of the kind is necessary?"

The young attorney's clerk summed up his opinion of the whole in a vigorous " Bah ? "

"Still, there are worse people," he continued, within himself, "oh, much worse. His sins are of omission rather than of commission, after all. Very little is heard against him, even in the fierce light that beats upon so influential a position. His occupation is useful to men. He is not one of those, at any rate, whose life is a mere setting of traps, and their wealth the spoils of the unwary. One should make allowances. Perhaps I make too many allowances. I dare say, however, that that is what one who needs them should do."

Musing thus, he came up again with Ottilie.

The central part of the serried procession had been checked at the point where it debouches into Union Square. The bronze Washington was there on horseback, extending a majestic arm above, as if to marshal it. The bronze Lafayette, holding his sword and cloak to his breast, bowed to it with a courtly grace. The gaunt, plain-visaged Lincoln, let it be fancied, regarded it with that "Charity towards all, and malice towards none," which was the motto of his blameless career. Sonorous commands resounded. Could it indeed be that the bronze Washington was ordering which columns should deploy to the left, which to the right, which should keep on through the Park, with its leafless trees, its benches preëmpted by tramps, and its fountain, around which, though boarded in for the winter, the nursemaids still trundled their charges?

A cab-horse had fallen, and a great pair of wheels carrying, slung in chains, a mammoth building-stone, stopped the way. The stalwart police of the Broadway squad endeavored to clear the chaos. The clamor was theirs. The fallen cab-horse sank back supine under the efforts to raise him. The affair seemed vastly more that of others than his own. The drivers clutched their whips, and muttered curses in impotent rage.

In the midst of all this Bainbridge caught sight of her with whom his thoughts were still more or less occupied. She was looking out pensively into the confusion. The top of the carriage had been put up, and the square opening inclosed her like a frame. Her white skin, and hair, under the brim of her black hat, were illumined upon the dusk interior like an old portrait of the Flemish school. She did not smile again at the young man, but bowed gravely as he doffed his hat. Then, by an onward movement of all the wheels, she was once more swallowed up.

Rodman Harvey, checked in this stoppage like others, sat in his buggy at a point where a political banner had been stretched across the street. It was adorned with rude portraits of the candidates, and was riddled, a cynic might have said, as a device for baffling the wind, with as many holes as their reputations might expect to be before the campaign was over.

The merchant prince looked up with interest at this banner. He hoped that similar ones were to be hung out for himself in the near future.

"Do you hear anything of interest about my prospects for the Congressional nomination," he said, suddenly reminded by this, and turning to his son, who sat at his side, "in the talk that has been set going of late?"

"I have happened to hear Dr. Wyburd"—

"Wyburd goes everywhere and sees everybody. He is a repository of universal information. I suppose his opinion ought to be good for something. Well, what does he say?"

"He honestly thinks that your having moved into the district and put up so expensive a residence in it, will conciliate public favor to your side much more than formerly. He thinks that Burlington will try for the nomination, and, failing to secure it, throw his influence for a third person the same way as before; but this time the programme will be less successful."

"So say Hackley and Hastings," coincided his father. "Of course, it is very far in advance, but it is well to take time by the forelock. Burlington is a hard fighter. We shall have to look out for him. Ever since he returned from his foreign mission he has been looking for office. He is needy; that is the trouble. If it were not for that Burlington would be well enough."

"It does not seem to me such a very great office," said the son.

"You do not understand it. To represent in Congress the district of principal wealth and social standing in New York is a very respectable thing, and something that easily leads much higher."

The merchant prince felt vaguely that he should be more comfortable in his mind if only with the letters M. C. after his name. It would put him on equal terms with his correspondent, the French deputy, whose silks and velvets of Lyons he imported; and the maker of his English woolen cloths, who was a member of Parliament. With both of these dignitaries he sometimes exchanged letters and small gifts of personal courtesy, apart from business dealings. For the founding of a family, too, all those things which pass reputably into tradition, were useful as well as money.

"But now a little as to your own affairs," he said presently to Selkirk, leaving this subject: "Mr. Minn tells me that you are not as attentive as you might be. You were away recently for a couple of days."

"I ran over to Philadelphia for a book-sale. It was something very important. There were volumes I wanted for my collection, which I could get nowhere else."

"Nothing of that kind is important to a person in your position. How often must I tell you so? Your old books and China plates may be well enough in their way, but not for one who has something to do in the world."

Selkirk murmured a protest.

"No, I tell you. I observe with grief your tendency to be led away by what is not to the purpose, in your direction, just as your brother Rodman is by an incorrigible recklessness, in his. Here are letters from this new military school, for which he pretended such a fancy, showing that he is as bad as ever. It is a question whether they will be able to keep him there at all. But you are to be the nominal head, at least, of the new firm which I design to establish, with Mr. Minn, Mr. Hackley, — who wishes to come in, as you know, — and others, as your assistants. It should be your pride and duty to be its real head, both for the purpose of adding to what I may legitimately call the glories of the old house, and to the sum of the fortune which I shall leave to your charge. It may be that I was wrong in sending you to Harvard. I was put into the traces at fourteen, and perhaps I should have done the same with you. But it is too late now. You know well the main purpose for which I leave you this fortune."

"Yes," responded the heir.

"Anybody and everybody founds a library, a hospital, a university, nowadays. They are often browbeaten, or flattered into it by the newspapers. It seems to both your mother and myself much more desirable to try to perpetuate our name by establishing a line of descendants in the community in such a way as to always hold an impressive position. I myself have no claim to pride of birth. I am self-made. Whatever we have of that kind is on your mother's side. But the idea seems to me, too, a good one, and it is not, like that of the hospitals and colleges, overdone. Our laws, of course, as compared with those abroad, are not framed to aid in carrying it out. Still, something can be done. I have arranged the whole in this manner. The will has just been re-drawn to-day."

Selkirk gazed about with a rather wearied air, as if he had heard much of this before.

"I have given to your mother all my plate and household effects, my horses and carriages, her own apparel and personal belongings, my house at Newport, my farm at Brompton, Massachusetts, where I was born, my residence now in course of erection at the corner of Fifth Avenue and West Blank Street, — all these for her natural life, without impeachment of waste. I have devised her, in lieu of dower, twenty-five thousand dollars a year, to be paid out of the residuary real estate. I have made liberal provision for both my daughters. I have made a liberal provision, also, for my second son, Rodman, Jr., this in the hands of trustees, to guard against the development of further unruly tendencies, which give me already serious concern."

"All the rest, besides such reversions as there may be, is yours," the speaker continued, after a short pause, during which the buggy narrowly escaped collision with another vehicle; "all the rest is yours. That is to say, it is yours to hold in trust for posterity. One half of the personal property will be yours in full ownership; the other half, together with the real estate, will be handed down. I have expressed my earnest hope and entreaty that when the proper time shall arrive, you will follow the same policy and aid to make the tradition of as binding force as possible."

"I shall conform to your desire," said Selkirk.

"There is another, connected, matter, about which it does not, of course, become me to hurry you, but I trust you give it your attention. It begins to be time that you were settled in the world. If such were your disposition, I should have no objection to your taking a wife."

"Yes," said the son, "taking a wife. Still "—

"You should have no great difficulty in choosing, with all the interesting young women there are in society. What do you think now of Goldstone's daughter? or Miss Ada Trull? You will want good looks, I suppose. Or there is Lehigh Cole's girl. She will have a very pretty fortune; and your mother would approve of her, or of any of these, in fact"— said the merchant prince, bringing the matter down to a practical issue.

Selkirk showed but languid enthusiasm over these young women. When pressed, he said in a hesitating way that he was not sure he greatly cared for any of " the regular kind."

The up-town procession spread out once more into the opening of Madison Square. It was reduced now by constant depletion. Still, the bronze Seward at the edge of the grass-plots, whose business it is said to be to keep the tally of the passers-by on his tablets, had enough and to spare to do. The trucks and drays had rattled away east and west over the broken pavements of the remote side streets to near the rivers. They would stand for the night in front of high, dingy, brick tenement houses, and serve as tribunes for the sports of ragged urchins. The honest beasts which had drawn them, which had once known the sweet air and herbage of farm pastures, were led to ill-smelling, make-shift stalls where it was much if they could stand upright.

The steaming dinners were served now; the anxious housewives had met their spouses. The formal waiters at Delmonico's, the Brunswick, and the rest, had uncrossed their arms, and were flying hither and thither with orders. Through the windows their elegant patrons could be seen smiling in their talk across the small tables. The gas began to flare brightly before the theatres, and leisurely persons to lounge there filliping small bundles of tickets in anticipation of the coming audiences.

Ottilie, in her railway train, was bowling along, in the early night, by the shores of the stately Hudson whose high palisades reëchoed to its rattling. A telegram had been dispatched, that she might be met at her journey's end. The many-winged many-storied institution to which she returned twinkled with lights. A feathery snow had begun to fall, adding to the carpet of white which lay before it broken by dark clumps of evergreens and trees denuded of their foliage.

She was kissed and embraced on this side and that, and sank down at last in a dazed way in her room. She wished, in a homesick mood, that this need of roaming the great wearisome world did not exist, that the allotted term of her stay were over, and she need never again leave dear old appreciative Lone Tree. Unable to sleep at once, though tired, she wrote a letter to acquaint her family with her safe arrival. The missive expanded considerably beyond its projected limits. She had taken many a note of novel things on the way, which she wove into it. She had passed Niagara in the night, having come by this route for the first time. She had opened the window of her berth, as they crossed the Suspension Bridge, and heard it roar, and *even seen the mist rising*. Rarely, perhaps, had the venerable cataract roared and shaken its hoary beard for the pleasure of a more brightly appreciative young person.

The staple matter of the letter was naturally the unexpected meeting with her uncle. She described his manner, at first fierce, then conciliatory. Ah, if he only *were* what he ought to be! It was a way of speaking they often had at home. In early times the children had been given to making great use of this rich uncle as a *deus ex machina* in their projects. Her brother Paul had figured him as leading by the bridle a pony of the most desirable size and breed for him. She herself had thought it probable that he would walk into their abode some day and ask her to put on her things and travel with him several years in Europe.

A young man who had formerly planted oranges in Florida, and was now an attorney's clerk, was not mentioned in this letter further than as "an odd, patronizing kind of person who overheard part of my interview with Uncle Rodman."

Mr. Klauser having discharged his duty at the central railway station, took his way back, with a feeling of relief that the hardships of another campaign were at length over, to his comfortable chambers at Mrs. Proudfoot's boarding-house, in Harvey's Terrace. At the dinner table, Mr. Mahaffey, ex-alderman and now a functionary of the comptroller's department, with Dr. Gaffin the dentist, and Dr. Reinboldt the druggist, welcomed him gravely, inquired after the success of his journey, and fell to comparing notes on the respective merits of the Erie, Central, and Pan Handle routes to the West.

His young fellow employees, the clerks Cutler and Whittemore, who were posted at an end of the table in the near vicinity of the comely school-teacher Miss Speller, and her bosom friend, Miss Finley, were much less serious in their tone. They ventured upon certain freedoms with Klauser by reason of long acquaintance.

"Aha, we saw you this afternoon," began Mr. Cutler. "Sly rascal! This thing of bringing back fascinating young ladies from the West will bear looking into. If I might advise Mrs. Proudfoot, a rather sharp eye should be kept on the doings of Mr. Klauser."

"She was the daughter of the old man's brother," replied Klauser. "And a mighty nice girl she is. You don't find many such nowadays: a scholar, accomplished, kind-hearted, no airs about her, and good-looking into the bargain. I was proud to have her in my company, I can tell you. She made everybody in the parlor car like her, in the two days we were coming on from Chicago."

"They say her father has n't a cent to bless himself with; never knows where the next meal is coming from."

"Nothing of the kind! Not so bad as that!" returned Klauser with heat. "They have a very pretty homestead, and, as the principal merchant of the place, Alfred B. Harvey has a neat business, which with good management ought to yield him very fair returns. Still, he is not the best calculator in the world, and he probably gets as little out of it as anybody could."

"Whatever took him off there to such an outlandish place, when he was at one time a partner in the firm, and engaged in big affairs?"

"Bad management, obstinacy, unpractical ideas. He went into the coal business once, and failed. Then he tried leather, and failed again. Finally, when he was all broke up, his brother happened to have this store at Lone Tree, which he had taken for debt, and put him into it as a resource for supporting his family. A. B. worked hard till he had paid for it and made it his own, then went to wrangling with his brother, as he had done pretty much always. He is one of the most independent fellows you ever saw. In some respects it seems as if his daughter took after him."

Bainbridge meanwhile was putting himself in evening dress for a social engagement, a meeting of the Harmonic Club, of which he was a member, at musical Mrs. Clef's.

III.

AT MUSICAL MRS. CLEF'S.

Mrs. Clef, a scion of the old so much esteemed Knickerbocker stock, was a lady of excellent social standing. She had had losses, and had reconstructed her circle. She had contracted it to moderate dimensions, and based it upon her ruling taste, which was music.

She had the faculty of enlisting in her service the leading professionals who appeared in turn. These came willingly to a hostess of cordial, unconstrained manners, a person of intelligent sympathy, and a performer, besides, of no mean skill. She was said to have played before Liszt and Thalberg.

In her pleasant apartments at the Brandenberg, a fashionable semi-hotel on Madison Avenue, she had old family portraits, and furniture of an elegant antique sort, which was a reminder of a former more stately and expensive style of living. A famous violinist, in a freak, had been allowed to write his name across one of the door-jambs.

Mrs. Clef was of an easy liberality of views, and encouraged ease in her guests. She was fonder of young than elderly company, perhaps to keep off intrusive suggestions of advancing age. She made a delightful chaperon for certain young women, who were accustomed to come often in search of her for that service. She was usually ready at the shortest notice for their excursions.

Most things were treated of here with a humorous cynicism that nothing greatly shocked. Mrs. Clef made a pretense of throwing off tiresome caution with which the world is stifling itself, and said sharp, bright things of people. It was generally with the implication, however, that she thought little the worse of them for it, and that she herself was subject to the same sort of treatment, as a matter of course.

The graceless Huyskamps, who fell with a sort of helplessness from one sin and folly to another, came in for hardly more disparagement than the upright Walkills, who, with large wealth and not a little fashion, professed a strict evangelical piety. To the fine large houses of the Walkills, in fact, a certificate of church membership was almost a prerequisite of admission.

The air of refined Bohemianism, together with the excellent music, had attracted Russell Bainbridge among others. In a desultory frequenting of society, — in which he was to be but irregularly counted upon at best, — he sought by preference those places which promised variety. The worldly tone prevailing, too, was that which he was pleased at present to call his own. After an experience of life which had not answered to his sanguine wishes, he considered himself a rather hardened person. Still, it is probable that it would have much troubled the conscience of which he sometimes made very light, to have greatly injured any human being.

To many of the ambitious, after the long miscarriage of favorite plans, there is apt to come a period of revolt. Since all that had been deemed sufficient and of binding authority has proved so unpropitious to cherished aspirations for happiness, perhaps there are other systems, other directions, in which it may now permissibly be sought.

Bainbridge was passing a life, now unlikely, he deemed, to be of special importance to any one, in an attitude (if the contradictory traits may be joined) of calm recklessness. "At least," he said, putting his experiences together, "I shall have lived; I shall not have stagnated."

A volatile spirit and susceptibility to humor, not wholly repressed by any adversity, played above this tragic substratum, so far as it was genuine, just as will-o'-the-wisps are said to dance cheerfully over black and dangerous pools.

Mrs. Clef, in person, sang, swelling out her ample throat and bosom in the process. Signor Banderoli gave a comic duet from "Don Pasquale," with his pupil, Miss Stella Burgess. He made that young lady herself smile with his droll grimaces, though she knew them so well of old.

Among those who played the piano with a noticeable degree of skill, was a Miss Emily Rawson. She captured Bainbridge afterwards, as it seemed she had sometimes done before, and led him away to one of the chintz-covered sofas.

"What a stranger you are! I had to put up my glass before I knew you," she began. "Are you never coming near me any more? What *made* you drop out of the reading club? As to that poor German class, you have set such an example that we are quite in despair. Professor Blauvelt says we must have fines. We think of going to the German theatre in a body, a week from to-morrow night. Will you not come?"

She spoke in a high-pitched, agreeable voice, which

conveyed in itself fashion and refined prosperity. She was of plain but lady-like aspect, and richly attired. A dot of court-plaster coquettishly aided her complexion. She appeared of a rather frail and nervous type, and perhaps not far from Bainbridge's own age.

This was a young woman who, in her native city, had "outgrown her set." Experiencing a certain mortification to see all her friends married about her, she had set off, with an unenergetic, widowed mother, upon her travels. They went first to Europe, where they sojourned in numerous pensions, and the daughter perfected her music; then to the health springs of Colorado and Florida. They had settled, finally, in New York, as a portion of that star-dust which the great city gathers, part come to seek its fortune, part to spend it in the greatest variety of ways.

The mother had a feeble motto, "Whatever is to be will be," but her daughter had latterly taken the disposition of her own fate and of all their affairs very much into her own hands. She was ambitious both of the married state and a social career. Thus far she had had no great success in any plans she may have laid for either. Without money sufficient to impress itself upon so great a city, though a snug amount in itself, she had been able to draw around her only a somewhat miscellaneous circle, composed of acquaintances of travel, the watering-places, coteries of music, the languages, decorative arts, and religion, — into all of which she had plunged in a craving for excitement and new opportunities.

She had secured a great deal of Bainbridge's society by a pertinacious ingenuity of invention. They had been associated in the pleasant intimacy of private theatricals, of musical duets, and classes in reading and the languages. She had even asked him to come and *smoke to her*, ingratiating herself on the side of his comfort. She believed in him, or affected to, and predicted fine things of his future. When he grumbled at ill-luck and poverty, of which he made no sort of secret, she said, " We are all poor in a genteel way." She professed simple and domestic tastes, but at the same time artfully dangled before him, under pretext of taking his advice on the price of certain stocks and bonds, glimpses of her private fortune.

Bainbridge, since his losses and the affair of Madeline Scarrett, hardly looked upon himself as an eligible person from the matrimonial point of view. He would not have been averse to continuing a platonic relation with a person so prepossessing in many ways, and one who had the good taste to appreciate his merits so highly, but further than that he did not wish it to go.

Miss Rawson secretly thought otherwise as to his eligibility. She made her own estimate of the value of his connection with the Hudson Hendricks, a family of the first prominence, whose near kinsman he was. With her income and the social advantages open to him, she would have counted on making a bold push to the front rank in society.

From certain signs, — he hoped it was not a mere masculine vanity, — the young man had regretted to suspect her of making what is called a "dead set" at him, and thought it prudent to rather withdraw from the intimacy. He yielded himself now to her old air of *bon cameraderie;* he could hardly do less, but whispered to himself at the same time, "*Suaviter in modo, fortiter in re.*"

"I really fear I shall not be able to. An engagement" — he began, in reply to her invitation.

"Oh, always some engagement; always something! You do not wish to."

"Oh, really" — he protested.

She began to question him as to the doings of late, which could have kept him away from her. What was the McMurray-Bourdon wedding like?" she asked. "Were there as many guests at Mrs. Antram's ball as usual?" She had the names and descriptions of leading society people at her tongue's end, having acquired them from the position of a very near observer.

He had gone to a Turkish bath instead of the wedding, he said, and an unconventional evening at the Rembrandt Sketch Club, to which he had been asked, instead of the ball.

This neglect of such choice opportunities in favor of something very ordinary and "common" seemed to Miss Emily Rawson little short of sacrilege. The Antrams' ball was the principal event of the winter. A team of wild horses could not have kept her from either that or the McMurray-Bourdon wedding, if the chances had been hers.

"Society and I neglect each other very much," said Bainbridge. "I wonder it doesn't cross me off its books more than it does. I suppose people forget. Mrs. Rifflard, for instance, must be in a very pretty muddle, among her list of a thousand invitations. I tell her my name when I go in. 'Mr. Bainbridge.' 'Ah, Mr. Bainbridge! It is so good of you to come.' I doubt if she knows me from Adam. My Hudson

Hendricks were good enough to start me very fairly in that sort of thing some years ago. I have cultivated it about as little — it really seems amusingly impudent to say so — as the greatest snob in town, — young Kingbolt, or Austin Sprowle, or Sprowle Onderdonk, for example, who assert that it is only strugglers for position who make dinner visits, or show any particular recognition of civilities offered them. In my case, it is partly a native apathy, I suppose, and partly — I could hardly tell you what. If I am treated ill, that stands for itself; if well, I consider it a case of false pretenses. There is attributed to me, no doubt, a bank account and other advantages I don't possess."

"You think money then of so much consequence?"

"Lack of it is the only crime that is not forgiven. Its possession is the one thing interesting to hear about. What is done in courts and camps is of no moment nowadays. It is what is done in a bank."

"For my part," said Miss Rawson, with a rather meaning air, "I consider family of vastly more importance."

To vary from a line of discussion which was not uncommon, Bainbridge next told in an easy way, as of an indifferent person whom she would never be likely to see, of the visit of Ottilie to the store, and of the interview at which he had been unwillingly obliged to be present.

"Is she pretty? You men always ask that. Nothing less will serve you."

"Oh, she is pretty enough. I should not call that kind of looks particularly imposing. It all depends on the character and manners. I should think she might have rather nice manners when not too much out of temper.

"Since she is so very fine, I should think her uncle would treat her better; perhaps do something for her. But he is a hard, disagreeable man, as I have heard. I doubt if he ever did anybody a good turn in his life."

"I have come to have a considerable regard for anybody who does not do you a bad turn."

"Oh, yes! you stand by him. I dare say you hope, in time, to become his principal attorney."

"Perhaps that might be a good enough reason, if it were so. But I hope I am candid enough to judge of people somewhat apart from their relations to me. I should say that affection was not Rodman Harvey's strong point; but that he was a very regular and upright person in his dealings. I should say that he would cherish a high ideal of commercial integrity, if only for the neatness and symmetry of it."

Later on the same name chanced to be under discussion in another group. Miss Rawson called to Bainbridge vivaciously, —

"*Au secours!* Your beloved Harveys are in danger."

Mrs. Clef was dissertating in her candid way on an engagement, not long since made public, between Angelica, the daughter of Rodman Harvey, and an extremely well-connected, though, according to her, stupid young man, Austin Sprowle. Sprowle had been at one time a secretary of legation at Paris.

"They say they were engaged, or at least that there was an understanding between them, for some time before it was formally announced," said musical Mrs. Clef. Some of the girls were rather ridiculing his appearance, at Mrs. Bloomfield's kettle-drum, and Angelica Harvey all at once broke out, ' He is of the very finest family in America, and — I am engaged to him ! ' She happened to be in one of her domineering moods, I suppose, that day. They say it was positively dreadful, the way her eyes flashed ! However, that does not prevent her flirting with other men I see, and notably with that young Kingbolt of Kingboltsville. The match was made by the two mothers, at Pau. Family is Mrs. Harvey's hobby. Having married as she did, she thinks that that is the direction in which they chiefly need strengthening. Her daughter shares the taste."

"I suppose the Sprowles are expecting something very handsome in the way of dowry from Rodman Harvey," said a divorced Mrs. Whipple, " but I should be inclined to think, with this fancy of his for piling up the largest sum possible for his eldest son, they might be disappointed."

"The Sprowles are far from poor, of course," returned Mrs. Clef, " but people who have so many generations behind them unconnected with trade cannot expect to compete with the vulgar modern style of fortune. Young Sprowle is *not*, in fact, fine-looking," she continued. " One always has to think of the *knobs* of his body. His feet stick out at an awkward angle, and he has one of those large, gourd-shaped heads with nothing in them which ought to be the despair of the phrenologists. It looks topply ; his neck is so slender. He never said a good thing in his life. I wonder how she puts up with him, she who is so ready with her tongue ; though she is a vixen of a girl, too, and he has no great treasure in her either."

"As to his doing anybody a bad turn," said Miss Rawson, returning to the subject of Rodman Harvey, "you know how excessively disagreeable he has been to our friends, the Hasbroucks, about their property."

"The newly arrived niece would agree with you. She took an early occasion to mention it."

Mrs. Hasbrouck has been here lately on a visit, from Baltimore. She thinks of taking a house or flat, in the spring, so as to be near her children."

"Why did you not tell me before? I should have liked to go and see her."

"How can I tell you anything when you never come near me?"

IV.

A SUNDAY ON THE AVENUE.

THE high board fence which had so long obscured the works in progress on the new mansion of Rodman Harvey was at length removed. On the day following, which was a Sunday, the fact became one of general notoriety.

Upon the letting out of the churches, at noon, there streams along Fifth Avenue — chief thoroughfare of the elegant quarter of brown stone and plateglass inhabited by the wealth and fashion of the city — a procession unique of its kind. In the charming early spring days after the severities of the winter, it becomes swollen to its fullest dimensions. Then even very exclusive people, who properly consider a promenade so open to all the world as beneath their usual countenance, are often wooed to take part. The Sunday in question was not only in the genial springtime, but it was Easter, the great festival of the Christian year, and a recognized occasion besides for the display of new feminine fashions.

Now that the fence was down the new house of Rodman Harvey, at the corner of West Blank Street, was seen not to differ greatly, except in size, from others in the neighborhood. It was of brown or red sandstone, fifty or sixty feet in front, and perhaps two hundred, with its various appurtenances, down the side street. It had three liberal stories, and a mansard, topped with a gilded railing. A row of classic window heads in its first story were of curved form, those in the second triangular, and in the third straight. A stone balustrade inclosed a low "area" in front, and the basement windows were protected by gratings with gilded spear-heads.

A broad flight of steps, curving hospitably outwards, led to a porch with a couple of Corinthian columns. Within this were heavily carven doors, a paved vestibule, and lighter doors, with stained glass panels. The long stretch on the side street was broken up by a bay window reaching through the several stories. Then an expanse, relieved by panels, with a sky-light above, indicated a picture-gallery. Next to this a brick wall, higher than a man's head, extended to two tall posts, topped with stone balls, — the gateway to low brick stable buildings.

The passers-by, who had long been alarmed by blasting, and made to walk the plank over yawning chasms, hailed with relief the end of their disquietudes. The sudden disappearance, too, of the high fence, blazoned with its advertisements, was almost as striking as had been its first initiation. It had blazoned in the most florid style of art, complexion renovators, velocipedes, the winter route to Florida, and the "Evening Meteor," which, it is well known, has a larger circulation than all of its contemporaries put together.

It had blazoned, also, the attractive investment system of the "Prudential Land and Loan Company," which combined the savings of many to the advantage of all. "For prospectus address the management, Fletcher, St. Hill & Co., in the Magoon Building, lower Broadway."

A SUNDAY ON THE AVENUE.   49

Whatever matters formed the topic of discourse elsewhere, at the corner of West Blank Street and the Avenue it was surely Rodman Harvey, just as the same light cloud always hovers about a tall mountain peak, though the particles of which it is actually composed are flying past at the rate of sixty miles an hour. Such as knew him little were now glad to learn more; and those who knew him better were glad to tell all they knew. One could have obtained a very tolerable idea of the aims and history of the merchant prince by no more than lingering awhile, and paying heed, in front of the mansion he had reared.

Aureolin Slab and the young architect, G. Lloyd, went by, and stopped and looked up, and regretted that what they saw should be in none of the new, artistic styles, but simply a great nondescript monument to a wasted opportunity.

"He was of mere farmer origin, of course," the severely aristocratic, Roman-nosed dowager, Mrs. Sprowle, was saying to her stalwart kinsman, Sprowle-Onderdonk, who walked with her a little, on his way to his breakfast at the Empire Club; "but I must say he has conducted himself in quite a praiseworthy manner. His first wife was one of his own sort,—a wise Puritan virgin, who knitted stockings, sang psalms, and quoted Cobbett and Poor Richard. But the present Mrs. Harvey is one of the old Muffetts, and all that could be desired, from that point of view. Her first husband was thrown from his carriage and killed, early in their marriage. He left her little, and her own family, who had the habit of spending everything, could not add much to it. She inherited the Muffett place, however, which

Harvey built up into blocks of houses. She lived in it when she first met him. I dare say she was having a stupid time. I remember that it was thought quite a piece of presumption, his aspiring so high, as he was not as rich as he is now, and nobody had ever heard of him socially. However, as I have said, he has certainly used his money in a very commendable way. I have no adverse criticism to make either upon him or his daughter. Your cousin Austin, my son, seems very happy in his choice of her for a wife, and, as you know, I have not withheld my consent."

Dr. Wyburd — diner-out, dabbler in literary and scientific matters in addition to the medical profession, depositary of universal information — spoke of the beginnings of Rodman Harvey's fortune. "He made most of it during and after the War of the Rebellion," he said. " Previous to that he had catered largely for the Southern trade. His credits were extended over the South at the breaking out of hostilities, and his losses were heavy. The Southern merchants continued, and even increased their trade with him, when they had withdrawn it from others of more radical opinions. That was all very well for the time, but when secession came and debts were repudiated, it was quite another story. He was lucky, I fancy, to pull through that scrape."

The dashing Cutler and steady-going Whittemore, of the merchants' clerks, went by in their turn.

" The old man is a fearful obstinate person, when he once starts in," said Whittemore. " They tell of a bank at Bridgehaven, when he was in business there in a small way, which refused him some accommodation. He went to work and bought up its bills, and presented the whole issue for redemption. The officers apologized humbly, and begged him not to wind up the concern, but he went on and did it."

"What I like," said Cutler, "is to get him on the subject of the economies he used to practice in those times. He lets us have them occasionally as a reward of merit, when he comes around in his snooping way and finds everything all right, instead of skylarking going on. This thing of getting a capital together by walking to save your car-fare, never taking a drink or a day off, cannot be done nowadays. Trade is too large. Look at our place!— a hundred and twenty employees, sales of ten and fifteen millions a year. It takes a good many car-fares to equal that, eh? The retail trade is worse, if anything. The big concerns eat up the little ones. It is no time for small fry."

"But a man would expect to go into the country, somewhere, to begin," said Whittemore.

"No country for me! none of that in mine! I stay here. Where will you find anything like this in the country?"

Two slow divisions passed each other, one up, one down the sidewalk, almost touching shoulder to shoulder. The individuals composing them gazed into one another's faces, nonchalantly, amiably, haughtily, impertinently, admiringly, distrustfully, according to the mood and character of each. There were modish young women and young men without end; old beaux, gray, experienced, and distinguished-looking; stately matrons; children in plushes and velvets, like young princes of Vandyke. A sweet-faced girl, afflicted with lameness and walking with a rose-wood crutch, aroused a kind of pathetic interest. Mourners lately from the cemeteries, seemed yet to carry in their garments airs from the laurel and cypress dells where they had laid their dead. At one point a tramp, his torn clothing held by a girdle of rope, crossed from a side-street, like a wild beast from its jungle, and gave the whole concourse a momentary check.

The first parasols were out. Some of these were in pure crimson; others — such was a fashion of the time — in concentric rings, black, scarlet, and gold, like targets for archery practice. Bluish shadows streamed from the figures along the pavement. The sunshine, filtered through a slight haze, arising from the burning of stubble in the country, had a quality like a mysterious smile. The first leafage flickered on the willows and maples in the squares like a tender yellowish flame. The generative feeling of the time was in the air. Small housewives planned to buy of the dealers, who would come about in their wagons, pots of geraniums, and sods of grass for the little city door-yards, tramped out by the serving-maids in the winter.

"For my part," Mr. Cutler went on. "I shall not stick to dry goods any longer than I can help. Look at McKinley! He has drawn the same salary for the last fifteen years, and he will go on drawing that and no more if he lives to the age of Methuselah. I was down to see a Mr. St. Hill the other day at this new Prudential Land and Loan Company. He offered me a place if I only had a little money to put up as a guaranty. I have got to get into something pretty soon. I don't mind telling you that I shall probably marry Miss Speller, and then there will be two of us."

Whittemore thought it odd that Cutler, who so insisted upon worldly wisdom, should be going to marry the quite impecunious public-school teacher, Miss Speller. But she was very pretty, and no doubt, like other would-be prudent men, he had yielded to fascinations which he had not properly estimated.

The sweet air seemed yet full of the chime of bells, the notes of organ, harp, and viol, and of the clear voices which had been singing anthems; and it was yet perfumed with the scent of all the lilies and roses clustered around the fonts and chancel rails.

The Resurrection had naturally been the theme in most of the pulpits under the line of steeples following one another interminably down the Avenue. But Mr. Haggerson had managed to combine with it the fourth in his series to young men. The Rev. Mr. Goswin found means to attack Romanism, the Rev. Mr. Telfair to demonstrate the absurdity of supposing a connection between ideas of supernaturalism and morality. Mr. Dillman had drawn the lessons of the City of Trebizond disaster. The Rev. Mr. Gambit had taken up the parable of the barren fig-tree, dividing his subject into three heads. The Rev. Mr. Bashan had utilized the blowing down of the walls of Jericho by the ram's-horn trumpets. How simple, how apparently contemptible, were the means; yet how, at the fated hour and the final note, the walls of the wicked, derisive city had crumbled to inevitable ruin. An analogy, he thought, to this might be found in the terrible force of public opinion upon a reputation falsely enjoyed, and undermined by consciousness of it.

The pastor of Rodman Harvey, the polished Dr. Miltimore, hewed down no barren fig-trees, and blew no rams' horns of judgment. He softened the asperities of theology. He had a scholarly air, as of a person delivering addresses before a historical society. He devoted himself somewhat to reconciling a supposed inconsistency between the temporal and spiritual welfare. Rodman Harvey had had one of his sermons put in pamphlet form, and kept copies of it by him, which he sometimes presented to new acquaintances, saying, "My good minister preached a sermon the other day which pleased me so well that I had it printed;" and this by no means did his business relations harm. Watervliet, the club wit, was in the habit of complimenting the gentlemanly tone of things at Dr. Miltimore's.

"He never touches on politics, — or religion," said Watervliet. "He offends the susceptibilties of no man."

Should Dr. Miltimore, then, have harrowed up the feelings of his parishioners, on their sole day of rest? Why, the responsibilities of Rodman Harvey alone, sitting there with his family around him in his crimson-lined, oaken pew, were something incredible. He was a stockholder and director in the Antarctic, Cosmopolitan, and Union banks, the Alien-Mutual and Planet insurance companies, the Western Mail line of steamers, the Devious Air-Line, Rio Bravo and Willamette, Onalaska, and Maumee Central railways, the Vulcan Rolling Mills, Franklin Telegraph, Metropolis Gas, and Featherstone Hay-Scale companies; the Chamber of Commerce, the Union League Club, the Academy of Music, the Historical, Agricultural, St. Nicholas, and New England societies. He was treasurer and first director of that excellent society for the purification of municipal politics, the Civic Reform Association. And even these, with his mines; his great business house, involving the calculation of effects of climate, seasons, and changing political conditions on goods purchased in distant lands, to be sold at distances as remote; his family; and the supervision of his new mansion, were but a tithe of the burdens which called for the extension to him of a more than ordinary freedom from other annoyance.

Rodman Harvey issued from the porch of Dr. Miltimore's church, accompanied by his wife, his younger son, Rodman, Jr., and his younger daughter, Calista, a tall girl of ten, with dull, blue eyes, a profusion of yellow hair, and a languid, complaining way of speaking. The younger son wore the uniform of a military school, from which he had lately been dismissed,—a circumstance which seemed by no means to weigh heavily on his spirits.

A handsome landau, with the front half let down, awaited the family. There were two men in livery on the box; the strong, dark horses had brass-mounted harness and small blankets of dark green, embroidered with monograms, under their saddles. The footman, Alphonse, called the attention of the coachman, Joseph, who was gossiping with the coachman of General Burlington, although there was a coolness between their masters,— and the landau promptly drew up to the curbstone.

"Let us walk, mamma; I am so tired of riding," pleaded Calista.

Quite unexceptionable people were going by. "Very well," said Mrs. Harvey, putting up a little parasol above a plump face retaining a certain middle-aged prettiness. "Joseph, nous allons nous promener jusqu'à la nouvelle maison. Attendez nous là!"

"Parfaitement madame," replied the careful Swiss Joseph.

One of his merits was that foreign languages could be practiced with him. He drove decorously before to the new house, and there took up the family and conveyed them to the Bayswater Hotel.

The elder son, Selkirk, was not present at the service. He passed his Sunday mornings over Herbert Spencer, or in arranging his books, or he called upon one Aureolin Slab, to whom he exhibited new acquisitions in Banko and old Kiyoto wares.

Nor was the brilliant elder daughter, Angelica, present. She found Saint Barnabas' better adapted to her spiritual needs. She had no great fancy for historical society discourses. The service at Saint Barnabas' was more like what one was used to abroad. She would have liked to walk down an aisle with a footman behind her carrying prayer-books, as is done in England, but had hesitated as yet to put this innovation in practice. At Dr. Miltimore's, at any rate, there were not even prayer-books to carry.

While her family were being driven to their hotel, Angelica Harvey was walking up from Saint Barnabas', attended by two young men, one on either hand, engaged with them in lively talk. These were recognized by the set which knew them, as Austin Sprowle, her affianced husband; and Arthur Kingbolt, heir to that great property, the Eureka Tool Works of Kingboltsville, Connecticut.

V.

A MAN OF FASHION DRIVES OUT A FRIEND.

YOUNG Kingbolt, of Kingboltsville, had the fancy that morning to take a turn up the road in his dog-cart. He had invited to a seat beside him his friend, and *protégé*, though a man much older than himself, — Mr. St. Hill, the manager of the new Prudential Land and Loan Company.

A large, high-stepping gray horse, with a quantity of silver chains rattling about his harness, drew along the box-like vehicle, with a light rocking motion on its single axle. The master of this conveyance, half standing, half sitting against its high cushioned seat, with one hand well forward, the other near the breast of his snug frock coat, with its bunch of violets at the lapel, was as fine a picture of supercilious young patriciandom as one would wish to see. He was of a type not uncommon in the well-looking American race. Almost any change in it must be for the worse, and he might not grow old as gracefully as some others of a lesser perfection of features. His expression denoted petulance and self-will. There was something terrier-like (of the best breed, be it understood) in the trimness of his cut, — his small ears, his close-cropped hair polished with brushing, his slight, dark moustache, and his glistening white teeth.

While this one was perhaps twenty-six, his companion must have been forty. He was a much stouter man, blonde, with a round, red face, above which he wore a hat of the smallest size permitted by the ruling mode. He had a glass in one eye.

The contribution of these two to the prevailing discussion of the merchant prince was of a somewhat unusual character.

"I am thinking of giving him a twist some of these days," said Mr. St. Hill.

"Giving him a twist?"

"Yes, if a man won't pay you what he owes you in one way, I suppose you have a right to make him, in another. I have a lot of his letters, which he would not be at all anxious to have see daylight, especially about these times, when he begins to have political aspirations. I think I shall have to crowd Rodman Harvey for about twelve thousand dollars."

"He ought to be good for anything against him in the regular way. If you have a claim, why do you not put it into the hands of a lawyer?"

"Oh, this is an old matter, and barred long since by the statute of limitations. He owed my father for cotton at the outbreak of the war. When we applied for payment, after it was over, he refused in the most abusive terms. He said he had lost enough by the South already, and we might see how we liked it ourselves. At the same time, he was remorselessly following up those who owed *him* there, even though they had hardly a cent to bless themselves with."

"But you could have made him pay you then, you know; the five years' limitation was not out."

"It was pretty nearly out. Both my father and myself had had the misfortune to be rather actively engaged in what you call here the "rebel" cause, and thought it advisable to go for a time to Europe, finally to Egypt. We did not quite understand what our rights were. When we did it was too late. I wrote to Harvey from London, and it was then that he sent the response I have told you of. I did not have his letters then, nor have I had them, till within a few days past, or I should have given him a turn before."

"And these letters, what are they?"

"Well, they show him up, you know, on the slavery question. He used to take niggers on chattel mortgage for goods, or own them outright, and hire them to the plantations. We had some of them on a place of ours up the Ashley River. He and my father used to be very thick at one time, and carried on an intimate correspondence. The letters turned up only the other day, at the plantation on the Ashley, after having been lost for years. The place was racketed to pieces, by troops on both sides, during the war, and has been in the hands of the Jews ever since. The papers were picked out of a barrel, with some other traps, by an old overseer of mine, who sent them up here to me to see if they might be of interest."

"Now, see here! I've been a friend of yours, have n't I?" began Kingbolt, when the scheme for obtaining payment from Rodman Harvey had been well laid before him. "I don't say anything about what I did for you in Europe. You were rather down on your luck, and I got you over here and put you into the Empire Club, and gave you a send-off in some good houses. Old Mrs. Sprowle was cracking you up only the other day on the score of family. And now you have a big financial company in which you think there is a mint of money. And you have some of my money in it, too, have n't you? Very well! Now what I say about this bluff game is, Let it alone! Drop it! See?"

Perhaps the superior age of the *protégé* added zest to the domineering air assumed by his young patron.

"You don't want to stir up anything of that kind," he continued. "Your *rôle* is to go on and make as many persons as possible favorable to your new enterprise. You asked me, when you first came here, what kind of a reception you were likely to meet with, on account of having been on the other side during the war. I told you that New York was too big and bustling a place to devote much time to by-gones. I said it might make you a bit of a curiosity, and be a point in your favor, and so it has. But now, if you go to raking up those dead and buried issues that people had rather forget, if you go to attacking one of the few men who has not forgotten, but for some reason or other keeps up a peculiar grudge about it, it will not be to your advantage with the community. And as to getting money from Rodman Harvey, you may dismiss that idea at once. You would come out second best. Besides, I don't see that it would be right."

This was rather an unusual display of morality in one who was not known for squeamishness, but was rather known for a readiness in putting things at cross-purposes, if only for the sake of the sport. St. Hill cogitated whether there were not some hidden motive inclining his friend in Harvey's favor.

At this moment Rodman Harvey's beautiful daughter went by, with Sprowle, to whom she was engaged. Kingbolt acknowledged her bow from the sidewalk with effusion, and glanced back after her when she had passed.

"It is too good a thing to give up. It is too much money to forego," persisted St. Hill, in his argument.

"You'll have to choose between him and me, then," said Kingbolt sharply. "See here! I think I'll get down. You can take the trap up by yourself. I believe I won't ride to-day."

St. Hill saw him go back and join Angelica Harvey. A sudden theory flashed into his mind as a solution of his meditations. He put together eulogies he had heard paid by Kingbolt to the beauty and style of this girl, with attentions he had witnessed, engaged though she was, and securely fixed in her choice by her own wishes, the plans of two prominent families, and the respect due the usages of society.

"Oho! is that it?" he said to himself. "He is a little gone on the young woman, and so takes the family under his protection. It is like one of his whims. Well, we must wait a little for the wind to blow round. It can't sit long in that quarter. The prospect is altogether too slim, even for him."

It is not too much to say that Mr. St. Hill was considerably disappointed. He had not even arrived at the subject of a small loan he had intended to propose, on the basis of the profits to be derived from Harvey. And further than this, an interdict had been laid on his scheme itself, which he could not disregard without the loss of a friendship from which he expected many substantial favors in the future, as he had received them in the past. But he had occasion to know something of his friend's vacillation of purpose. He was encouraged to believe that in a brief period Kingbolt would have forgotten Harvey and his daughter, even to the bare fact of their existence, and that he could then proceed again with his design, for the present postponed.

There was not a group on the Avenue that drew more admiring attention than the trio consisting of Miss Angelica Harvey and her two cavaliers. Not that the one to the right, her accepted suitor, was a model of perfection in looks. He had, indeed, something of the aspect pictured by Mrs. Clef in her lively description. On the other hand, there was hardly any mistaking his air of fashion, and of membership in a certain circle. He affected a choice elegance in costume. All of it, down to his gaiters, was black. He wore a weed on his hat. He carried his arms at an artificial angle, and balanced a small stick between a thumb and finger. "Commonness" was understood to be the chief avoidance of Austin Sprowle. When under-secretary of legation at Paris, he was said to have spoken of a number of ministers who came and went above him in turn, as "common."

But the one on her left was a very handsome young man. And then the young woman herself! She had fine, large, dark eyes, which she rolled about vivaciously as she talked. She had a small dimple in her cheek, and a smile which, in showing her fine teeth to the best advantage, caused some little wrinkles to appear around her quite enchanting nose.

Her costume was of some drab or pale yellowish cloth, which fitted almost as closely as her skin. Two distinct triangles of daylight appeared between her arms and the contours of her shapely waist. Her skirts waved off the hips, first this way and then that, in the undulations of a walk which was divided into syllables, as it were, like her name. At her breast was a nosegay of yellow flowers. Kingbolt always noticed in her some subtle touch of distinction from the crowd. Yellow flowers, now? It was a small thing, but nobody else yet wore yellow flowers. And be assured that when, through her example, they should have become the mode, she would be as far in advance again with some new bit of tasteful ingenuity.

It was upon these two, Kingbolt and Angelica, that interested glances were principally directed. So perfect in every artificial appointment, so elastic in tread, so comely and blooming, so airily free from trace of self-distrust, a young Diana and her brother, Phœbus Apollo, of upper society, they radiated around them, as it were, a kind of awful splendor.

"I got down on your account," said Kingbolt. "I saw you walking. I was going for a turn up the road after my breakfast."

"How very good of you! I have not seen you for a long time. What is the news?"

"I am bringing over an English tilbury. I like to have something a little different now and then, you know," he said, twisting a finger in a nonchalant way into the front of his collar. "It has a rumble, you know, for one's man. The horses have a silver bar across their backs, and are harnessed up in this way." He indicated with his hands.

"You must take me out in it."

"I think I'll get a tilbury, too," said Sprowle, not to be wholly relegated to the position of a listener, merely because he was less fluent in talk. As to the tilbury, he may have intended to get it, but probably not till after his marriage. The standing of the Sprowles, fortunately, depended upon something besides a lavish expenditure of money.

Being of those who did not often take part in the procession, the group set to making satirical comments, as on some display of curious manners and customs of aborigines.

"I am told that many of these persons who make such a fine appearance are mere clerks," said Sprowle. "Indeed, I have seen some of them in the shops."

"I never go to shops," said Angelica. "I send my maid. I order things directly from the manufacturers, and get original designs for myself. Thus you have things that the crowd cannot tiresomely imitate. There ought to be some special dress for the lower classes,— for all that kind of people. Simple caps and aprons, say, for the women, and blouses for the men. Then mistakes could not be made."

"Yes, there ought to be a law, you know," said Sprowle.

The clerk, Cutler, who prided himself especially upon his dapper attire, and was hardily scanning the fair proposer of the measure herself with an air of connoisseurship, from the steps of the Windsor Hotel, would scarcely have relished a proposition to put him in a blouse, as a mark of his social station.

"I suppose you will be going out again a great deal, now that Lent is over," said Kingbolt, suggesting a new train of thought.

"Yes, I suppose so. I am back from abroad only so lately that I do not find the novelty exhausted. Besides one is so uncomfortable in a hotel. It will be such a blessed relief when our house is done. I went to two or three places every night last winter, and was hardly ever in bed before two in the morning. I sometimes wonder how I stand it."

"You are made of *i*-on," exclaimed her affianced, admiringly.

"I have done my share of all that," said Kingbolt. "I used to lead the German continually, chiefly while you were abroad; but I have given it up. I recollect going to ten young people's dinners, followed by ten large balls, in succession. New York did not content me in those times, either. I used to take in the country also. I made it a point to know every society belle from here to St. Louis. I thought nothing of running out to Cleveland for a wedding, or Cincinnati for private theatricals. You would hear about me out there, I dare say, even yet. But I am not going in for that now. I shall just give a theatre party or so pretty soon, — may be a dance, at Delmonico's, or the club house up at Jerome Park, — and then clear out."

"Where shall you go?"

"To my place at Kingboltsville." He would have liked to hear her protest against it; but she only said,

"What do you do there? It must be very stupid."

"Oh, I have my horses. I speed them on a race-track of my own. Then I get some fellows up from here, you know. We are close to Bridgehaven, which is quite a city. We shall probably be taken in as a suburb. Then there is a social club of which I am president. They have made me president of a railroad, too. They make me president of almost anything, you know, if I like. I have a lot of trustees who expect me to be around part of the time, and be nagged at about my property. And there is building going on."

"Yes, I recollect when I first met you at Pau, that you were traveling with your architect, to get up plans for some industrial museum, or library, for the improvement of your tenantry. I suppose it is finished by this time."

"Oh, that rot! No, I abandoned it long ago. You can't do much for that kind of people; they wouldn't appreciate it. Besides, I could not stand the person, that Lloyd, whom I took along with me. He was an acquaintance of mine, and I thought I could depend on him to do as I said. But you would have thought that *he* was the one who was going to do the building, and had hired *me!* I had to turn him adrift. — No, my sisters, — two widows, a good deal older than I, — are tinkering with a church and a new wing to the house. They make me subscribe to the church, though I started it originally, and half finished it. That was another of my ideas. The house has more wings than it knows what to do with now. They went over awhile ago to the Maximoff sale, — at Florence, if you remember, — and brought back a lot of vases and things to put into the house and the church."

"I used to go to school with one of the little Maximoff princesses, at Geneva," said Angelica, by way of reminiscence. "She had some trouble with her spine. She took a fancy to me. They were enormously wealthy. They had one of their residences there. When they sent their great lackeys to take her out for an airing in the carriage, I was often asked also."

They were continually passing, while engaged in

such discourse, the people they knew. The two young men were never done doffing their hats and putting them on again. The old beau, Robert Rink, sometimes spoken of as "the gray deceiver," Judge Chippendale, Watervliet the wit, and Dr. Wyburd, all looked with not less interest than their juniors for the bow of the young beauty. Baron Au, of the Pomeranian legation, and Bulbul Effendi, the hideous little Turkish secretary, whom women tolerated as a kind of bricabrac, chuckled over it audibly. De Longbow Rowley, upon failing to receive it, though he was perfectly well known, — it was a trick Angelica had, occasionally, by way of keeping them on their good behavior, — said to Whitehead Finch, —

"*I* don't see that she is such a howling belle."

When Angelica met Ada Trull, whose blonde hair, cut upon her forehead to an even line, resembled a cap of gold, these two exchanged several sprightly nods, in bright recognition of many things in common between them. But with Alice Burlington, between whose father and hers there was a feud, only glances of a far-off pensive criticism were exchanged.

"She has the knack of making herself the most distinguished figure in the company," said Kingbolt, walking away after leaving her at the Bayswater Hotel. "She would do any man credit. Had I been a marrying man in season, I could have found no one who would have served my turn more completely. She is haughty. I do not mind that. We would have been haughty together. Why did I not see her before?" he said. "Or rather, why were not my eyes opened? I had the same chance with her at Pau as Sprowle, if I had wanted it."

Was it possible, after his large experience of life, the atmosphere of sighs that had been breathed, the swath of damaged affections he had left behind him in his course around the world, that he could have come to the absurd pass of being inconvenienced by one irredeemably beyond his reach?

"What in the world," he cried, "can she see in that muff of a Sprowle, at any rate, to take up with him?"

Then he scoffed at himself for the unprofitable speculation, and went down to join a group of his friends, ruminating in the large windows of the Empire Club, with their sticks under their chins.

VI.

SOME PERVERSE OPINIONS OF MR. BAINBRIDGE.

RUSSELL BAINBRIDGE also joined the Sunday procession, which he had called the dress-parade of the drill down town. He lapsed into a querulous mood, as he went along, and began to inveigh against the spring as an unsettling season.

"I dare say I shall be laying violent hands upon some of these prosperous people next, out of pure spite," he said to himself.

He met Bentley, with whom he had formerly been intimate, leading his charming boys by the hand. "Perhaps I should have made a very tolerable family man myself," he said again.

But, immediately afterwards, meeting Madeline Scarrett, with her invalid capitalist, Elphinstone Swan, he reflected that, whatever turn fortune might now take, this form of happiness was of course for him impossible.

Well, perhaps it was better to have been disillusioned early. One is wiser for such experiences. They are useful in the heavy play of life, which comes later. But had he been in search of that kind of wisdom? He could well have spared it. Why had not his beliefs been left to him? Why could not his modest ventures have been crowned with success, as he saw those of others about him crowned? "I had the economic virtues," he said,

"I was not afraid of work, and I think I should have made a fairly exemplary use of success. — Ah, these eternal Whys!"

He checked himself, to inveigh also at Sunday, when one is cut off from the duties that keep his mind profitably employed during the week, as the most unsettling of days, just as spring is the most unsettling of seasons.

Well up towards Central Park, he encountered Miss Emily Rawson, with a companion. This companion he recognized, with a movement of surprise and interest, as no other than Ottilie Harvey. The two had just issued from the ornamental iron gates of Saint Adrian's.

"Will you not join us?" asked Miss Rawson, in her high-pitched, agreeable voice. "You and Miss Ottilie have met before. I borrowed her this morning. She came to hear me sing. I am going to put her in a horse-car, at the end of my street, to get back to early dinner at the Regina Flats. She is stopping with the Hasbroucks, and they insist upon it. I have been singing in the choir this morning. Would you have come if you had been aware of it? I *know* you would not. You have not been at church at all this morning. One sees that with half an eye. Oh, you young men! you young men! You need looking after."

She had an almost affectionate air in her banter. She would not have been at all averse to looking after this one herself.

"What were you sitting up so late over, last night, that you could not have come to church? Bishop Caxton's sermon was something quite remarkable — even if you cared nothing about *me?*"

"Perhaps I am a little sermon proof. And to tell the truth there was something a little out of the common. I have dissolved my connection with Chippendale, Bond & Saxby. You see before you Russell Bainbridge, Esq., Attorney and Counselor-at-Law, Notary Public, Commissioner of Deeds for several States, and so forth, and so forth, all on his own account. I spent a good part of last evening in my new office, down among the ghosts of lower Broadway. The watchmen too flashed their lanterns at me and wanted to shoot me for a burglar. It is up in the mansard roof of the Magoon Building. As it contains but two chairs, a table, and book-shelves, the problem of producing a gorgeous effect became a rather difficult one. Have you no cases you want undertaken, no unlucky debtors you want persecuted? I know you are in need of a first-class bond and mortgage, — no commission to the lender. I have reason to believe that, unless this opportunity is taken advantage of, there will never be any others."

"Oh, yes, you shall have all my litigation. I shall try to become as quarrelsome as possible. How long will it take you before you are Judge?"

"It may not be this week perhaps, nor even the next. The law is proverbially 'slow, but sure.' It sometimes happens that the proportion of slowness to sureness is rather large."

Whether the meeting had acted as a stimulus or he had the faculty of putting his unpleasant moods under control, at will, Bainbridge now conducted himself with quite his usual animation.

They drew near in their turn the house of the merchant prince.

"Why do we not build *palaces?*" said Bainbridge,

in an impatient tone. "It is high time. Somebody estimates three hundred fortunes of a million dollars each, and plenty of these of from five to a hundred millions, in New York. What are they expecting to do with their money, these Crœsuses? Does experience show that their children spend it to any better advantage than themselves? I should say not. Here now is one more big, genteel house, with no idea above that of a wretched little comfort. No breadth, no grandeur, nothing monumental. Wherever there is a chance for an honest space of blank wall in an American building they punch it full of windows."

"I trust you are not forgetting Miss Harvey's relationship," interposed Miss Rawson.

"Not at all; but that need not trammel our explorations into the pure realm of the higher arts. Besides, these opinions are eternal verities, as it were. I get them from G. Lloyd and Aureolin Slab."

He directed a pleasant questioning glance at Ottilie, on the other side of Miss Rawson. He was wondering what resentment, if any, she cherished for his part in their peculiar first meeting now two months ago.

Ottilie raised her eyebrows at some of his views. She heard, for the first time, for instance, that comfort was so very despicable an ideal, but she found him amusing, and had no idea of taking further offense.

"Sardanapalus, now, Lucullus — that kind of person — understood the thing," he went on, confessedly with the extravagance of one whose theories were never likely to be put in practice. "For my part I should have a house as big as the Sub-Treasury, or the

Post-Office. I should have perfumes burned at my banquets, slaves with pots of jewels on their heads, roast peacock with the feathers on, and a pearl or two dissolved in everybody's wine-glass."

" And you would ride out in a circus chariot, I suppose, drawn by twenty-four white horses with nodding plumes? "

" I do not know but I should. On the whole, I think I should, — just to show that I was not to be browbeaten by other people's ideas of what was right and proper for one with so much larger opportunities than themselves."

" The people about you would be very insincere."

" I dare say I should not be very sincere myself, but we should try to have a glorious good time, all the same."

" You are dreadful to-day. I wonder we listen to you. — But here is our street. Good-by! Can you not come up on Friday evening? Ottilie and the Hasbrouck girls will be with me. Bring your violin. Out of order? Oh, well, come without it, then. *Good*-by ! "

" Perhaps Miss Harvey will let me put her in the car," volunteered Bainbridge. " Or," deferring politely, " perhaps she may even feel like walking down, — though I fear that would be too fatiguing? "

" I am an excellent walker," said Ottilie, hesitating.

The delightful morning and the many novel sights and sounds about allured her. If she had borne resentment it did not survive these fascinating influences. She did the young man a tardy justice. After all, perhaps it was not his fault that he had been present at the disagreeable interview.

" Thank you ; I will," she concluded. " One hardly knows what distance is, in this entertaining New York."

The arrangement may not have met with the most perfect approval of Miss Rawson. She repeated her farewells graciously, however. They saw her disappear down one of the blocks in the numerically entitled cross streets. Its collection of red sandstone façades, with their projecting porches, cornices, and window heads, seen in profile, had somehow the aspect of cliffs or palisades, the flights of heavy steps serving for the bank of débris, at the customary angle of forty-five degrees.

Ottilie said to Bainbridge that Mrs. Hasbrouck had lately come to take up her abode at the apartment house on the French plan, known as the Regina Flats, and that Amy and Lulu Hasbrouck had brought her down to spend the short spring vacation with them. " They would not take No for an answer," she said.

Bainbridge speculated as to whether she might have quixotically refused for this some invitation to visit her uncle's family instead. But she had not in fact been subjected to the temptation, though she may have somewhat expected it. The estrangement, so far as she was concerned, remained as before.

"Are you as great a Westerner as ever?" The young man inquired, when they had gone on some little way, discoursing with gradually decreasing formality.

" Oh, *bigoted*," she replied, laughing.

She was dressed this morning in black silk, of a soft character, fitting her neat figure excellently. She had crossed a white handkerchief, bordered with lace, over her shoulders and waist. In facing towards her companion, she was obliged to turn the upper part of her body, as the satin bows of her bonnet held her round chin a little stiffly. They might be fancied to take a certain pleasure in the embrace. The sun, shining directly from the south, as its way is at noon, was sometimes a little incommoding. To shade her eyes, she held up a small morocco prayer-book, pressed against the fringe of hair on her forehead, and looked out at him from beneath it.

They went down, past the unfinished Cathedral, the Moorish synagogue, the Egyptian reservoir; the castellated dwellings opposite, on the battlements of which an Ivanhoe, or a Sister Anne, might have appeared? They went down past the church of the Heavenly Rest, with the angels trumpeting to the heavens from its tower; past the tall hotels and apartment houses, past the random shops of tailors, confectioners, and jewelers, recommending themselves to neighborhoods where they were not greatly wanted, by a profuse display of Eastlake decoration.

A few tender flowers were seen in the beds along the base of the massive granite reservoir. In a dooryard, a peculiarly warm and sheltered nook, a magnolia shrub had already opened some of its large creamy blossoms, though the leaves had not appeared.

Ottilie exclaimed at the lovely sight.

"Such a tree might grow in the courts of Paradise," she said.

"There is a lesson in it. It is very young and simple," responded Bainbridge, affecting cynicism at the expense of the poor plant. "It will find that such a splendid effusiveness will not do. After it has put forth all its flowers, you will see it adopt a foliage more in keeping with the conditions of a cold and heartless world."

"How many interesting faces one sees in such a crowd!" said Ottilie, turning to it again.

"There are faces, occasionally, that almost give one a pang. He is never to see them again. They pass and that is the end of it. But no doubt it is better that it should be so."

"You do not think they would wear, then? You think they would not prove worth your knowing?"

"Perhaps I should not prove worth their knowing."

Bainbridge made himself her cicerone, and told her what he thought might be interesting of the people who went by. They met some of the upright Walkills, and the wicked Huyskamps. They met Watervliet the wit; young Stillsby, whose latest inanity goes the rounds with Watervliet's latest gibe; Blithewood Gwin the journalist; Wrye the banker, who was thought to carry Blithewood Gwin in his pocket almost as easily as a copy of his journal; Mrs. Stoneglass, whose literary receptions are so highly esteemed; Mrs. Eglantine, who turns her social position to account for the benefit of strugglers, and entertains her friends at other people's parties; the Hudson Hendricks, the Antrams, the Schinkos; Hackley and Hastings, two intimates of Rodman Harvey. They met Daisy Goldstone, Ada Trull, Alice Burlington; and the Misses Gilhooley, daughters of the ex-state senator of that name, who had laid the foundations of his fortune at a corner grocery in the "Bloody" Sixth Ward.

"What a variety of people! And how do you come to know about them?" exclaimed Ottilie.

"Oh, I have been at the Misses Gilhooley's parties as well as the Bourdons' and Antrams'. There are no nicer nor quieter girls now, since their convent education. It is an interesting class, that of the immigrants who have arrived at prosperity with their native traits unchanged. Refinement of speech and manners is mingled with dialects and boorish coarseness. Gilhooley did not wish to leave the Sixth Ward even after he was rich, but was prevailed upon to do so by these daughters, who insisted that they wanted their house on Madison Avenue while they were still young, and not when too old to enjoy it. They engage more or less in politics, and hold offices, — the wealthy ex-plumbers and liquor-saloon keepers. They wish their children to have educational advantages superior to their own. This often results in heart-burnings. They are purse-proud, too, and sometimes cut their children off in good old country style, for 'misalliances.'"

"You are a student of types and characters, then?"

"A student very backward at his lessons, if so. I have seen a random collection of people and places, while drifting along; that is all."

When Kingbolt and St. Hill were seen riding up in their dog-cart, he had something to say of them in their turn.

"Is it not severely disapproved of," inquired Ottilie, — "their parading up like that, just as the churches are letting out?"

"As likely as not they take some credit to themselves for going up with only a single horse, instead of, for instance, Kingbolt's tandem, of alternate bays and grays. As a matter of fact, nobody is better received in society than he."

" They put up with his bad qualities in consideration of certain good ones, I suppose ? "

" I think they rather put up with his good qualities in consideration of his bad. But nobody ever seriously disapproves of a person with such a property. Why, it must be five millions."

She gave him a reproachful glance.

" What is his occupation in life ? " she asked.

" Spending the revenues of the Eureka Tool Company is a very pretty occupation."

" Well, how does he spend them ? "

" He has numerous caprices. He went abroad with young Lloyd, the architect, to get up plans for model buildings, but quarreled with Lloyd, abandoned the project, and brought back this St. Hill with him instead. He spent a hundred thousand dollars on a church at Bridgehaven; then left it. His latest hobby, I believe, is the English sport of fox-hunting. He has his friends in red coats, corduroys, and top-boots. They go flying over the stone fences in Westchester County in the most picturesque and dangerous fashion. He has corresponding whims in his personal appearance. Sometimes he is very simple. Again, he will wear gold buttons on his dress coat, half a dozen rings on each hand, and bangles, like a woman, and pack up a dozen suits of clothes for a two days' visit. When he first went to Bridgehaven, in all his magnificence, the good people held up their hands in holy horror. They had never seen a 'swell' before, he said, and he thought he would show them what one was like."

When this person alighted, as described, and came back in company with the others, Ottilie had her glance of interest for the trio.

"What a beautiful girl!" she exclaimed, quite innocently referring to Angelica.

Bainbridge, embarrassed, found her looking at him inquiringly. "Your cousin, Miss Angelica Harvey," he said. "Mr. Austin Sprowle, to whom she is engaged, is the other one."

Ottilie was more embarrassed. Fate seemed to force a confidence between them on this basis. But she adopted the policy of entire frankness as the best.

"There have been disagreements, as you know, in our family, and I have seen little of these relatives," she said. "My cousin is very accomplished, I suppose, as well as beautiful?"

"I have the pleasure of but a slight acquaintance with her. She 'speaks every conceivable language,' as our friend Miss Rawson would say. That means French and German very well, and Italian enough for use in singing. She has visited titled people, and been presented at court. She rides, dances, and converses. She does not always converse too amiably. Some of the young men are said to be afraid of her on account of the sharp things she says to them. *She is a student of character, now.* She considers me, for instance, an extremely matter-of-fact person."

"And Mr. Sprowle, what is he like? What is *his* profession?"

"He is a genteel idiot, as I think. His profession is the same as Kingbolt's, though he has not the same money to carry it on with."

Ottilie was not wholly pleased. She would have preferred her kinsfolk to be left to their attitude of dignity, at least.

"I should hardly think my uncle would like such a match," she commented more distantly.

"They take him for his family. That is what the ladies want, and Mr. Harvey lets them have their own way. Sprowle is the sixth in descent from an ancestor who was a governor, or something of that kind, before the Revolution. Sometimes he is quoted in the fashionable intelligence as Austin Sprowle, Sixth, as though he were a part of a regular dynasty. You cannot do better than such a connection in the way of aristocracy in America."

"But do you not think that every young man should have some useful work to do?"

"That is one of those things that come under the head of 'Important if True.' Why should he? If the young millionaire were going to have a tremendous business talent, together with the power that his money gives him, where should the rest of us be? No! Polo, pigeon-shooting, racquets, coaching, yachting, fox-hunting, are his proper field, unless he can go into the arts. He should aim to hand down the best possible constitutions to the next generation or two. They will surely need them in the work of accumulating fortune anew, when it has slipped through their fingers in the natural course. — Sprowle does a little of all these things, but he is not very good at any."

"He might at least do them well."

"Why, so he might; but he does n't. It is a fine, hearty, natural existence," he continued, in a moralizing way, "like that of your Pottawatomies at Lone Tree." Ottilie frowned momentarily at this. "The polo mallet is the noblest implement of husbandry in the world, unless we except, perhaps, the hickory oar or the Creedmoor rifle. The wild young aborigine of civilization, instead of going down town to an office desk and a dyspepsia and a hectic flush, is off to the chase in the glades of the forest. Ti-*ra*! ti-*ra*! the rabbit, the quail, the snipe, the New Jersey woodcock! Back he comes at night, his sinews strengthened, his pulses bounding. He throws down the spoils at the feet of his primitive spouse. A few friendly savages of the vicinity, in evening dress, gather around the frugal mahogany to compare notes on the prowess of the day. And so to well-earned repose, on silken mattresses and eider-down pillows."

"But if he be as stupid as you say? A bright, intelligent girl might be capable of so much more under better circumstances."

"Oh, if the wise married only the wise, and the beautiful the beautiful" —

And with this they were at the Regina Flats.

Ottilie saw that much of what he had said was, on the face of it, drollery. But it was impossible at the same time to decide what part also might not have conveyed his own sentiments. She did not like such a confirmed tone of ridicule. And she did not like it in a person that he spoke of himself as one who had drifted in life, and had not squared his doings to a fixed plan.

VII.

PROSPECTS FROM HARVEY'S TERRACE.

The Regina Flats was near Madison Square. It was a very tall, red brick apartment house, with picturesque balconies and a slate roof of many stories. Bainbridge, whose own lodging was not far distant, renewed this morning the acquaintance of the Hasbrouck family, and began thereafter to make somewhat frequent visits to their elevated quarters in the Regina Flats.

He devised, also, some plans for the entertainment of his friends and of Ottilie, their guest. He took them to the opera and the theatre; and again to a dinner at one of the better restaurants kept in the foreign style. With the novelty of this last Ottilie was especially charmed.

The young man esteemed his income at this time as too paltry to be husbanded in the least, and spent it freely. He gave himself, in his association with these girls, somewhat the air of a mature person ministering to the pleasure of ingenuous youth. Perhaps he deceived himself with this view, but it was one in which the three Vassar undergraduates (who had no small idea of the importance of their ages and station) would hardly have coincided. He found in Ottilie an enthusiasm, an unhesitating belief in the possibility of doing anything and everything, whereas, by virtue of his own cynical enlightenment, he knew perfectly well that little or nothing could be done, or was worth doing if it could be. He said to himself that this was an amusing contrast and a distraction.

They two had plenty of opportunity for talking together. Mrs. Hasbrouck was of a social nature. Though she could entertain now in but a poor way, she soon had numbers of her compatriots who came to see her and her daughters, and engaged their attention.

These were largely Southern *émigrés* who, tired of stagnating at home, had at last gravitated to New York, to try and repair their broken fortunes. Most of the men had titles derived from the land or naval service of the extinct Confederacy, and a certain military way of carrying themselves, though now engaged in civil pursuits, often of an unpretending character. Among those of the other sex who came was the poetess, Mrs. Anne Arundel Clum. She had written, in the heat of the struggle,

"Will ye cringe to the hot tornado's rack,
 To the vampires of the North?"

but was now the fashion-and-literary editor of the "Saturday Evening Budget."

Ottilie learned something, in this way, of the Southern element in New York; something of persons who did not come as well as those who did. She took occasion to repeat to Bainbridge stories of battles and sieges she had heard, which gratified her taste for the marvelous. She expressed an interest, also, in some taciturn young men with traditional Virginian names, who showed themselves occasionally. They were studying medicine and engineering upon scanty means. Whereupon Bainbridge strangely found them of just no interest at all. She said that

Mr. Dinwiddie had related to her instances of a touching fidelity and devotion between slaves and their masters. Colonel Roanoke, in depicting the ruin of the war, had shown how the valuation of the State of Georgia, for example, had shrunk from six hundred millions of dollars to but one hundred and fifty millions, through the abolition of property in slaves alone.

"How singular it would have been," speculated Ottilie, "had the South succeeded instead of us. Supposing it were now alongside of us as a foreign country, with separate flag, and uniforms of its own, and a long line of custom-houses! It would have been interesting to travel in, would it not? And both sides would probably have gone on growing more and more unlike as they got older."

"It might have partly taken the place of Europe," said Bainbridge, "only we should not have regarded it with quite the same abject reverence which is the normal attitude of every good American."

"I do not wish to listen to any such sacrilege. Europe is my dream."

"Oh, I shall not do Europe any harm; but let it keep to its own side of the water."

Ottilie talked, being led on by her listener to do so, of the things of greatest moment in her present life. She spoke of her studies, her friends, the routine of the school. The characters in books she had read, it also appeared, had taken a strong hold upon her. She considered them worthy of not less animated discussion than real persons. There were secretly those among them she would have liked to imitate. She would have wished to be like Ethel Newcome, generously giving away half her property, herself remaining unknown; or Romola, attending upon the footsteps of the blind old scholar, her father; or Theresa, in "Picciola," softening the lot of the poor prisoner of Fenestrella.

Whatever was magnanimous quickly moved her. She was responsive, too, to music and fine poetry, and had a capacity for getting pleasure out of simple things. A shop window, an odd figure or an animal, furnished material. With a quick observation, too, she was sometimes rather ingenious in reflection.

Looking down into the street, for instance, from their balcony, she said, "How strange that the whole traffic should be for the purpose of supplying material wants! First a dry-goods store, then crockery, then millinery, then shoes, jewelry, drugs, hardware, groceries. Only once in a long time, books, pictures, or even flowers. Do you suppose, when we are sufficiently advanced, there will be just as many banners hung out, wagons going along, clerks behind the counters, and crowds passing in and out — all shopping for something for the higher faculties instead of the lower?"

But she was by no means an oppressively serious person. Bainbridge was privileged to see her in moods of a breezy playfulness, that bore out the forecast of her illuminating smile. She carried her hands in the pockets of her jacket. She sometimes whistled a little to herself, over a piece of embroidery. Seated at the piano, she threw out her arms in wild despair or disdain over certain music.

There came up some of those discussions on verbal points so common by reason of the want of logic in our language. Should " either " be pronounced *e*-ther or *i*-ther. Should one say *ac*climated or ac*cli*mated, or spell certain words with double letters or single? These were the problems mooted. Ottilie secured the large dictionary in her lap and bestowed herself in an easy-chair. She had placed an ottoman for her feet, the better to sustain its weight; and this afforded a glimpse of small slippers and pretty, blue, clocked stockings.

"I say *i*-ther when I am afraid of people, and *e*-ther when I am not," she announced, as her ultimatum on that point.

"Webster gives but one *l*," declared Bainbridge, arguing a question of spelling.

"But *I* give two," she asserted with intrepidity.

"Do you mean to say that you don't believe in Webster?"

"I mean to say that I believe in Ottilie Harvey."

But when she was forced, by general pressure of opinion, to consult the authority, it was found against her. She refused to announce the decision, shut the covers abruptly together, and endeavored, by flagrant subterfuges, to disguise her defeat.

The balcony of the apartment commanded an extensive view. There could be seen from it the interior of a city block, with occasional vines, a metal statue or urn, in the depths of the small yards, divided by high fences, like bins. There was a glimpse of Booth's Theatre, the Grand Opera House, and a bit of the heights of Hoboken.

Ottilie had excellent eyes, and was pleased to make tests of their ability. Her companions were sometimes skeptical as to these. She read, for instance, on the high wall of a distant manufactory, the inscription, "Hackley & Valentine, Church, School, and House Furniture." But Bainbridge scoffingly declared it to be "Coffins, Millinery, and Assorted Railroad Ties" instead. He pretended further to discern the monogram on the seal ring of a man leaning out of a window at the other end of the block. When the glass was brought, however, it appeared that she was right. She endeavored to give the credit for her good vision, somehow, to her much-maligned West.

One afternoon she went out with Bainbridge to visit studios and picture galleries. She was to be left afterwards at Harvey's Terrace, where she wished to call upon Wilhelmina Klauser, now returned from her musical studies at Leipsic. The Klausers would see to her safe return in the evening.

They went to Tenth Street, and Twenty-Third Street, and thence to the well-known gallery of a dealer in works of the best class, of the modern schools of Paris, Munich, Rome, and Madrid.

Hardly had they entered this place when Ottilie recognized her cousin, Selkirk Harvey. He was in company with a richly dressed lady, and a man who, though quite bald, was of a figure still young. This latter spoke in an effeminate voice. The three were grouped about a salesman, who expatiated on the merits of canvases before them. Selkirk came over presently and shook hands with her. Then he led her back to make the acquaintance of the lady, who was his mother and her aunt. She made, also, the acquaintance of the gentleman with them, who proved to be Mr. Aureolin Slab.

Mrs. Rodman Harvey stared at her niece in a way no doubt permissible "in the family," and complimented her broadly, as if it were a surprising circumstance that she should be so presentable a person.

"I have heard of you. Your uncle told me about you," she said; "but I have been so busy — I have so many cares — Nobody who has not been through them can have the faintest conception. We are decorating and furnishing the house now, and it seems as if every mortal being connected with it had conspired to annoy me. We are looking at pictures for the gallery." She paused, as if for some observation.

"Ah, indeed!" murmured Ottilie.

"What we had in Union Square are but the merest item towards filling up," continued Mrs. Rodman Harvey. "Mr. Slab has been kind enough to give me his assistance. What do you think of that?" pointing very close with her parasol. "Isn't it too dreadful? Here, Mr. Bainbridge, perhaps you are a critic. Did you ever *see* such sheep in your life? One would not have them at any price."

She waited for no replies. Ottilie thought her style of conversation very fragmentary, and also that it must be rather unpleasant for the dealer and for Aureolin Slab.

But the dealer was used to people of many kinds, and led on with unwearied patience from one to another of his Bouguereaus, Gérômes, Jacquets, Knaus, Von Marckes, Pasinis, Michettis, and Madrazos. He dwelt on their desirability as investments, and enforced his argument with anecdotes of the remarkable advance in price of certain names.

As to Aureolin Slab, this gentleman was never so happy as when selecting a work for a friend. He had lost the fortune he once possessed, and was no longer able to do it for himself. He spoke now of broken and pure colors, "mass," "focus," and "sympathies of lines, radiating and converging." He spread his open palm at times before a picture, without other comment, as if paddling deliciously in its combined excellences.

"If I had only thought, I could have sent for you just as well as not," said Mrs. Harvey to Ottilie later, when they were a little apart from the others. "Can you not come to me now for a few days? With whom are you staying? What Hasbroucks? Oh, those must be the people who have made your uncle so much trouble!"

"And I hardly think you ought to go about with a young man alone," she added, glancing at Bainbridge.

Ottilie departed, having refused this invitation, and not over-pleased with the scrutiny to which she had been subjected, nor the unpleasant allusion to her friends. Nevertheless, she had seen the purchase by her aunt of an actual Gérôme, — the photographs of which alone, in the window of the principal picture store at Lone Tree were esteemed a choice artistic treasure, — and she was deeply impressed.

Her companion took pains to sound her as to what change of sentiment, if any, had been operated by the meeting. He found her more warmly devoted to the Hasbrouck cause than ever.

"And you," she said, after some impartial remark of his, "I do not understand how you can be friendly to both sides."

"In international quarrels — and this had a kind of international aspect, you know — the justice of the cause is considered."

"I do not see that there is anything equal about it. The Hasbroucks paid once, and now my uncle wishes to make them pay it again. He has got the courts to decide in his favor, and it is only some minor delay that keeps him from taking everything they have. Meanwhile they have had little use of their property for years. The Confederate government passed a law that debts of its own citizens to Northerners were to be confiscated. This was one of them. But it seems that after the war the Confederate laws were not considered binding."

" Well no, hardly," said Bainbridge.

" And so they must pay twice. *I* think it outrageous ; that is what I think."

" The courts do not seem to think so, as you admit."

" But they *had* to pay it," insisted Ottilie, impatiently. " They may not have wished to; I know they did not ; but their government made them."

" It was their misfortune, then, to have that kind of a government. I fail to see where that benefits Rodman Harvey. It simply raised a forced loan from them, to that particular amount, whatever it was, and matters between them and Rodman Harvey remained as before. We are sorry, of course, that it is our friends the Hasbroucks, but the thing is perfectly just. Your uncle, besides, has never had any means of knowing what agreeable and deserving people they are, and he cherishes a peculiar bitterness towards the South. Perhaps if there were anybody to put the case to him in a very persuasive way he might be induced to relent."

Ottilie may have been more impressed by this suggestion than at the moment appeared. But she said, perversely, " I should not think lawyers would want to practice their heavy arguments on mere ordinary persons, unversed in legal technicalities. My aunt said I ought not to go about alone with you, and I do not think I will."

"*Did* she say that, now?" he exclaimed, in a hearty way, with a laugh. "Has it reached that point? Well, you and I know better. This is the chaperon business, the latest great American problem. A matron must be on hand everywhere, to play propriety. Perhaps it is an indication of our growing wickedness. At any rate, since communication with Europe has become so easy, in these last years, European manners are rapidly making their way here. The amusing thing is to see aspiring young women forcing it, as a pure piece of fashion, upon their dazed mammas, who would never have thought of it of their own accord. It has considerable vogue already, however. If you lived in New York I dare say you would come to it, since it is often convenient to follow the mode, even when it is based upon absurdity. But let us not begin yet. Mrs. Hasbrouck is a sensible woman, and she has not enforced the rule. Besides, it has scarcely touched the interior yet, and you and I well know what can be done there."

This view seemed to Ottilie wholly reasonable. She recalled so well the entire freedom prevailing at home, and was met by this restriction so almost for the first time, that the puzzling caution of her aunt had seemed adapted to no other purpose than to be used, as she had used it, as a pleasantry.

By some favoritism in early times the rocky site of the old Muffett mansion, now Harvey's Terrace, had been exempted from the general grade. It rose close by the East River, a kind of domestic Ehrenbreitstein. All of its sides but that of the sloping ascent from Second Avenue, were precipitous. At one end of the *cul-de-sac* formed by the houses on the top was the gate to a German garden and pavilion, which was utilized for Turnverein and Saengerbund feasts, balls of the Dennis J. O'Mulligan Association, the Box-makers' Union, the Lady Violets, and the Happy Seven, for political caucuses, and Father McIntyre's lectures on the Ancient Greatness of Ireland. Near the centre of the Terrace was left, between the houses, a small space closed by an iron railing, for a promenade and lookout upon the wide river view.

Harvey's Terrace was very quiet and genial on the April afternoon when our friends entered it. They took the wrong turning at first, in seeking their number. As they passed, something of the blue prospect, and the sails moving in the river, could be discerned completely through the outer line of houses.

"It is like looking into the magic crystals in which the old soothsayers used to pretend to read the prophecies of fate," said Ottilie.

They stopped by the railing, as they retraced their steps, for the enjoyment of the view. There lingered near it, also, a shabby old person, whose only object seemed to be to warm himself in the early spring sunshine.

A wooden oriel, projecting from the side-wall of the house abutting at the left of the space, held, as it were a bird in its cage, a blonde young woman, sewing.

The river below was blue. It was ruffled by the breeze, and the swift passage of steamboats, and ships dragged in and out by tugs. The ships' masts came nearly up to a level with the eye. An interminable expanse of red and black suburban city, bristling with steeples, spread around the farther shores. In the midst of the ruffled blue river lay a number of islands, with singular buildings upon them. These were explained to Ottilie to be the institutions for the poor, sick, and criminals, housed by the great city in the stern charity of self-protection.

It was the penitentiary that especially fixed the young girl's attention, and exercised a kind of fascination upon her. A long, low, sullen, granite building, lying there under the great light and air, it blasted the sight. A gang of convicts came out of it, and marching in lock-step, moved like some strange sort of reptile life across the ground, from which it was hardly distinguishable in color.

A guard-boat, manned by convicts, and carrying a keeper, armed with a rifle, was patrolling the island, in the stream. There might also have been noticed a yawl, which had put out from the shore, and, clumsily handled, as if by inexperienced persons, was drawing near the guard-boat.

Something as it were bitter rose in Ottilie's throat, and a tender pity in her heart.

Bainbridge also was serious. "Great heaven!" he exclaimed; "that there is but one life to live, and some human beings must pass it like that!"

"No, there is, there must be, another!" said Ottilie, with fervor. "These inequalities convince one of it more than anything else."

The shabby old person lounging in the sun, not quite so inoffensive as he had at first seemed, noticing the object of their momentary interest, began by way of overture at conversation —

"There's them in it as shud be out, and minny a wan out as shud be in it, so there is."

Bainbridge at first returned him a careless monosyllable, but finding that he came so close as to annoy Ottilie, said sharply, "Go off, will you! We don't want you here."

"I will not go off, then," said the man defiantly. "Has any wan o' yez a better right? Used n't it to be me own house and home? Used n't I to be livin' here aisy and paceful, wud me neighbors, till Harvey kem wud his lyers, and his police, and his sowljers, and evicted us out of it?"

"Oh, if you are going to set up for the Last of the Mohicans, or Philip of Pokanoket, — brooding over the ruins of empire, and that sort of thing," said the young man humorously. "I dare say you have heard of the Last of the Mohicans?"

"I *have* not," replied the man sullenly, "nor the first of them, nayther, — wud your Geo*h*egans, and Poky-Woky."

Ottilie could scarcely contain her laughter at his discomfited air. But the movements of the awkwardly managed yawl in the river were becoming very peculiar, and she turned to watch them. It had approached quite close to the patrol-boat, and the armed guard seemed to be warning it away.

The man drew off somewhat farther, and, having meditated his grievance, turned back with —

"I did not hear o' thim, but I heard tell o' chatein' a poor man out of his bit of a house and ground. And I heard tell o' yourself, that was wan o' thim that was helpin' wud it. And I heard tell o' chatein' a bank, what is more," he added, after a pause, bending out his head in increasing excitement. "Harvey's Terrus, is it? It's over beyant, on the Island, Rodman Harvey shud be, be rights."

"What *does* he mean?" asked Ottilie, turning back, with an anxious expression.

"Nothing at all. He was one of the squatters, who were put off when the land was wanted for useful purposes, and naturally feels sore over it. I recollect him as particularly violent at the time. His name is McFadd. They say he was a bank messenger once, but lost his position through shiftless habits, and finally drifted to this place, where it cost him nothing to live.

"See here, McFadd," he appended, for the benefit of that person, "worse will probably happen to you than being put off a piece of land that was not yours, if you do not keep a civil tongue in your head."

"Others was knowing to it, besides meself," persisted McFadd, — " plinty more. The prisident o' the bank was knowing to it. A party be the name of Hackley was knowing to it. A party be the name of Gammage, of the same Antarctic Bank, was knowing to it. Did n't I go to the prisident meself, thinkin' I'd get a bit o' satisfaction be rayson of it, but divil the satisfaction did I get. What was the word o' the likes o' me agin the word o' the likes o' him? But was n't I the missinger o' the bank meself? and did n't I carry the tillygrams? and did n't I bring Harvey to it, affrighted out of the life of him?"

Bainbridge recalled that Gammage was an elderly, broken-down personage, once an occupant of positions of respectability, for whom he had of late obtained an employment in addressing circulars at the office of the Prudential Land and Loan Company. He recollected having heard from Gammage, also, some formless hints to the detriment of Rodman Harvey. These were nothing more, he was convinced, than the mouthings of an impotent malice with McFadd, and of a mind disordered by excesses with the other. But the coincidence of the mention of the name made him determine to question, at a favorable opening, the old clerk who had become his *protégé*, and draw from him whatever he might have to say, in more definite form.

He was anxious now, for Ottilie's sake, to check this flow of abuse. Before he could take any step to do so, however, she uttered a little excited cry. It was doubtful if she had heard the latter remarks of McFadd at all.

The yawl from the shore had collided with the patrol-boat, and capsized it. The armed guard, losing his rifle, which sank to the bottom of the river, was forced to swim to secure his own safety. His convict crew were soon helped aboard the marauding boat, and supplied with fresh clothing. Their now openly discovered friends at once turned back for the shore, and pulled this time with the sweep of trained oarsmen. So sudden and bold had been the manœuvre that they reached the covert supplied by the freighting schooners, the coal and wood yards, the shot tower, and the breweries fringing the water's edge at Harvey's Terrace, before anything could be done on either side.

McFadd was greatly excited. He raised and lowered himself on his stiff knee-joints during the spectacle, and cried, "Heaven be wid ye, boys!"

He now hobbled down from the Terrace to the concluding scene below, where heated policemen, with clubs and revolvers drawn, had begun to beat a grand battue among the lumber yards.

Ottilie, in trepidation lest the runagates should appear in her own vicinity, now made haste to her destination, and took leave of her escort. It proved to be the very house next at hand, and the bird-like young woman in the window no other than Wilhelmina Klauser. The unusual incident they had witnessed together became the basis of an animated acquaintance at once. At the boarding-house dinner, at which Ottilie also took part, since Klauser had not yet returned from down town, the whole subject of the escape and of the prison in the neighborhood was treated of, in but a facetious light. The sentiment of McFadd was also heard repeated, to wit, that there were many outside the prison who might justly be in it.

The humorous tone was that which generally prevailed. The lively Mr. Cutler made many sallies. The newest piece of gossip in the house was his engagement to the teacher, Miss Speller. It had just transpired. They would be married within the month, Ottilie was told. The quiet, plain Miss Finley, Miss Speller's inseparable friend, would go to live with them.

The waitress, Sarah, offered the guests such alternatives as "roast beef or boiled mutton," "baked dumpling or boiled Indian pudding."

"I will take a little boiled tea, Sarah," or, "Some baked bread, Sarah," said Cutler, by way of parody.

To which the flustered Sarah, unable to cope with him on his own ground, said under her breath, "I suppose you think that very smart. Well, *I don't.*"

This afternoon made a deep impression on Ottilie. The escape of the prisoners was an incident, indeed, to be taken back to school and narrated among the experiences of her vacation. It proved to have been a case of collusion with an influential prisoner. He was in the boat, and the apparently ill-used keeper had been well paid for his ducking. The rescue of the others, some of whom were subsequently recaptured, had been merely incidental.

Her active mind and sympathies opened quickly to a subject with which she had never before been confronted at close quarters. She asked both Bainbridge and others many questions about it. A party was made up to visit the city prison, "the Tombs." She talked with hardened malefactors, and accepted their versions of the malice and errors of others, which alone had placed them there, with great ingenuousness.

"Why is nothing *done*," she inquired, "to make such people better, — to prevent its going on? If women, now, had the authority, it seems to me *they* would *do* something."

"I am sure they do a great deal," answered Bainbridge. "They send all the first-class murderers flowers and quail-on-toast and their photographs, and try to get them out and introduce them into the best society."

But she was serious, and desired to learn what steps had been taken for the permanent reformation of criminals. He could think of nothing further than a plan at Valencia, in old Spain, where forty-three distinct trades are taught in the prison, and the inmates allowed a share in the proceeds of their labor; and the Maconochie plan, by which convicts of good behavior are finally left almost free of supervision. But he had some pamphlets which he could send her, on her return to school.

"Only you must tell me, when you have finished

them," he said, " which plan, on deliberate reflection, you like the best. Will you not write me a purely philanthropic note, setting forth your system for the final settlement of these vexed questions?"

It was not etiquette, at Lone Tree, to be hasty in opening correspondence with young men, although one might walk or ride with them to her heart's content.

"I am sure I shall not have any opinion," she replied; "but if I should — Well, I will see."

A considerable part of the pleasure of her vacation had been due to him. She thought it a little odd that he should care to be so considerate to her, when his way was to scoff at everybody and everything else. He seemed to delight in representing himself, too, to the worst advantage. One would have thought that he was in favor of famine, flood and pestilence, arson and house-breaking, and opposed to all civilized observances.

As to money matters, he said, "What you have spent, and that alone, you have had." And again, "It is better to live rich than to die rich."

He perhaps put the climax to his preposterous sayings with the statement, —

"It is more heroic to be a martyr to error — conscious error, — than truth. Then you have nothing at all to sustain you, and it is pure, solid heroism."

With his apparent absence of convictions on all the important matters of life, matters as good as settled beyond dispute, Ottilie thought him a person to be looked at with serious misgivings, from any other point of view than that of a very superficial acquaintance.

Miss Rawson thought it odd, too, that he should care to interest himself in an immature school-girl, "a mere bread-and-butter miss," when he so rarely came to see her. He presented himself on the Friday evening when Ottilie was at her house. She took occasion thereupon to compliment Ottilie to him in an artful way.

"You see at once that she is not a New Yorker," she said. "There is a certain lack of something — But I *like* it, you know. It is such a pity that her uncle is so hard! There is not the slightest possibility, I suppose, that he will ever do anything for her. And her family, in that obscure Western hamlet, — perfectly upright and honest, of course, but so poor. — He might do so much for them also."

And to Ottilie she said of Bainbridge with a meaning smile, which the young girl took to indicate a kind of proprietorship, "Is he not charming? You must like him very much, or we shall quarrel."

VIII.

A FLAW IN A CORNER-STONE.

THE merchant prince had alighted from his buggy, on his way down town, every few mornings, during the building of his mansion, and become a familiar figure in the neighborhood. He had peered into corners, turned over bits of loose material with his boot, and put sharp questions to his workmen, lifting his hand to his ear, in his awe-inspiring way, to catch their replies.

When all was complete he paid off those engaged, having first beaten them down to the lowest point, and they departed in such contentment as they might. To the general harmony there was one exception.

The stone-mason, Jocelyn, had grumbled for some time, claiming to have taken his contract too cheap, and to be carrying it out at a loss to himself. There had been no relief for this, however. He had been obliged to acquiesce in the brusque opinion of Rodman Harvey, that it was altogether his own affair and he should have kept a sharper lookout.

But now, at the last moment, an off-set of some hundreds of dollars was also demanded from him, for a bit of defective stone-work. This, he thought might have been spared him in consideration of what he had already suffered. It was the last straw, and it broke the camel's back. Jocelyn went away in a rage, vowing never to do another stroke of work for so hard a task-master. He obtained such poor satisfaction as he might from retailing everything he could learn to the disadvantage of Rodman Harvey. He did not disdain even the scurrilous stories of the shanty tenants, which he had heard while engaged in building the houses in Harvey's Terrace. He talked in his abusive way among other places, at a Nassau Street restaurant, where he was accustomed to lunch when coming to deposit funds in his bank.

Jocelyn, in his irritation, was disposed to deny the plainest evidence of the senses. There was, in fact an imperfection, in the corner-stone of the house itself. There began to appear at once a scaling of the surface — a defect to which the red sandstone of which New York is so largely built is subject, but only with time, and hard usage by the elements. This scaling continued. One day a lamina as thick as a clap-board detached itself, and disclosed below a very singular thing.

There was seen one of those large fossil bird tracks found in the Connecticut River formation, from the quarries of which the stone was derived.

"Anything connected with birds, you know, is dreadful," Mrs. Rodman Harvey declared. She chose to profess a superstitious awe at the occurrence, as if it were a kind of harpy clutch of destiny upon the house. "If a bird flies in at your window, now, — nothing could be worse. I have known so many instances."

But Dr. Wyburd held learnedly that it was not certain that this was the track of a bird. It was as likely to be that of the *Otozoön Moodii*, a reptile of the Labyrinthodont order, and the Triassic period, which had often attained to a height of twelve feet.

Selkirk approved of the odd foot-print from the curiosity hunter's point of view. Angelica fancied it more like a hand than a claw, and was pleased to find in it a certain resemblance to the Muffett crest, in use on their note-paper and carriage panel. It might be taken as a testimony to their distinction on the mother's side, come down expressly from the Mesozoic age.

The block was therefore neatly surfaced again, and the singular mark allowed to remain. As it began to attract attention from passers-by, a magnolia shrub was set out to partially disguise it.

After Harvey had finished his series of visits to the house, he was followed by his wife and daughter, who had taken the matter of decorating and furnishing particularly into their own hands. It may be fair to say that Miss Angelica devoted her chief attention to her own apartments. She succeeded at last in getting a sitting-room done to her satisfaction, in pear-wood and gray silk plush; and her bed-room in flowered silk chintz and gilt, this last of a charming general pink effect.

Mrs. Rodman Harvey summoned this popular arranger of interiors, then that. She gave a room to each; then got one to going over the work of the other; and embroiled herself more or less with all. She was aided by the suggestions of Aureolin Slab, who, though pained to the heart by the exterior of the house, deemed it his duty to save it to what extent he could from a similar vandalism within. Then came the dealers in the smaller objects of art, who filled the rooms as full as they could hold of their elegant wares. The result was of a magnificence that the inexperienced in New York houses would hardly have inferred from without. It was finished so as to be ready for occupation by the family somewhat before the opening of the watering-place season.

There was time, for example, for a notable entertainment which took the form of a reception to the President of the United States. The merchant prince considered a house-warming, to which the world should be invited on a liberal scale, a promising means for the increase of his popularity. It happened that the President was to be in town for the dedication of some public monument, and accepted his invitation.

If Mrs. Rodman Harvey had cares beyond the ken of most mortals even at ordinary times, it may be conceived that they were not diminished now. Her husband, hearing her complaints, suggested, as he had suggested before, that the experiment of taking Ottilie to write her letters, and otherwise assist in lightening her burdens, should be tried.

"Oh, you cannot have relations," objected the brilliant Angelica, impetuously. "There are their dreadful feelings; and they always expect to be treated as equals."

The idea apparently did not meet with Mrs. Harvey's favor, perhaps because it had not at first been her own. She was led by it, however, to include Ottilie in the long list of guests for the "reception." She sent up to Vassar for her, asking her to come down the Saturday before — the entertainment being set for Tuesday. It would be an easy way, at any rate, to discharge obligations the niece might fancy them to be under on the score of kinship.

Ottilie's invitation came late. She was asked to reply by telegraph, and to start immediately. Could she have had the option of writing, she might have framed excuses; but a refusal by telegraph must be curt and ungracious at best.

She had had repeated instructions from her mother that it was a Christian duty, as it were, both to herself and her family, to receive in an affable spirit any overtures that might come from this influential source. She remembered the arguments of Bainbridge, and she remembered the real Gérôme she had seen purchased. The Hasbrouck girls themselves, who surprised her meditating over the letter, urged her to go by all means. The opportunity to meet the President, they said, was not to be neglected. She set out, therefore, and the feud in the family was to this extent healed. She knew very well what she should do for the Hasbroucks, could she ever gain sufficiently the confidence of her uncle, their creditor.

The grand mansion proved for her a near realization of the rich properties she had dreamed of in her histories and romance. "The bedstead in my aunt Alida's room," she wrote home, ministering to the eager curiosity that would naturally be entertained there, " is of carved teak-wood, with a canopy of velvet and lace, and it stands upon a platform. I am told by her French maid, Rosine, that it cost six thousand dollars. All the toilet articles in my cousin Angelica's chamber, are of ivory and silver," etc., etc., etc.

There was a fire-place in the wide entrance-hall, with vases and plates of Italian majolica above it, warm rugs before it, and on each side a vase of *cloisonné*, taller than Ottilie's head. A flat porphyry bowl, standing on a pedestal of old Japanese bronze, as large as a baptismal font, was for the cards of visitors.

She climbed a stair-case so broad and easy that the climbing was hardly an effort. It had lamps alternately of silver and porcelain, upheld by bronze figures, and it had tubs of tropical plants along its platforms. In the picture-gallery her Gérôme, with plenty of other masters who pleased her even better, when she came to know them, was now securely established. The immediate approach to the gallery was by two short flights of marble steps, with a marble balustrade between. On the way you passed the soft bather, Musidora, in marble, faced by a twisting Samson Agonistes.

The principal drawing-room, upholstered in silks and plushes, in sulphur yellow, was in the lightly severe yet elegant Louis XVI. style. It had a small gallery projecting for musicians. A lesser drawing-room in damasked rose-color, was fantastic with the gilded rococo scroll-works of Louis XV.

It was her cousin Selkirk who interested himself to go about with Ottilie and explain the puzzling variety of styles. She found a gravely rich Henri II. library hung in old tapestries. The dining-room had straight chairs and dark Italian cabinets, so rich with carving that no vacant space of the natural wood was seen. Besides the regular collection in the library, there was in a small reception-room a series of choice volumes in white vellum, inclosed in ebony cases.

There were wrought and embroidered tissues of silks and wools, crystal chandeliers with wax tapers, porcelain lamps, their light softened by colored silk shades, and tables to contain them covered with velvet and bordered with Venetian lace. There were screens, clocks, musical boxes, statuettes, objects of ivory, pearl, ormolu, blue China, and Limoges enamel. The whole was one revel of glowing color and luxury unstinted by thought of expense.

Ottilie was impressed, too, by her cousin Angelica. She saw her first leaning, in a becoming attitude, on the back of a fauteuil, in one of the rich parlors. She bowed down in ingenuous reverence before the many accomplishments of this young woman, her costly education, her travels, her reception at foreign courts. So many advantages, such beauty, and so high-bred an aspect could hardly consist, it seemed to her, with any but the most dignified and worthy character.

She did not quite understand how her aunt need really be so agitated over the management of her servants, and all the rest. She thought one of the first privileges of wealth would have been to purchase immunity from vulgar cares. "Aunt Alida" took her on her tours of inspection about the house, bustling now with preparations for the festival. She made her a sharer in many confidences, and found here a jewel and there a ribbon which she forced upon her with a lavish open-handedness which proved one of her traits.

"There are times," she confided to her hearer, "when it seems as if I must put on my bonnet and leave all. I would fly to the ends of the earth, in search of but one moment of blessed, blessed peace. Fourteen mortal servants, the last thought of each of whom is to do what they were engaged for, and the first to persecute me."

The tasks of the bond-slaves of Egypt, it appeared, the sufferings in Dante's Inferno, were but a bagatelle to her own.

Yet Mrs. Rodman Harvey retained a plump comeliness. Though often threatening, she did not put on her bonnet for any more desperate purpose than to go out with it wherever it was needed conformably to the usages of the best society.

Nor did Ottilie reconcile herself at once to the full-grown men in livery. They seemed clumsy and out of place in-doors. She would have preferred, for her simpler tastes, neat, trim maid-servants. The English butler, William Skiff, with his baldness and false teeth, was as imposing as a bishop. Alphonse, the footman and waiter, had a sort of grenadier aspect. He should have presented arms when you came in at the door. If he had, that would have been something worth while. The family had brought him back with them from their last tour in Europe.

Angelica had a cultivated taste in servants. She declared the most simply horrible thing in the world to be a waiter with a moustache, instead of the conventional side whiskers and shaven lip. This view of the horrible did not strike Ottilie as quite of the profundity to be expected from such a source.

On the evening of Ottilie's arrival there came in to play billiards with the merchant in his sumptuous new billiard-room, his friends Hackley and Hastings. These two men were cronies of Rodman Harvey, so far as so staid a person could be said to have cronies. Both, as it appeared, resided in the vicinity. With Hastings came his wife, who was young and pretty. She tripped up-stairs to the boudoir of Mrs. Harvey for a confidential chat, while their husbands were knocking about the ivory balls below. Ottilie was presented to her. Quite an intimacy sprung up between them, which was increased the next day by the young girl's admiration for two pretty children whom she was accorded the privilege of seeing put to bed. It ended in her being practically given into the charge of this lady for the entertainment. Her aunt and cousin were to have their hands extremely full. She was not to receive with them, but to be simply a minor guest among the great number invited, — an arrangement that suited her taste exactly.

IX.

"TO MEET THE PRESIDENT OF THE UNITED STATES."

The list of invitations, "To meet the President of the United States," as the inscription on an impressive large square of pasteboard ran, was sufficiently large to include Russell Bainbridge. The young man considered it desirable to appear at the reception of a patron, who might be a more useful patron yet. He had a certain interest, besides, in the new chief magistrate of the country, then but lately installed into office.

He first paid a call or two, dropped in at a regular weekly reception of the same date, and arrived at Rodman Harvey's at about eleven o'clock. A fine, drizzling rain was falling. The glowing roof of the picture-gallery could be seen from a distance, lighting up the humid atmosphere above it. A striped canvas awning stretched down from the portal of the house and across the sidewalk. Similar awnings were out to-night at the fashionable restaurants and theatres.

By the awning's mouth lingered a few spectators, kept in check by a policeman, watching patiently under their umbrellas the arrival of the guests. The elegant men got down, with the collars of their great-coats turned up and silk mufflers about their throats. Wonderful creatures, in voluminous draperies of white, pale pink, blue, and saffron, followed. Their skirts were gathered close about them, and they alighted upon the carpeted stone with dainty rebounds. The carriages were ranged in an interminable file on either side of the street. Their wet varnish glistened in the gas-light. The gas-lights themselves were reflected mysteriously from the wet sidewalks, as if black streams of fathomless depth, somehow curiously solidified to bear the weight of the figures which trod them.

The gloom without gave but the more effect to the brightness within. Two orchestras were playing: one in the music-gallery of the principal drawing-room; the other in a spacious temporary apartment formed, for the convenience of the dancers, by roofing over the yard at the rear of the mansion. The banisters of the grand staircase were adorned with a wreathing of smilax and roses. A deep cornice and wainscot belt of white flowers, starred with others in color, extended around the small drawing-room. Over the spot where the President stood, with the hostess and her daughter beside him, hung a mammoth ball of violets.

No expense had been spared, as the saying is. Some elderly guests, brushing up their mature whiskers at the mirror in the dressing-room, endeavored, in a practical way, to compute it. There were those who said, —

"Harvey is not doing all this without an object, either. He has his designs upon the distinguished guest of the evening. He hopes to obtain from him the office of secretary of the treasury. He has long intrigued for it. This, chiefly, is what his late political activity means. He considers a seat in Congress from the foremost district of New York, as a stepping-stone. No doubt his not having taken part in national affairs before has been construed against him."

"The health of the present incumbent is not good," said one speaker. "In case of the appointment of a successor, it is eminently proper that a secretary should be chosen, for once, from the commercial metropolis of the country. Who more suitable, in that event, — so Harvey thinks, — than himself?"

"He knew the President of old, it seems," said another. "He employed him in some railroad case in the West. Well, I do not say that Harvey would be my choice, but stranger things have happened than that he should get it."

"I see that General Burlington is here," remarked another. "He and the President were in the war together. I suppose he has laid aside his difference with Harvey for the time being, to come and pay his respects. He is quite right. He is a level-headed person, Burlington."

These elderly gossips were not above comments, also, on feminine points, and on the current social scandals. They retailed two late Huyskamp escapades. A granddaughter had run away with an adventurer, whom she had been in the habit of meeting in Central Park, instead of going to Madame Bellefontaine's school, for which she started with her books regularly. The second Mrs. Huyskamp, Mrs. James, had also been seen coming out of a cemetery with her head on the shoulder of Northfleet, a man much younger than herself.

"That I deny *in toto*," said Watervliet, availing himself of an opportunity to repeat a witticism which had met with success at the club. "It stands to reason. You cannot have old heads on young shoulders."

The indifferent feeling with which Bainbridge had come to the party changed to something much more like pleasure when he unexpectedly found Ottilie there. That young woman colored a little on meeting him. She was reflecting as to what he would think of her vacillation of purpose.

She was with Mrs. Hastings, who had presented to her a number of young men. Among these was young Stillsby, whose repute for wisdom was not of the most profound. She had been impressed at first by this person's air of fashion, then wondered, and been amused, at the character of many of his sayings. The new acquaintances hovered about her, and Bainbridge at first could have her to himself but little.

"You did not write to me, as you promised," he said, seizing one of the opportunities. "I have lived for nothing else ever since."

"You have lived very well then, apparently. *Did* I promise to write? Well, I have been busy. It is but a short time now till our Commencement. And by the way, since you remind me of it, I have used your pamphlets in the preparation of my graduating essay. It is to be 'The Reformation of Criminals.'"

"Bravo! At last we have the matter settled. So you are to graduate. And then —?"

"I return to my home in the West. Glad enough I shall be to get back to dear old Lone Tree again."

"I am sorry for that. — I thought perhaps you might be intending to come here. — Your uncle would not leave you a great fortune, I dare say, but he would not be bad to live with. If you should get on as well with the rest as with him, I think you might count on a very tolerable existence. Why not return?"

"Nobody has axed me, sir," she said, misquoting the old ballad. Then, as if the subject were not a wholly comfortable one, she changed it, with " Well, you cannot deny that *this* is palatial."

"Oh yes, I can. Do not limit my capacity for denying too hastily. In the palace there should be a noble poverty of effect. They understand it in Italy. There should be a few handsome things along the walls, and the central spaces left free, for the noble occupants to walk up and down in, with their hands behind their backs, planning statecraft, wars, and matrimonial alliance, with the princes, their neighbors."

They were favorably posted for observing the guest of the evening.

"I think I should wish to be like that," said Ottilie, contemplating him. If I were a man I should want to be very ambitious, and have as many bowing down before me as possible."

"Oh, the point is to *be* something; not to make a lot of people think you are," said Bainbridge.

It was a fine and somewhat startling sentiment, from him, but he delivered it with an air implying that the object was of course impossible, and nothing less was worth striving for.

The President was in some sense a type of his kind. He had risen honorably from humble beginnings. He had been farmer's lad, school-master, general in the civil wars, representative, governor of his State, and diplomat. He was a person of sterling worth; yet he was hardly of merit sufficient in itself to command the imposing recognition he had received.

He had been chosen rather as a compromise candidate, in the discords of greater leaders, who often destroy one another, under our system, and rarely attain the coveted prize. His whole presence disclosed a calm, well-regulated life. He was of a good, robust figure, and neat and plain in attire. His dignity was of a genuine, simple sort, arising apparently from consciousness of his exalted success, but it had traces of angularity. He gave all who were presented to him a somewhat stiff shake of the hand. He had no great fund of ingenious or gallant discourse at command, but uttered now and then one of those mild pleasantries, which pass on such an occasion and from such a source as brilliant scintillations of wit.

As the pressure of new arrivals slackened, Rodman Harvey, the host, was to be seen conversing with him confidentially, and even giving slight taps on his sleeve, by way of emphasis.

"Ah yes, indeed," said lookers on, "he will have his secretaryship, sure enough."

Angelica, slender, erect, with a long, simple "train" of rich material stretched out behind her, stood like some rare proud bird. Mrs. Harvey was in brocaded satin, its front embroidered with seed pearls, garnets, and other precious stones. From a collar of large diamonds of the purest water depended a splendid ornament of opal and diamonds. Her full bosom, heaved with the pride natural to such an occasion. She was all smiles and comely condescension. When the guests had finally been received, she took the arm of the President and walked through the rooms. Angelica, had withdrawn with Kingbolt of Kingboltsville, to take a turn in the dancing-hall.

It was at such times that Rodman Harvey was

especially content with his spouse. This was her element. It was what he had had in mind when, at a certain stage of his increasing prosperity, caught by the subtile taste for fashion and display, he had married the widow of the elegant Charles Battledore. Perhaps, as he contemplated her, his thoughts may have gone back to an earlier helpmate in the day of small things, — to her with whom he had trodden ingrain carpets, and sat upon horse-hair furniture. Conference with that wife had always been a matter of the calmest reason. *She* had had no petulances of a spoiled child, no preposterous stormings-about, arising from slight cause and abating as easily. She had been inclined to look upon his growing wealth as a delusion and a snare, and had hardly increased her scale of personal expenses to the last.

The young children by that marriage were dead, with her. He thought of the group buried away together in the rural graveyard of his native place. He had been accustomed to alight from the train there, on summer days, at long intervals, to pass an hour beside their graves. There were wooden urns on the posts of the gate, through which you entered from the village green. The head-stones were stained now and awry, the low mounds grown over with tall grass and wild flowers. How very far away that earlier life all seemed! Could it be that he had ever been bound in such intimate ties with so different a circle? Was it to be that in some vague future state the relation was again to be renewed?

The dancing-hall afforded Bainbridge, also, a pretext for taking Ottilie away. Dancing was an exercise which he disparaged with some other things, but his partner found him, to her surprise, no mean adept in it. He even aided her in a new step, of which she had got an inkling from the girls at school. In consideration of this she could almost have condoned some of his errors.

They found seats afterwards in the picture-gallery. It so happened that it was under an orange-tree, by the marble balustrade. Ottilie had an unusual animation and color, and fanned herself vigorously. The painter Millboard, wandering about, with little to do, having few acquaintances in the assembly, made a furtive note, on his thumb-nail as it were, of her appearance as she reclined in a fauteuil with her fleecy white draperies scattered about the nucleus of her slim waist, arms, and head.

"Do *see me!*" she said, admiring herself whimsically. "One would think I had always been used to such magnificence, I take it so calmly. And as for my poor dress, for the last hour I have quite forgotten it."

"You will find that the fashion reporters, if they be worth their salt, have not been so remiss. It will certainly appear in the papers."

"That shows how little you know about such things. It cost—but never mind what it cost; and I had to make a good part of it myself. If you want to see dressing, look at my cousin Angelica. I am glad if you think it pretty, though. It is what I am to wear on Commencement day. By good luck it was just done, or I could not have come."

This was a further touch in a Cinderella aspect of her situation, which had pleased him from the first.

"Oh, an orange-tree!" she babbled presently, catching sight of the boughs above her head, and raising her fan to touch them. "Do tell me something about the orange-groves and the manner of your life there!"

"Shall I tell you about the silver blossoms and the golden fruit which are sometimes both on the trees at the same time, when last year's crop has not been wholly picked? There was a tree on my place which bore one year seven thousand oranges. What do you think of that?"

"At that rate you must have made an immense fortune."

"It was not in my time, though, — no such luck. It was only a tradition. In the first enthusiasm of my venture I wrote some letters for a newspaper, which were complimented as one of the most practical treatises on orange-culture that had yet appeared. When I got back, I hastened to secure the *entrée* to Mrs. Stoneglass' literary receptions on the strength of it. Really, though, it was pretty grim satire, so far as I was concerned. I was like one of those geniuses who go about lecturing on 'How to Get Rich,' and have to jump out of the back windows of their hotels for lack of money to pay their bills."

"You did not succeed very well, then? I had inferred so."

"No, I did not succeed. One year a hurricane, such as had not been known for half a century, ruined me; the next a frost, such as had not been known for another half a century. You might have heard a ton of coal fall — but scarcely anything less — on this last occasion, as I woke in the morning and shouted to the hands to rush and apply restoratives. But it was all to no purpose. I took my leave of Florida."

"And then? — as you ask of me."

"I came into some more money presently, on the

death of my grandfather. Did I ever happen to tell you that I was brought up by my grandfather? He bore me no grudge, it seemed, for the failure of the orange speculation."

"It was n't your fault," interrupted Ottilie.

"It is n't for your faults that people generally bear you grudges. I went next into the manufacturing of a lawn-mower. I put one half of the money in that and loaned the other half, as a temporary accommodation, to a very dear friend. The lawn-mower was embarrassed by a crisis that overtook certain industries about that time. The temporary accommodation extended to my friend, for whom I would have done anything under the sun, and in whose equal devotion to me I had implicit confidence, proved of such permanence instead that not only was it not returned when it would have saved the lawn-mower, but I have never seen it since. This dear friend was hopelessly insolvent, and knew it at the time. He cleared off to Colorado, and that is the last I have seen of him from that day to this. And now you have my whole financial story. It is a little monotonous, is it not, — three such mischances? Nevertheless, it was as I tell you."

"That, then, is what makes you so cynical?"

"I do not admit that I am cynical; but naturally experiences of the kind hardly improve one's temper."

"You do not think, perhaps," she suggested, "that business may not have been your strong point?"

"No, I cannot say that I had thought so. My idea, on observing the countless thousands pouring into the professions, was to try and do something more distinctly practical and useful in the world. Where was the fault with that?"

"Well, you must try again, and a great many times more."

"At my age one does not try very much more. He takes what is sent him. There are certain advantages in the law, however. It is a way of getting even. It affords delightful opportunities for rascality."

"At *your* age?" Ottilie exclaimed, "Why, you are a very young man!"

Indeed! Was it thus he impressed her? They were fast approaching terms of equality, truly. This came of being betrayed into gravity, and making confidences. He had not made them before, he could not tell when. By way of recovering ground he became as flippant as possible.

Ottilie could hardly credit the occurrence, in this society, of doings which would better have suited her idea of the times of the Borgias. The suiciding, dueling, opium-eating, and eloping Huyskamps, of whom she heard, were of the most excellent stock, if that counted for anything. The grandfather, from whom their money was derived, had been a beau in two hemispheres, the companion of Louis Philippe and Ludwig of Bavaria. And that the actors in these dramas should still be welcome on terms of equality seemed to her monstrous.

"You must know that this putting down of people is not so easy," said Bainbridge, in his worldly tone. "We good ones are not strong enough. The bold and bad override us, and there is nothing to do but to take it out in browbeating the weak and timid. At the same time, I think it doubtful whether the upper circle of society is so much worse than those below."

"Worse?" exclaimed Ottilie with ardor. "Ought it not to be a hundred times better? With every comfort and luxury, with opportunity to travel, to be educated, to be cultured and perfected on every side, it ought to admit of no comparison."

She put back some strands of her hair from her temples and leaned forward, in the earnestness of her argument.

"That is a point of view worthy of note, but I doubt if you will find wealth and luxury to have ever worked that way. First, there is the period of hardship and striving; then, when the end is attained, the splendid efflorescence, the decadence. For my part, I ask, 'Why is this prejudice against decadences?' They are the autumn, the legitimate fruition, of all that has preceded. Why is the battle so much better than the victory? The poets and orators are continually giving us to understand that the struggle for freedom is particularly fine, while the peace and plenty by which it is naturally followed are of no account whatever."

"Oh, can you never be serious?" said Ottilie, looking at him half wearily.

Mrs. Hastings now came to find her charge to take her to the supper-room. The tables were so heavily laden with the plate and viands of the costly banquet as to have required to be sustained, so the rumor ran — by extra braces underneath. Haricot's men, in unexceptionable evening dress, responded calmly to the demands made upon them.

"*Deux glaces!*" they cried, "*Trois glaces,*" passing over these delicacies to the thicket of reaching hands.

From time to time others made their way through

the throng, bearing aloft new supplies of game, oysters, and salads, with deprecating cries of "Please! please!"

Mrs. Eglantine approached the discreet financial magnate, Bloomfield, taking his salad by himself at a corner of the mantel-piece, and said, " I want you to do something with my Missouri 6's. It is the only chance I ever have to get at you. You know everything. And do you think Devious Air-Line is going higher?"

Mrs. Sprowle said to Mrs. Clef, finding that lady by chance in a chair beside her, "Why do we never have a *gentleman* for President?" To which Mrs. Clef replied good-naturedly, "Why, indeed?"

Then Mrs. Sprowle, stopping Kingbolt, who was hurrying by with some refreshment for Angelica Harvey, asked him a question about his friend St. Hill. "He is such an agreeable man," she said, — "of the best old Southern stock, which I have always highly esteemed. I do not see him here to-night."

"He does not come here, I believe. There is some misunderstanding, some difficulty of a business sort between him and Harvey?"

"Ah! indeed? I must ask him about it," she said, and Kingbolt passed on.

Next, Austin Sprowle, who appeared to have the most liberal leave of absence from the side of his betrothed, came up to pay compliments, by way of passing the time, to Mrs. Clef, who received them as affably as though she had never said a disparaging word of him.

"How delightfully you are looking!" he said. "We have hardly met since last year, at Saratoga. Saratoga is very good for us New Yorkers. We need something of that kind, a certain — a — er — variation; but we must *not* drink the waters, — we must not, really." His tone was almost tragic.

"When are we going to have another of our little dinners at the Four-in-Hand?" Mr. De Longbow Rowley was asking of Ada Trull.

"*Sh!* All that is over for the present. Somebody has been telling mamma that from eleven in the morning till eleven at night is too long for us to be out with the drags. She has heard that Mrs. Calloway, our chaperon, was younger than most of the girls; and that some of you young men drank too much champagne."

Bainbridge managed to bring about another meeting with Ottilie later in the evening, just before the young girl's departure. Her prospect of going home after her school days, and probably returning to New York no more, was again touched upon.

"Of course I could never get you to write to me, on any pretext?" said the young man.

"No," said Ottilie.

"Suppose we agree to think of each other? Suppose we fix a certain time and hour when you are to think of me, and I of you. Perhaps some mysterious electrical influence will pass between us. Remarkable scientific phenomena may take place. It is worth trying."

"There is a difference in longitude. I should have to remember you at eight forty, or nine twenty, or something, when it was ten here. I could never calculate it."

"This is a very sad and solemn occasion, then. As likely as not I shall never see or hear from you again," he said.

"N — ever," with a mock melancholy waving of the head from side to side.

Bainbridge murmured, by way of parody, —

"Two souls with numerous different thoughts,
Two hearts that beat as two."

"But perhaps you think I do not care," he concluded.

"Of course I do not. Why should you?"

"I think I had begun to take a great liking to you."

Ottilie would perhaps have been touched by this had she thought him sincere, but she knew his raillery too well. "I wish I could say that I returned the compliment," she replied.

"Why can you not?"

"Well, you have tried to patronize me a good deal, for one thing," she said, casting about for reasons. "And then, I have hardly ever heard you utter a sentiment I knew to be in earnest."

"Oh, is that it?" reflectively. "But in your case I assure you I am earnestness itself."

"So much the worse! Nothing is less defensible than to be heavy on a trifling subject."

In such tantalizing fashion, and with a bright smile and a shake of the hand, she was gone. It had been a pleasant acquaintance, and this was the end of it.

The thoughts of Russell Bainbridge drifted after her not a little, from his office, up in the mansard of the Magoon Building, where his new-fledged law practice was developing. He was of course as incapable of foolish sentiment now as the Magoon Building itself. But she had been a bright, piquant person, with excellent traits. Wherever she went, he wished her well.

Meanwhile, — for we need not leave at once the scene of rare festivity at Rodman Harvey's, — the *tête-à-tête* which the daughter of the house had granted Mr. Kingbolt had been in progress. The young man had made, it seemed, but a short visit to his estates, and then, for reasons best known to himself, returned. The painter Millboard could hardly fail to include Angelica in his hovering admiration.

A curiously simple skirt of lustrous, cream-white satin fell down over her limbs, which its folds delicately outlined. The waist had no other support than a small strap over each shoulder; but she wore above this a jacket of rare lace, amber-hued with age. She had cast loosely about her neck a gossamer scarf, which she drew together from time to time as it became slightly disarranged. At some places the leaf and snow-crystal patterns of the lace seemed daintily printed upon the smooth, firm flesh. Her arms were of a more pinkish tinge than her face.

They were lovely arms. They seemed capable of weaving dangerous spells, even from a distance, and Kingbolt of Kingboltsville had ventured into fatally close proximity.

"I don't know when I have enjoyed a waltz so much before," he protested, passing a cambric handkerchief over his forehead. "I had about given up dancing, to tell the truth. I have hated to ask an American girl to dance this long time. One does not reverse abroad, you know, and I had quite got out of the way of it."

"To what shall I ascribe this exemption in my favor? Your reversing is perfect; I have no fault to find with it."

"Oh, you would turn anybody's head. And of course a man is not going to let slip the opportunity to put his arm around the most beautiful girl in two hemispheres, if he can help it."

Miss Angelica had two very distinct manners. She could assume, when she chose,—and she often chose,—a chilling dignity; but with her intimates she professed to like *natural* people, and to hate nothing so much as "the stiff kind." At this time, too, she was permitting herself, towards some favored individuals, a certain sisterly policy, warranted, she deemed, by her new situation. But this talk of Kingbolt's seemed trenching on the bounds of the permissible naturalness. She called him "Wretch!" however, and then inquired,—

"Why do you waste such things on an old engaged girl? Why do you not go and say them to Daisy Goldstone or Ada Trull? I suppose you know that I am 'another's,' as the novelists say?"

"Oh yes, I know it."

"Why! You say it as if you were sorry."

"I am,—damnably," he broke out with a changed manner.

The profane epithet had been half muttered, but his listener heard it. It appeared that she had led him too far. She had no objection to amusing herself a little while her freedom remained; but if it were possible, after all they had both seen of the world, that he were going to annoy her with an absurd earnestness, if he were going to look and talk in such a savage way as that, it was high time to turn over a new leaf with him, and that instantly. In the project she had formed for the disposal of her hand, she was fixed and inflexible.

Kingbolt had already begun some further words in the new vein. Angelica looked about for a pretext to repel them. It happened that Dr. Wyburd was holding forth near by. Mr. Hackley, who, on account of his intimacy with Rodman Harvey, assumed an unusual air of geniality and good-fellowship in this house, was his principal listener. The doctor was saying, —

"When you hear the first part of a good story, you are pretty sure to hear the last. It comes to you from different sources, and you finally put all the parts together. Now I recollect a certain" —

"Oh, an anecdote! an anecdote!" exclaimed Angelica, jumping up, and joining this group. She glanced back at Kingbolt as she did so, as a sign that he might follow if he would. She returned presently to her mamma. Whatever small contact she may have had with the misguided young millionaire during the rest of the evening was marked by the calmest indifference.

The mamma took it upon herself when the guests had gone, and she was alone with her daughter in her sitting-room, in the small hours of the morning, to complain of the character of the *tête-à-tête* the latter had allowed Kingbolt. She had observed it while moving through the rooms on the arm of the President.

"I could see," she said, "that Austin was not at all pleased. It will not do to go on so."

Angelica, nettled, through her consciousness of rectitude, refused to either explain or deny.

"If Austin is not pleased with what pleases me, so much the worse for him," she said. "I will *not* be found fault with. Leave me in peace!"

And she retired petulantly up the staircase to her bed-chamber in flowered silk chintz and gilt.

Mrs. Rodman Harvey murmured after her a formula to which she was much given. It was intended to convey a sense of an obstinacy out of the common:

"She is a regular Harvey."

X.

IN MAGOON BUILDING OFFICES.

The Magoon Building stood in that part of lower Broadway, near the head of Wall Street, whose imposing structures loom nearer heaven every day.

In the Magoon Building were the offices of coal, brick, cement, salt, and silver-mining companies; offices of attorneys, architects and trustees of estates, offices of locomotive, sleeping-car, iron, and dynamite works. There was the branch office of the Devious Air-Line Railway, and of the Eureka Tool Works of Kingboltsville. Young Kingbolt was sometimes met with coming to this latter.

"What are you doing now, Russ?" he asked Bainbridge, whom he had known at college, and passed on, without waiting for an answer.

There were offices that seemed never to be entered but by stealth, others, as that of the Prudential Land and Loan Company, always widely open, to show their elegant mahogany counters. Feet were never done clacking over the tesselated pavement, nor the elevators flitting mysteriously with their human freights from story to story.

The day after we saw him last, Bainbridge returned from lunch an hour later than usual. He stood a few moments at his office window, gazing out at the view. It commanded a corner of Trinity church-yard, the historic graves of which, robbed now of gloom, are invested only with a sentiment of gentle melancholy. The striking of the clock, and the chimes in the belfry, which rang for service daily at three, came across to him at that height almost on a level. An expanse of roofs beyond, studded with innumerable chimneys, like another cemetery in its way, was terminated at the water's edge by a palisade of masts and spars. Over in the Jerseys could be seen the steam of a locomotive or two, speeding out into the country, thrown up in solid puffs, like clods produced by a rapid burrowing.

"The tempter no doubt puts us young and needy ones up into these high places with an object of his own," mused the young man. "Nevertheless," he went on presently, "the kingdoms of the world and the glory thereof, though interesting, certainly do not offer from here overpowering attractions. So get thee behind me, Satan."

A knock came at the door, and a senatorial-looking man, with a dome-like bald head, gray moustache, and clothing, which, though shabby, had a touch of surviving gentility, entered. It was one Gammage, of whom a mention has been made. His figure at a desk in the Prudential L. and L. Company's office was worth much more than the small stipend it commanded, from the pure point of view of dignity. It was a very decayed dignity now, however. A roving eye, an unsteady gait, and an unusual lightness of speech in one who was habitually serious, oppressed by a sense of his position, told the pained eye the story of a relapse into a ruinous habit. The face of this man, instead of being flushed, was of a marble pallor, as though his drams and opiates took hold upon his very vitals.

"Purely social call. Don't dis — turb yourself," he said. "No business on hand. Just dropped in to see how my young friend was getting along." He seated himself without being asked, and appeared in no haste to go. He had lunched, he said, with a very pleasant fellow, Jocelyn the builder. Jocelyn, it seemed, had been again abusing Rodman Harvey, apropos of the account in the newspapers of the entertainment to the President.

"Jocelyn is right, too," said Gammage. "Rodman Harvey is a bad man, — a hard man, if ever there was one."

"What did he ever do to you, Gammage, that you should speak of him in such a way? What do you know about him?" Seemingly this was the opportunity for securing information of which he had been in search.

"He would not give me a situation, when I was first down. May be I'd have been different then. He knew me when I held my head up with the best. He was not always so easy in his circumstances, either, nor so high and mighty and strait-laced. Certain things came under my obsiv — my ob — servation. Because things are passed over, that is not to say they are forgotten. I suppose he could afford to pay me for keeping quiet, Rodman Harvey could. You would not want to go into it, would you?" he proposed, in a maudlin way.

"Go into what?" inquired Bainbridge, with an injudicious sternness.

"Oh, of course, I did not mean — I am too high-toned" — the shattered visitor apologized.

He rambled thereupon from the subject and was only drawn back to it with difficulty. The questioner heard then a story in which, as in that of McFadd, the names of General Burlington and Hackley, now of "Hackley and Valentine," occurred as persons who knew something to the detriment of Rodman Harvey. It was incoherent and fragmentary and highly improbable. Not to give it in the inebriate's mind an exaggerated importance, he abandoned any attempt to make a lucid system of its obscurities, proposing to defer inquiry into these, should it seem desirable, till Gammage could be met with in a sober mood. He only asked whether the story had been repeated to any others, — to his employer, St. Hill, for instance.

"No, not as I know of, not lately. Talking with Jocelyn brought it up. You don't suppose I talk to Mr. St. Hill, anyway, do you? He's too super — psilious. He takes no interest in poor folks. — Besides, I have my suspicions, also, as to the usefulness of the business transacted in that company's office. I would not wonder, what is more, if there was a purpose afoot to supplant me in my clerkship. What does he mean by advertising for young men with small capital, to put up as deposits, I'd like to know?"

"I advise you not to go back in your present condition," said Bainbridge. "You will certainly lose your place. You had better go home and return tomorrow, with the best excuse you can offer."

"Why do you not take me to task? Why do you not plead with me?" urged the wretched man, breaking into a kind of luxury of self-abasement under the cold demeanor of his friend.

"It is too late for that now, Gammage. Your most solemn promises are of no avail. I must give you up."

"Don't say that! Don't say it yet! You were the only one to give me another chance. You took hold of me when I was ragged and starving. You told me there wasn't one man in a thousand looked as well as I did and that the streets was no place for me. Didn't you say that? You put me out among the farmers of Westchester to sober off, and I did odd jobs and writing for them. After that, at last, you looked about and found me a place — and I — I lost it, and then you got me this. Didn't you do it? Weren't you the only one who would trust me again?"

"Well, and this is my return for it."

These were certainly illogical doings for one professing so wholesale a bias against charity, and even the ordinary humane impulses.

"But this is the last time. Something will stop me yet. Don't say it is too late. Men have been stopped. You will see." And Gammage, partially sobered, shambled away overwhelmed with dejection.

In the course of a fortnight he had not again appeared. An inquiry for him at his office by Bainbridge was answered by Fletcher St. Hill in person.

"We had to let him go. Frankly, we had to 'bounce' him," said the manager, emerging from an inner, private room, and airily dusting the sleeve of his coat in a consequential way with a handkerchief as he talked. "He was away two or three days every now and then, and always came back in a beastly, shaking condition. He was of little use to us at the best. He had warnings enough and this time we decided to put an end to it once for all."

Bainbridge was led also by sympathetic interest to

Charlton Street, where the man had lodged. The people there said that, as well as they knew, he had gone back, after a deplorable debauch, to the Westchester farmers. He had told them that he wished to put himself out of harm's way. The details needed to complete Gammage's story in case he had had a mind to verify them, were thus placed effectually beyond his reach, with that of others.

A new incumbent was shortly installed at the desk which Gammage had occupied. Mr. Cutler, formerly with Rodman Harvey & Co., was now seen lending the splendor of his crimson braces, his ornate scarf-pin and sleeve-buttons, to the service of the Prudential Land and Loan Company. He was said to be a young man who had lately married, and come into control of some little property.

Though Mr. St. Hill had dusted his sleeve with his handkerchief airily enough, he was a prey at this time to unpleasant reflections. His company had advertised itself, throughout the small country newspapers and elsewhere, as being the only one offering investments which returned from two to four per cent. a month, and the only one always standing ready to buy in its own shares, at par, on demand. There had been at one time a considerable stir of interest in response, but this had gradually subsided. One annoying circumstance after another had happened, and the enterprising manager saw himself, as he had unfortunately often seen himself before, beginning to be in uncomfortable straits.

If we may be let into a secret, too, the responsibility in the company was not so divided that great aid and comfort could be sought elsewhere. The impression ran that Fletcher, of the firm name of Fletcher, St. Hill & Co., was an elderly capitalist, of high character and great wealth, residing in London, and attending to the company's affairs there. The "Co." was thought to indicate partners of a corresponding sort. As the fact was, however, the Prudential Land and Loan Company consisted solely of Mr. F., or Fletcher, St. Hill. The fictitious London nabob had grown up out of no more substantial basis than a comma. A comma had unfortunately crept in — as errors will happen even in the best regulated companies — between the two names of the advertiser, and somehow got itself perpetuated. As to the "Co.," that is a common enough assumption, to give a fuller roundness and completeness to a firm name and style. It is often for the satisfaction of such as feel themselves vaguely more comfortable with the idea that they have a number of persons to look to instead of one.

Mr. St. Hill took out to-day some yellow old letters to which reference has been made. Harvey's desire for the congressional nomination was making talk, and, as bearing upon this, he found them highly satisfactory.

"It is true that Kingbolt has not recovered from his absurd passion for Angelica Harvey," he said, "and would make a precious row if he knew of my using them. But, on the other hand, why need he know? The chances are twenty to one that, whether I succeed or fail, the secret will rest between Rodman Harvey and myself. He cannot afford to spread the scandal about, and whether *I* should care to or not would be a matter to be determined afterwards."

His meditations resulted in a conclusion. "Yes,"

he said, "I will make them serve my purpose. But now as to the means?"

He cast about for the most desirable means from day to day while driven up town in his coupé, riding his friend Kingbolt's saddle-horse "Jim" in the Park, while calling at the fine houses on the Avenue to which he had obtained the *entrée,* or dining at Delmonico's or at the Empire Club. His accomplishments, his knowledge of the world, his *risqué* stories, and an impressive habit he had of permitting himself always the best of everything, had gained him much consideration. It was a consideration, however, which had been warmest at first, and was of a declining order.

His reflections upon this matter were of such a deliberation, however, and one delay after another so interposed, that he had taken no step up to the departure of the Harvey family, with the exception of its head, to their villa at Newport, and till Kingbolt had set off in his yacht for the coast of Labrador, leaving him, St. Hill, in possession of his bachelor quarters and other comfortable appurtenances.

When the coast was thus clear he dispatched a short note to Rodman Harvey reopening the subject of his claim.

"The animosities of the war," he wrote, "have now so far passed away, such time has elapsed for mature reflection, that I trust my application may be met in a different spirit. Since the validity of the debt has never been disputed, I venture to hope, from a person of such recognized standing in the community, from one to whom his reputation must be dear, a voluntary reversal of your former judgment."

Very delicately, like fingering the hair trigger of a deadly weapon, the matter of the late receipt of some old letters from the plantation on the Ashley River was touched upon. "It is the pleasant interest I find in these," he continued, "as recalling the cordial relations that had once subsisted between yourself and my father, General Rockbridge St. Hill of Savannah, which has especially moved and encouraged me to a renewal of this appeal at this time."

Rodman Harvey returned much the same kind of blunt refusal as years before. "I know of no such claim valid in law," he said, "and I must decline to be interested in any personal circumstances or reminiscences of the writer whatever."

It was apparent, St. Hill thought, that he did not remember the contents of his old letters with sufficient distinctness, or that he did not believe in their existence at all. Could it possibly be, though, that he meant open defiance?

Under the influence of a slightly more favorable turn in his affairs which relieved his pressing needs, he allowed more time to elapse. Autumn arrived, and the election was at hand. Should this, too, be allowed to pass, his opportunity would be lost to him for good. Too wily to put upon paper what might be construed into the criminal offense of threats with the purpose of extorting money, he sought and obtained a personal interview with the merchant prince at his Broadway store.

Meanwhile Harvey had been enjoying the society of a modest young person, some casual information from whom, as it happened, was to have an important bearing on the interview in question when it should take place. This was no other than his niece, Ottilie. She had read her essay, and been on the point of starting for home, when she was met by the entreaty, almost command, to come and aid in taking charge of her uncle's house for the summer. The invitation was conveyed by the hands of the butler, William Skiff. Ottilie's father, a more thick-set and belligerent-looking copy of Rodman Harvey, who was present at the Commencement, stoutly refused at first, then gave a grudging assent. He accompanied her to New York, and spent a night or two under his brother's roof. During this visit Ottilie being, as it were, a hostage, an unbroken truce reigned between the brothers.

It was Harvey's desire to entertain in the new mansion, during the absence of the family, some persons of a minor sort necessary to him in his political campaign, who could be flattered so much in no other way. His wife and daughter, had they undertaken such a mission, would hardly have abstained from a disdainful air which must have been fatal to the end in view. He wished Ottilie, therefore, to preside at his table instead, and have a general oversight of the house with its reduced force of servants, Mrs. Ambler, the housekeeper, still remaining.

Ottilie imagined in the faces of the Hasbroucks — who were to spend the summer economically at a farm in the Catskills — a mute reproach, when they learned of her own destination. The very first use she made of some slight influence over her uncle, which she fancied she possessed, was an attempt to conciliate him in their favor as she had proposed. He peremptorily refused and denied all the positions she assumed. But it was in a description that she gave him of her friends, what they had suffered from others as well, and who it was that had injured them, that some items concerning St. Hill came out, which proved of value in the interview, as has been said.

XI.

EMBITTERED RECOLLECTIONS OF OLD SLAVE DAYS.

ADVANCING a little the pace of our story, — for the events of the summer must again be returned to, — let us see what the manner of this interview, which took place in late October, was.

The merchant prince had breakfasted that day as usual, before the rest of his family, whom he seldom saw at the morning meal. The semblance of pillage was actively in progress at the store on his arrival. A cannel coal fire burned in his office grate. He thrust his feet into a pair of slippers, of a handsome sort, which his daughter Angelica had embroidered for him in advance of some heavy demand upon his purse.

He dictated letters to San Francisco, in reference to waste lands he was redeeming; to Cincinnati, to resist the opening of a street through suburban property; and to Chicago, to foreclose a mortgage. He saw Mr. Minn about sending an order for Merrimac prints at once, in anticipation of an ease in money which would enhance prices.

His friend Hackley dropped in and brought reassuring news of his, Harvey's, prospects in the election set for the first Tuesday in November. He then spoke casually of his own proposed connection with the new firm to be constituted upon the retirement of Rodman Harvey. The talk was that Hackley should raise a sum larger than Mr. Minn, in order to outrank Minn in the order of importance.

"I cannot afford, of course," he said, "to play second fiddle to a person who, however well up in the details of the dry-goods trade, has always taken so much less conspicuous a stand in the community than myself. The firm name must be Hackley, Minn & Co., not Minn, Hackley & Co."

Harvey had put a number of advantageous things in the way of Mr. Hackley at various times, and the latter had flattered and fawned much upon him in return. Perhaps he secretly cherished a belief that it might not really be necessary to secure the whole of the sum proposed, in order to take precedence of Mr. Minn in the partnership, after all.

Harvey received, next, a man who offered him large gains for the use of his name in the directorship of a new mining scheme. He declined. He could not afford to be mixed up in anything of a problematic character. He bought then of a dealer, in such property, a new lot of defaulted bonds, of Western towns and cities. With ability to wait, this was a very profitable investment.

Over a luncheon, brought in from a down-town branch of a fashionable up-town restaurant, he glanced at the financial column of his newspaper. A report of a serious illness of Rodman Harvey had served to depress stocks, notably Devious Air-Line, of which he was the principal holder. Happily, it had proved a *canard*. A trifling touch of vertigo at his broker's office had been magnified into a paralytic stroke, and used with effect until the fiction was exploded. The shares had recovered, and even advanced beyond the point of decline. Such notices, in his regard, were not infrequent, and perhaps in no other way was his sense of power and self-importance more keenly gratified. These were the capitalist's pleasures, — to see his least movement, an indisposition, a journey, any fugitive taste or whim, of a potent influence in the weightiest affairs of men.

A visiting-card was now brought in by a boy who sat without, to answer the summons of his sharp little bell.

"Show him in," said Harvey, after scrutinizing upon it the name of a person with whom he had lately had a brief correspondence, and Fletcher St. Hill entered.

The merchant prince scanned his visitor with a keen interest which changed so quickly, into a cool impassiveness, that one would have hardly said that it had existed. Yet the glance had served to recall a type of features which he had once known well.

"I had the honor of sending you a communication, some little time ago, on the subject of — a — an indebtedness," Mr. Fletcher St. Hill began, after having taken a seat indicated.

"I had the honor of returning you an answer."

"It was naturally a disappointing answer." The caller brushed his hat gently with his sleeve. "I ventured to hope that, with the freer discussion of a personal meeting, there might still be hope of change."

"You had not proposed to undertake legal proceedings. That is satisfactory to know. You would have been several years too late for that. You understand, of course, that you could have done so, had you availed yourself of your privileges. War suspends but does not annul indebtedness, unless confiscated by special enactment, and this was not confiscated. You base your application now upon grounds of "—

"Simple justice and consideration, as between man and man. You do not deny the original validity of the claim. I find, on lately arriving in this community, that you have the repute of being the support of many worthy enterprises, a church member, and a person of integrity. I was inspired with a lively conviction that you would not permanently take refuge from an honest obligation behind a legal technicality. You have yourself demanded from debtors at the South what was due you there under the same circumstances. May I call attention, too, to the fact that I personally was but little identified with the — with our "—

"Rebellion, if that is what you mean," supplied Rodman Harvey, sternly.

"As you please. I was very young, and passed much of the time abroad. I will further urge as a reason for consideration at your hands the situation in which I find myself involved at this time. I will trust in your discretion as a man of honor, and admit that I have met with unexpected and serious difficulties in a business enterprise which I have undertaken here. I am, in short, sir, at this moment, almost without means."

He spread both hands wide open, by way of showing their emptiness of resources. He did not yet display resentment. He did not bluster. This was not at all the Southern fire, as traditionally understood. He was keeping himself in check, essaying first a policy of ingenuousness and humility, on the chance that this of itself might serve.

Rodman Harvey turned back in his chair, upholstered in Russia leather, in which he had turned a little away at first towards his desk, and gazed at his visitor with a level directness.

"As you were so young at the time," he began, — "though permit me to remark upon the expedition with which you have aged, — let me relate a small chapter of history. There was owing to me at the South, when it thought good to secede from the Union, about a quarter of million of dollars. I have never recovered so much of it as would pay the fees of collection. I had been of a conservative, nay, even more, of a friendly bias toward the South. I had never assailed your 'peculiar institution' of slavery."

St. Hill received this with a certain significant expression.

"I was one of those," the speaker continued, "who knew that slavery had not been established in our time, but had come down as an inheritance. As to authorities, texts of Scripture, and the like, there were almost as many on one side as the other, in those days. I did not hold the present generation guilty, and I looked to see the difficulties settled by constitutional means. I liked the Southern people, and had confidence in them. I sent them my goods, on demand, up to the last moment. How was I repaid? By the basest ingratitude, — a treachery that no words can characterize. They betrayed me as unconcernedly as if I had been their most fanatic opponent. I became, with the rest, an 'alien enemy.'"

"'*The payment of alien enemies is treason to the state,*'" he read from a newspaper clipping which he hurriedly took from a pigeon-hole in his desk.

"'Millions and millions, if it be not prevented, may be sent to the enemy's country by Southern patriots, magnifying with a narrow and perverted honesty the duty of individual gratitude, over the holier obligation of national fidelity.' Do you know who wrote that?"

"No," said his hearer, wincing.

"Your father, the late 'General' Rockbridge St. Hill, of Savannah. It was sent to me. His initials are appended to it. Here! You may see. He had been my correspondent and intimate friend. None understood my condition more thoroughly, and none proved viler now than he. He it was, as I came to know, who, by speeches, articles, and private letters, organized a movement for the general repudiation of debts. He wrote to my debtors, dissuading them from any false sympathy for me, more than others."

"There may have been similar initials. I have never heard that those were my father's sentiments. I certainly recall newspapers which insisted that individual debts were on no account to be repudiated. And how many persons have there not been who have since come forward voluntarily and paid what they owed?" said St. Hill, making a show of argument.

"The time to pay was *then*, not now," cried the merchant prince, striking his fist violently upon his desk. "What does it avail that a few should have come whining, five years later, with the money in their hands, and a plea for new credits? I know not how others have fared. I tell you only what happened to me. It would have been 'a narrow and perverted honesty,' you see, to have sent me the funds for want of which an old and reputable house was tottering to its fall. I was made to suffer the tortures of the damned. I was well-nigh ruined, body and soul."

It seemed a curious violence for what had so long passed, even if there were conceded to be excellent provocation. Rodman Harvey possibly thought so himself, for he continued more coolly, though still with snapping eyes.

"Instead of payment, in those last days, when ordinary years of anxiety were concentrated into hours and minutes, came such newspaper clippings as I have shown you. The South having now both its crop and the price of it received in advance, was adjured to give of its fullness only to its own glorious cause.

"Instead of payment came the rhodomontade of your Barnwell Rhett: 'I would go to the fanatic,' he said, 'the manufacturer, the plunderer, who has fattened upon us like the vulture upon garbage, and I would tell him in thunder tones, *This Union is dissolved!* I would write on the walls of their banqueting-halls, *This Union is dissolved.*'

"Instead of payment came intelligence that attorneys would not aid in the collection of debts, that the courts were closed for collections against citizens of non-slaveholding States. There was news of the riding on a rail, and bare escape with their lives, of my agents. Instead of payment there were missions to Great Britain and the emperor of the French, to open free ports and ruin utterly the 'mudsill' merchants of the North. Instead of payment came news of default and disaster by every post and telegram. Will you see now how all this was crystallized into legislation? It is all here."

The merchant prince ran over with a mumbling

commentary another batch of papers, taken from his pigeon-holes.

"Montgomery, — Proceedings of first Confederate Congress, May, '61, — payment to alien enemies forbidden, — payment to Confederate treasury authorized: Richmond, — debtors to alien enemies held to give information to government receiver under penalty, — debtors to alien enemies held to pay receiver, — and so on, and so forth." He cast the papers suddenly aside, as if recognizing that the argument was not worth his pains. "And you," he went on, "of the people who have done this to me, who gave me a day such as "— But here he stopped with a final air.

"I am to understand then," said St. Hill, with a flickering, sardonic smile, "that my application is not favorably received."

"You are to understand that I consider it the supremest effrontery. Even had the claim been technically valid, I should have resisted it to the last. I would have spent twenty times the sum, before you, or any of your blood, should have benefited from my purse. As to your desiring to place yourself in the list of my private benefactions, I fail to see that you are an orphan asylum, a missionary establishment, or a worthy object of charity in any way whatever. If you are really in difficulties, with your fine new nondescript corporation, of which I have heard something, I cannot truthfully say that I do not rejoice instead of regretting the fact. Should your troubles be but a tithe of what I was made to endure, then you would know agony indeed."

St. Hill upon this changed his manner.

"I fear that you may not have sufficiently attended to my note concerning the letters of yours now in my possession," he said. "They were not destroyed at the time, in conformity with your caution contained in some of them. They turned up the other day, at the plantation on the Ashley. You know the old place well. There is not much left of it, but it had closet room enough, yet, it seems, to contain these. They say you dropped the hint to the regiment you fitted out to give the place particularly bad usage should they ever happen to fall in with it. They did fall in with it, and followed your instructions."

"I had attended to the remark, and had thought of offering you five hundred dollars for your pretended correspondence," said Harvey.

He was bending the caller's visiting-card into ellipses, or pivoting it by the corners between a thumb and finger, while he talked.

"You cannot yet have a distinct recollection of their contents to offer so little. It would be a ridiculously small sum for such entertaining matter. I must have the full amount of my claim."

"Then I have nothing further to say."

"You have given me an abstract of certain papers. Let me give you one in return," said St. Hill, disregarding this. "The letters are all complete and in order. They begin long before the election of Lincoln, extend through that agitating period, and up to the very brink of the war. Letter one — if you allow me to display a few of a typical sort — is a direction to lease out your slaves, 'House Molly' and 'Sue's Tom,' who have been with us, to a neighboring plantation. Letter two takes the position that the North and South are antagonistic in essence, and had better separate quietly, each going about its destiny in its own way.

"In letter three you are certain that there will be a peaceful separation, and you discuss a proposition of much interest. You think of removing to the South, to become the leading merchant of the new Confederate republic. Charleston, Savannah, and Mobile, when opened to the world as free ports, can perhaps, one or all, be made to surpass New York. As first in the field, with ample capital, and your large connections already established, you may confidently expect to monopolize the business of supplying the vast back country, at the unprecedently low rates to prevail under the new system. In letter four you are less positive of non-coercion. A violent sentiment is rising, the end of which it is difficult to foresee. But the conflict at the worst must be short, and can end in but one way, — the success of the South. You dally with the idea of removal still. Blockade-running seems to have been spoken of as a resource, during the brief continuance of the struggle, if come it must, with the scheme above indicated to follow. But to the former you are not quite favorable. Letter five relates to a shipment of arms, ' to keep down the niggers with.' This is the last in the treasonable series.

"You begin almost immediately upon this complaints, and then unsparing abuse, because some of our small traders, in a most strange and alarming crisis, have not been able to comport themselves towards you with quite the clock-work regularity of the piping times of peace. — All this would sound well in a gathering of your political friends, would it not?" concluded the visitor, by way of a summing up.

"You are a fluent talker, Mr. St. Hill. You have interested me in reminiscences to which it is long since I have attended. A thousand dollars for these alleged letters of mine."

"It must be the full amount of my claim, and nothing less!"

"Then, Mr. Fletcher St. Hill," said the merchant prince again, "I must remind you that you have met with a very obstinate person. Be good enough to take yourself and your black-mailing scheme out of my sight. There is the door."

He turned back to matters demanding his attention at his desk with a very offensive air, and as if the subject were finally disposed of.

"You will regret this. — I shall find another customer for them," said the visitor, after a pause, as he buttoned his overcoat irresolutely, and prepared to depart. Greatly chagrined at his failure, he was not sure that he should not have done better to accept the lesser offer made him. But the matter was to take even a worse turn still.

"No doubt," said Harvey, answering him, as he had not at first appeared inclined to do. "It is what I expected. They will make some little stir, in the heat of the campaign. It is an old calumny, however. I suppose I was not the only one who changed front in face of the wicked attempt to destroy the government. At the same time, I would consider, were I you, whether there are any circumstances in your own situation and career upon which it would not be well to have the full light of publicity turned. You know, in the first place, though perhaps that is not greatly to the purpose, that your father received from his own government the amount of this claim you come so impudently to thrust upon me. You know whether he and yourself were so well occupied to your private advantage, in the business of the Confederacy with which you were intrusted, that you were able to retire after the struggle with a handsome competency, the whole invested in the foreign funds."

"Tut!" he continued, as St. Hill gave a violent start of indignation. "Of course these things are not spoken of. A Southern gentleman emerging from the ruin of his country's fortunes with wealth despoiled from its very woes, is not at all a conventional figure. You know whether," he went on, "in spite of your alleged tender youth, you sailed at one time as officer of a slave-ship, taking advantage of the new situation of affairs to reopen the trade with the coast of Guinea. You may recall, also, some later transactions not altogether of a reputable sort, — the collection of moneys for a certain Hasbrouck family, and the like. You know, I say, as I do not pretend to, whether some such allegations as these could be worked up by a little investigation into a highly unpleasant form."

St. Hill, having no longer a grand stroke in reserve, clenched his hands in a furious temper. It almost seemed as if a bodily assault upon Harvey were imminent.

"You shall give me satisfaction for these outrages," he cried.

But the merchant prince, showing so little fear of violence that he still kept his back contemptuously half turned, replied, " If you mean a duel, it is not the custom here. Your own code, too, would no doubt interpose obstacles, on the score of difference in age. All the satisfaction, I can give you in this matter, I regret to say, you have already obtained."

Surely such a way of probing to the quick the sensibilities of people, even of an objectionable sort, could result only from a high sense of rectitude, a consciousness of a position altogether impregnable.

St. Hill took his departure, with a bitter personal hatred added to the annoyance of his failure. He did not at once market his wares elsewhere. He had found the means of offense he had counted upon comparatively idle, but he would search for others. If there were any rusted spots in the armor of Rodman Harvey's respectability, here was another person ready to apply to them the biting acid of an envenomed malice.

The clerks among their packing-cases without noticed in "the old man," as he departed, a somewhat unusual sprightliness. He had relieved his mind, to say the truth, that day, in a fashion that gave him much satisfaction.

XII.

OTTILIE HARVEY'S ROUTINE.

OTTILIE's position, upon becoming a member of the household of the merchant prince, some time after the middle of June, was of an indeterminate character. Her uncle treated her with the same consideration that he would have extended to a visitor of his wife or daughter. Her aunt proposed to draw out a regular schedule of occupations, but this plan, like many others of that remarkable woman, after having been postponed till her return from the country, was never realized at all. Ottilie had some scruples about accepting the moderate allowance that was assigned her before her duties should seem of a more tangible sort.

Her cousin Angelica was affable in a condescending way; but as the novelty of her presence wore off, tried to throw upon her a number of burdens which could hardly have been included in her duties by any fair construction. Secretly, this accomplished cousin would have liked to treat her as an upper servant.

"Why not," she said, "since my father pays her?"

She even appeared to look upon the allowance made Ottilie, small as it was in contrast with the magnificent sums lavished by herself, somewhat grudgingly. She had that trait of parsimony so especially odious and surprising in those who have never known either lack of money or the hardships by which its acquisition is often attended. It was a trait hardly likely to be known to her masculine admirers, whose business it naturally was to bestow and not receive. It was known, however, to small tradesmen, and inferiors generally.

Ottilie felt herself stung, too, from time to time, by intangible offenses of such a nature that she could not always convince herself afterwards, as a conscientious person, that they had really existed. The beautiful and accomplished cousin was like a large, lithe cat, which may scratch cruelly even when but stretching its claws. But much of this came later, though a hint of these small inconveniences is here conveniently set down.

Ottilie did not at all mind being condescended to somewhat, at first, by so superior and distinguished a personage.

"How accomplished you are!" she said to Angelica one day, in a warm admiration, which was drawn out by some new example of a deftness extending to a great variety of subjects.

"Well, I ought to be," replied her cousin, serenely accepting the compliment as her due. "I am sure I have had advantages enough. My father tells me that the European part of my education cost him twenty thousand dollars in gold, and gold was at a premium then."

The reflective mind of Ottilie, besides, would have pardoned much in consideration of a pampered and luxurious bringing up, new evidences of which she saw every day. Her aunt Alida showed her Angelica's christening robe and other effects of her tender years. The robe was of the rarest old lace, — there was also a tiny ring set with a costly pearl, which had accompanied it at the ceremony. The cradle was of ivory and pearl, and had been covered with an ermine quilt, having the infant's name in letters formed of the black tails. There had been two nurses in those times; one a steady-going Englishwoman, the old family nurse; the other a robust shepherdess, brought over from her home in the Juras for this especial purpose.

Then had followed a nursery-governess, with whom Angelica had acquired the French tongue even earlier than her native English; then an infantine day-school; and then the long course of education abroad, varied at one time by a short stay at a seminary of a select character at an elm-shaded Connecticut village.

Among other small properties about which she thought worth while to write home, though it would be tedious to set them all down here, was a costly gold bon-bon box, chased and enameled, which her cousin had carried to school in her pocket. "Alas!" said this correspondent later, "when one sees all that it takes to give us the few airs and graces, the petty smattering of things we can acquire at the best, of what obdurate material we seem to be made!"

"She certainly is of a lovely, what you might call artistic, taste in dress," wrote Ottilie. "At one time you see her brilliant and Amazonian-looking, in a cuirass flashing with bugles; again in jackets braided across the front, hussar-fashion. Or she will have a girdle bordered with gold fringe following around the lines of her charming figure, which she knows how to pose in so many graceful attitudes. Again, she wears India mulls, and other such textures, as soft as a summer morning on our dear Kewaydin Lake. There is one white dress, with embroidery of blue flowers, and another of gray satin with blue and pink forget-me-nots, that almost drive even poor unenvious me quite wild. Sometimes she appears with a Japanese touch; then like a court lady of the time of Josephine; and again, with hair rolled high and powdered, and a dot or two of court-plaster, like those German beauties you see in the pictures of the time of Goethe and Mozart.

"Her system is to get part of her costumes from Paris, and have the remaining, possibly, too, the most effective part, done here under her own supervision, or even — so far at least as some alterations and happy new inventions of the minor sort go — by her maid Cécile, with the aid of her own hands. She has a knack of leadership in these matters. She it is to whom is ascribed the first use of a bonnet made of natural instead of artificial flowers. When flowers are not the mode she wears at her belt an immense bouquet; when immense bouquets are in fashion she has none at all. She adopts certain stuffs which no one had before thought of using for costumes. She has some made to her own order by the manufacturers, and it is said they are told to break the loom afterwards, that the patterns may not be duplicated. These are her greater feats. She declares that if a striking hat or costume of hers were imitated she would burn it. But in reality she sometimes sells them to a dealer who comes by the back stairs, and is supposed to have a ready market for the cast-off finery of the upper classes among minor actresses."

Breakfast at the Harveys was a movable feast. The table stood, and William Skiff's services were likely to be in demand, by one or other of the family, till noon. Angelica took her light repast in bed, or in the intervals of dressing, assisted by Cécile. Nothing could be more charming than a view of her in her robes of lace and ribbon, as she reclined with a cup of chocolate in her hand in one of her pink silk chintz or gray plush fauteuils. Cécile did her abundant hair, which fell far below her waist, pointed and delicately stained her fine nails, laced her stays, and buttoned the marvellous boots which were to bear her about on her errands of pleasure and fashion for the day.

The time of the annual departure for Newport was close at hand, and Angelica spent some part of every day with Cécile, perfecting the toilettes which were to give her the usual *cachet* of distinction for the summer campaign. Ottilie, too, was drafted — not unwillingly, since it gave her the advantage of association with her cousin in so informal a way — into this service.

As they worked, Angelica was pleased to show her amiable side. She gossiped, in reply to Ottilie's deferential questions, on that European school life, everything in connection with which appeared so fascinating to the younger girl. She had a refined and beautiful manner of telling a story when she chose to exercise it. Ottilie listened as if to the reading of some delightful book of memoirs.

She complimented her cousin again upon this acquirement.

"We had much practice in narration at Paris," said Angelica, accepting it as before. "I perfected myself there. We used to have sewing and embroidering one morning in the week. A few of the pupils in turn were appointed to entertain the rest with stories. They must have prepared them beforehand.

Madame Batignolles-Clichy sat by and criticised. If there were any straying from the point at issue or drawling or hard drawing of the breath, or if there were too many *et puis, et alors*, and *lorsques* in the story, it had to be repeated till it could be properly done.

"At Geneva," she said, "we had such a lovely distant view of Mont Blanc, across the lake. Our school was an old chateau. The owner had rented it for economy's sake and gone with his family, to live in the orangery. He was a nice old gentleman. We often saw him. I have been back there since, and tested his recollection of me. There he sat, as if it were but yesterday, in his skull cap, on a stone bench, in the sunshine. I let him look at me a long time, when I came up, after alighting from the carriage.

" ' *Tiens!* ' he exclaimed, at length, ' *c'est la petite Angelica*,' — It is little Angelica."

"I left there when I was but fourteen. We used to play hide-and-seek in the garden, and run on the top of a wall along the lake front. A door opened through the wall and gave access to the shore. I remember how the water used to make a wavering on the white curtains of our beds in the summer mornings. Once we saw one of the lateen-sails capsize and three men drown."

"Were there many Americans?" asked Ottilie.

"I was the only one at first. The rest were of all nations, and many of noble families. Later other Americans came. There was Edith Wynn, of Philadelphia, who afterwards made a brilliant match with the Duc de la Tribord-Babord. I hear since that she wishes she had n't. There was Lilly Weidenmeyer, a very beautiful girl, who had lovely arms. She would hardly ever consent to have them covered. They were her death in time. She rested on a marble mantel when heated with dancing, felt an icy chill run through her, and died within a month, of quick consumption. Alice Burlington was there also. She ducked Madame's lap-dog in the fountain one day, and I told of her, I hardly know what possessed me to do it. I fancy that was the beginning of the trouble in our families. I never see her yet without recalling it."

"But now Paris?" said Ottilie, coaxingly. "I suppose Paris must have been the most interesting of all?"

"At Paris we were close to the eccentric Duke of Brunswick's. You never could tell, when you looked out of the window, what color his house was going to be next. Sometimes it was light blue, again dark blue, pink, green, or yellow. He used also to have his maid-servants ride his horses around the courtyard, in their ordinary dresses. There was another school, of a commoner sort, on the other side of us, so near that we could look over into its garden and see everything that was going on. The poor girls had to pass a regular muster every morning. We used to see each one in turn hold out her hands, to a teacher, to show her nails; smile — so — to show her teeth" (here Miss Angelica smiled in mimicry, displaying her own white teeth to excellent advantage), "lift her skirt above the tops of her shoes, and then swing around, with a flourish, to let it be seen that her dress was properly hooked up, and so pass on.

"At Hanover," these episodic reminiscences continued, "the young German officers used to walk past, by threes and fours, very sentimentally, when we were taken to the afternoon concerts at the Thiergarten. But any girl who showed a disposition to flirt was sternly made to sit with her face towards the shrubbery. Once a very bold young aid-de-camp dashed by the school on horseback, and threw a bouquet in at an open window. There could not have been a greater excitement if a bomb-shell had burst."

The narrator went on to tell of the steps she had taken in due course, in Italy, to acquire the true *lingua Toscana in bocca Romana*, and nothing less.

Returning again to Paris, she said among the rest, that school had adjourned, for the summer months to a villa at Etretat, and lessons had depended on the tides.

"A ridiculous proposal for my hand was made here," she said, "by the son of a rich Paris grocer. He had seen me walking on the sands, and sent his mother to negotiate. The girls used to ask me after that the price of sugar, and say, 'How is soap to-day, Angelica?'"

The comfortable sitting-room of Mrs. Rodman Harvey, on the story above the parlors, proved to be both the central focus of authority and something of a rendezvous for all the household. Angelica came there for criticism on her new apparel, the yellow-haired Calista to complain querulously of the difficulties in her studies.

This child displayed a curious shrinking — encouraged by neglect — from almost every form of mental effort. She seemed to cherish the idea that her instructors, being sufficiently paid, could somehow learn her tasks for her, as well as teach. But she was found by Ottilie, who took some pains to win her confidence, to be of a certain slow shrewdness, and of a generous and loyal disposition as well. The young girl thought her not likely, under competent management, to remain always as dull as she seemed.

Selkirk dropped in at his mother's room to report upon some commission he had undertaken, or, perhaps, to keep up an acquaintance which, with the varied habits of the several members of the family, often appeared in danger of lapsing altogether. Rodman, Jr., came to help himself liberally to fine stationery, and renew a nagging argument he had in progress for the privilege of a latch-key. His father refused this. His mother, more than once " for the sake of peace," lent him her own. He had entered the Columbia Grammar School now, and was supposed to be preparing for college.

" He may not be a *saint*" — Mrs. Harvey took occasion to say to Ottilie, but she paused there. Some kind of a saving clause seemed to be implied, yet it would be difficult to explain just what it was.

Conrad, the cook, came in white cap and apron, to confer on the day's dinner. Mrs. Ambler, the housekeeper, reported that she had been to market, and had given out the stores from the store-room — a place almost as large as a shop, and redolent of delectable odors like Araby the blest.

Mrs. Ambler brought the latest news from the servants' hall. John Welsh had come in from the stables in a flushed condition the evening before, and made himself very obnoxious at the dining-table. Miss Angelica's maid, Cécile, had again been making trouble in the laundry because her fine clothing had been washed with that of a commoner sort.

"That girl is an *image*, if ever there was one," said Mrs. Harvey.

She rarely ventured, however, upon further interference in the jurisdiction of her daughter. She was afraid of this daughter, as even irrational and strong-willed mothers may be of children stronger than themselves.

One day the majestic-looking Alphonse, however, it came about, slapped Mary Callahan in the face. Who would have believed it? Who would have supposed that so formal and irreproachable a person, to the view, could be so rude a barbarian underneath it? Mary Callahan was the trim parlor-maid, who wore pink calico and cleaned the mirrors and brasses, and was often seen on the upper window-ledges, her body half out, holding a sash in her lap while she polished the glass till it shone again. Mrs. Ambler brought the news that she was crying in her room, and dressing in haste, with the avowed intention of "going down to the court for a warrant."

It was a trait in Mrs. Rodman Harvey's character that you could never tell upon which side she was going to appear. Her judgments were sudden and remarkable. Mrs. Ambler was accustomed to receive from her all opinions alike with equal deference and freedom from comment or surprise. She said simply, "Yes, Mrs. Harvey," or "No, Mrs. Harvey," as the case might be. Instead of espousing now the cause of outraged beauty and helplessness, as might fairly have been expected, it was precisely the ungallant Alphonse, the rude aggressor, — a servant, it should be borne in mind, however, of a kind much in demand, and hard to replace if lost, — whom Mrs. Rodman Harvey supported.

"That Mary Callahan is a limb," she exclaimed. "You will have to go to her and quiet her now, Mrs. Ambler, to keep her from being ridiculous. But afterwards, just put on your things and step down to Galpin's, and see whom else he has got for me. Tell Galpin it is too dreadful of him to treat me the way he does! Tell him it is too terrible of him to send me such people!"

Mrs. Harvey seemed to have divided her servants into three classes, of her own, according to their relative depravity. If the short-comings were comparatively slight, the offender was only a "curiosity." A considerable degree below this was the "image;" while the most aggravated and heinous form of all was the "limb," whatever that might be. There was great rotation in office, in the household, and frequent recurrence to Galpin. Galpin, being well paid, shrugged his shoulders, and said little, as was the way of a number of other worthy persons whose fortune it was to have dealings with Mrs. Rodman Harvey.

The rows of servants sitting along the benches of the intelligence office knew her well, and exchanged philosophic reflections about her. She was spoken of as "a woman a bit too free wid her tongue."

At the same time some mind of more impartial scope among them might remark, "She do be over it as quick; and may be she'd be the first to be sorry after."

It was in virtue of irresolute and forgiving traits on both sides, no doubt, that many even of the worst "limbs," — persons whose departure from the house had been attended by throes and convulsions, — were found reinstated, even after more dismissals than one.

at their posts, and going about their affairs as though no cloud had ever troubled the serenity of the domestic sky.

When Mrs. Harvey had brought matters to such a pass that there appeared no escape, she threw off the direction helplessly upon Mrs. Ambler, and rested upon her own laurels till the way seemed clear again. She had had housekeepers, she said, who brought her too many complaints of the servants, which showed want of discipline; and others who brought too few, showing collusion. Mrs. Ambler, deferential in the presence of authority, was of a good deal of self-reliance when it was withdrawn. She indulged the mild vanity of speaking of " *my* servants," and " *my* kitchen." She seemed for the moment to have realized the happy medium.

Into all this Ottilie was initiated, as a part of her new experiences. Her aunt professed to expect much assistance from her.

" From no quarter, from no human eye," Mrs. Harvey declared, " do I receive even such a ray of aid and sympathy as might penetrate into the darkest caves of ocean."

She complained guardedly at first, then more openly, of selfishness on the part of Angelica, with the rest. " Angelica," she said, never too particular with her metaphors, " would walk over chaos, mountains high, and never raise hand or foot."

If an impulsive mother, however, she was also a fond one. She bore no apparent grudge for her daughter's selfishness. At the most trivial ailment of Angelica's she manifested a concern which had no fault but over-officiousness. She hastened to fetch and carry, prepared tea and medicines, and asked a thousand superfluous questions, which, sometimes met with but short answers. Ottilie once saw the charming patient dash away a teaspoon held by her mother's hand so vehemently that it fell clinking to the floor.

Good Mrs. Harvey had often occasion to repeat her favorite formula: "She is a regular Harvey."

The card of Arthur Kingbolt of Kingboltsville came up one afternoon, when the preparing of toilettes was going on as described. Angelica frowned at sight of it. She was beautifully dressed, as usual, and there was no ostensible reason why she should not have gone down. She handed the card to Ottilie, however, and said: "Please go down for me. Say that I am otherwise occupied, — that I cannot conveniently see him. — I wish the message to be rather uncivil; do you understand?"

Ottilie had considerable trepidation at the idea of meeting this grand personage, and especially as the bearer of so ungracious a word. But some plainly visible uneasiness of his own prevented his attending to hers. His countenance fell when he saw who it was that rustled down to him instead of Angelica. Ottilie softened the message to what extent she dared. Kingbolt babbled a commonplace or two about the June races, the kind of a season it had been socially, the increasing heat of the weather, and the like, and took his departure. He had hardly deigned to give her, she thought, a second glance.

"Little enough, poor I, just down from Vassar, knew of the kind of season it had been socially," she said afterwards, about this interview.

In truth, the numerous victims in a sentimental way — blonde and brunette, and in many lands — to the personal charms and the magnificence of Kingbolt of Kingboltsville might now have felt a certain sympathy for him. Rebuffed in advances of a vehement earnestness, which he had allowed himself to make to the betrothed of another, his affections, his pride, and his confidence in his own distinguished merits had all suffered cruelly. He was driven to despair. This refusal to see him completed the measure of his humiliation, and, as he said, of his folly. He had thrown himself into the scale against that dolt of a Sprowle — Yes, he had come to this, he had condescended to it, — and thus it had ended.

He put his yacht in order, bustling vigorously himself about the preparations, and set off for a cruise. At first in his misanthropy he was capable of flying a black flag, and becoming a terror of the main after the most approved pattern. But the winds blew, and the seas curled bravely round his prow. He took part in the manœuvres of a squadron in the Sound; put in at summer resorts along the New England coast; rose and fell on the great tides of the Bay of Fundy; made Halifax, passed into the Bras d'Or, and around Prince Edward's Island and the Magdalen Islands, and so home again.

Much before the end of his six weeks' cruise he figured to himself that he was entirely cured. He went to Newport in the end of August. It was by no means because She was there, but because it was the correct thing to do. Sprowle Onderdonk had marshaled the Narragansett Gun Club, for instance, and sport of many kinds was in prospect.

The day at length came when the family departed for their villa, and Ottilie was left to the duties for which she had been more particularly engaged. Harvey's campaign for the congressional nomination was now begun in earnest. The people whom it was considered desirable to dine were invited as proposed. Hackley, served, with a great show of activity, as a confidential agent, and procured the insertion of artful communications in the newspapers and the like. The reconciliation of coolness of long standing was effected. Sums of money were apportioned out and placed in an occult way, as the saying was, "where they would do the most good."

In the worst of the midsummer heat Harvey transferred his headquarters for a fortnight to one of the great hotels at Coney Island, then newly risen into prominence, and took his niece with him.

Ottilie did not send for Bainbridge, preferring that their meeting should come about, as it no doubt shortly would, in some natural way. Miss Rawson heard of her arrival and called upon her, partly perhaps in the hope of making the acquaintance of the principals of this important family.

So considerable a time elapsed, however, before a chance meeting with Bainbridge came about that Ottilie perhaps found the surprise he expresssed at finding her in town rather natural.

"I thought it possible that Miss Rawson might have told you," she said.

"I dare say she forgot it," he answered dryly.

Ottilie had inclined to anxiety, remembering the manner of their parting, but as he made no other advances than those of an easy, unsentimental goodcomradeship, this happily vanished, and they were soon upon their old friendly footing. Bainbridge, not at any time too much pressed with business, had more leisure than ever now in the dull part of the summer. He was employing a part of his time, he said, and adding a trifle to his income, by writing occasional articles for a newspaper. She insisted on his showing her some of these, and he allowed himself to be persuaded to do so.

It stood the young girl in good stead, now, to have been elder sister, and lieutenant of her mother in the management of a large family. She got on well with the servants and with Mrs. Ambler, the housekeeper. She presided at her uncle's dinner-table with a demure composure. More than one of the masculine guests regarded with approval the slender figure appearing above the board, against its high-backed carven chair.

The presence of Stoneglass, the editor of the "Meteor," among others, had been secured in some apparently informal way. He was a person thought to have peculiar influence with a party of independents in the district, who held the balance of power. His position on the nomination, with theirs, was not yet determined, and remained a source of painful anxiety. Stoneglass was pleased at dinner to compliment the merchant on his "little housekeeper."

"Few young women nowadays," he said, "know anything of the good old domestic arts, so becoming to their sex."

He recurred to the simpler days of his youth, when housekeeping had been as regular a part of education as all the others. Harvey, finding him in this vein, encouraged it with the anecdote about Ottilie — which he had heard from her father on his visit — that she had taken a prize, offered in her family, for the best loaf of bread.

Stoneglass turned to her pleasantly from the talk

on serious matters. What were the views of a learned young lady fresh from Vassar, he asked in banter, on the question of specie resumption?

Instead of the blushing disclaimer, which might have been expected, she made him, to his surprise, a little reply which was by no means wholly devoid of sense. Thereafter, whether Ottilie had anything to do with it or not, Stoneglass became, both in the " Meteor," and out of it, a firm adherent of Harvey's cause.

"Where in the world," her uncle inquired, when the guest had gone, " did you come to have an opinion on the currency question ? "

" I happened to have just read it in a newspaper," she explained, coloring. "Should I have told him that?"

But she did not appear to find it necessary to say that it was a paper brought her by Bainbridge with one of those occasional articles of his of which he had spoken, and that the article was his.

Harvey had his niece read to him, and now and then sing some ballad music for which he had a lingering taste, seldom gratified by his daughter Angelica. She read his financial column, with the incidental references to himself contained in it; or long reports which he had saved till evening, not having had time to finish them in the morning.

These were often trials, extending over several days, for defalcation, forgery, breach of trust, and other financial crimes. For these cases, especially when occurring among persons who had once enjoyed the confidence of the community to a notable degree, he showed a definite taste.

Ottilie ventured to commend his political ambitions. " There are so many persons of position and means," she said, ingenuously, " who remain selfishly wrapped up in their own affairs, and take no part in the government, nor aid in any way to improve the general condition." She said she had heard that nothing was so much needed in politics as good men.

It was at this time that she ventured to approach, with trepidation, the subject of the Hasbroucks.

"Your interest is creditable, but misdirected," Harvey replied to her appeal. "Let me hear no more of sympathy for them or any of that section of the country. Had it depended upon them, I should have been a beggar in the streets to-day. That I am not, that I escaped bankruptcy, is due — I hardly know to what it is due."

He proceeded to acquaint her with some of the particulars which we have seen laid before St. Hill.

"I *would* not fail," he continued, "for then I should have been impotent to resent the harm that had been done me. I could not bear arms, but I remained solvent, to strengthen the power of the government, and pay for those who could. I put a regiment in the field at my own expense. As my Southern debtors had forgotten, together with my dues, my favors and good will, I sent bayonets to prick their recollections. No, let me hear no more on this subject."

Why was he so bitter, and why so sweeping in his resentment? Ottilie asked herself. It had all been so long ago, and her friends were women, who could not personally have injured him. Others had escaped bankruptcy, and even fallen into it, she was sure, without cherishing such long and violent animosities.

She was humiliated and depressed at her rebuff

She enjoyed no such place in his esteem as she had foolishly imagined. She thought of going away at once, but this could hardly have been done with credit. It would not be understood. For the present she would stay.

One small event succeeding after another dimmed this impression. Her uncle Rodman certainly had had provocation, and different natures take things so differently.

He brought her one day a considerable sum of money, directing her to distribute it in such charities as she saw fit. He wished her to be assured that it was not niggardliness or insensibility to distress that caused him to withhold his aid from the Hasbroucks, but a settled principle.

At the same time, perhaps, the candidate did not forget that benefactions distributed from his house would much redound to his advantage in the political way.

XIII.

SHOWING THE PERFECT FEASIBILITY OF PLATONIC FRIENDSHIPS.

THE circumstances of their new situation — left in town together, when all the world had gone out of it — contributed to the growth of the intimacy between Ottilie and Bainbridge. There was no one to especially remark upon the young man's calls, frequent though they might be. Only Mrs. Ambler showed herself discreetly from time to time in the large rooms of the mansion. Bainbridge bid for her favor, also, by remembering her and addressing to her an occasional courteous remark. She had lived at one time, it seemed, with his relatives, the Hudson Hendricks.

She told Ottilie, " They are elegant people, so easy in their manners, that a body gets along with them as well as if she were one of themselves."

But a stray figure or two would be seen in these midsummer days on the whole length of the Avenue. The windows of the deserted houses were darkened with green shades, close-drawn. The entrance doors of many were battened up as if never to be opened again. A chance pull at the bell was answered only by some frowzy charwoman, who looked up with wrinkled forehead from the basement area. The grass grew long in the door-yards. Oleanders here and there showed their white and crimson flowers against some bit of brick wall. The impulsive magnolia shrubs were flowerless long since, and gave token of their advancing age and experience. The bay and rivers, around the city, were full of white steamers, fluttering with banners, resonant with music, and going on excursions.

"Do you not go out of town, also?" Ottilie asked her friend.

"Oh, I have been in the habit of taking a run to Fire Island, or Lake George, or the White Mountains," he replied carelessly; "but the fact is that New York itself is not the least desirable of summer resorts. You cannot exactly swing a hammock in Madison Square, nor cast yourself down with a book in front of the Astor House, but you can take a more comfortable lodging at half the price, walk in the shade of the tall buildings, listen to the spatter of the water-carts, and study the country cousin come to town."

"And of course you can make day excursions. There seems to be so many attractive places to go to."

"I cannot endure them," asserted Bainbridge. "What with the discomfort of the journey and the return again to town, more sultry than ever by the contrast, it is like eating the rind of a water-melon to get the pulp, and afterwards eating your way out on the other side."

Sometimes in the evening the pair sat in one of the chintz-covered parlors, by a window which opened on a balcony. The gas-light was not too brilliant. Fitful puffs of air stirred the soft material of the curtains. Strolling German bands played in the side streets, and the music was borne sweetly to the ear from a distance. In the side streets the women of families who did not go out of town till late, or not at all, sat upon their doorsteps in white toilettes, and held informal levees.

Bainbridge's visits were oftenest in the afternoon, and Ottilie received them in the large picture-gallery. It was a favorite resort of hers in the long, quiet, hot days. She liked to go there with a book and look up from it and let her fancy wander away to the endless variety of scenes and personages about her.

There were coquettes, madonnas, vestal virgins, and odalisques. There was Francis I. as taken captive at Pavia, and Hannibal swearing eternal hatred to the Romans. You drifted in a barge, with flower-pots at the stern, along a silvery French canal. You assisted at a harvest in a Normandy apple-orchard; a gay dance of Hungarian peasants; shrank in dismay from a charge of Thor-like cuirassiers; or looked down at night upon a snow-clad farm in Ukraine, white under the moon; and you might hear, as it pleased you, the faint sound of bugles, the lute of the troubador, or the pan-pipes of Daphnis and Chloe.

Bainbridge thought the living, intelligent Ottilie, as he saw her there, in her fresh, summer gowns, in patterns of blue and white stripes, or small sprigs, with her nice hair, her smooth skin free from blemish, and a little high light at the tip of her nose, which was made by the illumination coming from above, far prettier than any of the pictured ideals on the walls.

They talked naturally more or less of the works about them. These subjects led up to that of European travel.

"Ah, if I could but travel!" Ottilie exclaimed. "I wonder if I ever shall! — But what do I say? You see before you a person who is traveling. I am in Italy at the present moment, and writing back my experiences to an intimate friend."

It appeared, when this enigma was explained, that she had entered into the improving plan, with a classmate, of carrying on a correspondence in the same manner as if they were really journeying abroad. They were to collect information as to the places through which they imagined themselves to pass from books or any other sources accessible.

"My correspondent is Alice Holbrook," she commenced, "the one who"—

"Oh, yes, the studious one, whose family wanted her to marry her cousin. She did not wish to, however, and sent him back his engagement ring. Afterwards her sister took the young man," supplied Bainbridge promptly.

His companion gave him a glance of surprise and reproach. "You are very observing," she said, with a slight asperity.

"Bless you, I know them all by heart," he replied, shamelessly. "I could n't know your school-mates better if I had been born and brought up with them."

Severity seemed thrown away on such a person, so Ottilie went lightly on again.

"Alice is still in England," she said, "but I came to Italy the first thing. I could not wait,—I was at Florence at the last writing, and about to start for Rome."

Bainbridge was able to correct a few monstrous errors and impossibilities in her imaginary travels, at which both laughed gayly.

Perhaps a vague fancy of the pleasure of seeing all that again in company with such a charming young enthusiast may have passed through his fancy. A person like this, exclaiming over the picturesqueness which had pleased him in his time, and giving it new interpretations, leaning on his arm in becoming fatigues in the galleries and steep streets, — ah, perhaps, that might be even yet something worth while!

They stood one day before the patriotic Hannibal.

"Let us swear an eternal friendship instead," proposed Bainbridge, imitating melodramatically the pose of the young avenger of his country. He raised one arm to heaven, and extended the other towards the young girl. They were on excellent terms that afternoon. She took his offered hand, laughingly, with a becoming reluctance. Secretly she was pleased to have the character of the relation between them thus accurately defined.

They proceeded to talk of friendship, of the possibility of an enduring regard on the platonic basis between the sexes. Bainbridge quoted La Bruyère who asserts that it is possible. An understanding seemed to be arrived at that they were never to be anything more to each other than pleasant companions. They knew each other's circumstances perfectly. The pecuniary reason alone, were there nothing else, should be sufficient to put all thoughts of love and marriage out of their heads.

"Nobody shall marry me but Miss Golconda Harrington, whose income is a thousand dollars a day, — unless it be Miss Butterfield, who has five hundred," asserted Bainbridge, making open profession of the most glaringly mercenary motives. "Both of them have reached forty-five at least, and they are tortured with the dread that everybody who approaches them is after their money. I shall feign, however, some philanthropic or other crafty motive for getting at them."

"And I?" said Ottilie.

"You? you must marry one of the enormous young millionaires floating about on every hand. There is young Northfleet, who owns half a county in Pennsylvania. Or Kingbolt of Kingboltsville. Come, there is an excellent match. I select Kingbolt of Kingsboltsville. I give my consent. Bless you, my children," and he performed a benediction above this imaginary union.

"Very well, then! Enormous young millionaires, and this one in particular, will please look out for themselves."

"The fact is," he went on, "that after a certain age a person" ("the person" apparently meant himself) "rarely has magnanimity enough to wish to increase his burdens in matrimony. In his first romantic impulse, on the contrary, he would have been glad to double his hours of labor, wear shabbier clothes, live in a tenement house, or a wigwam for that matter, and consider himself amply repaid by the least of the dear one's smiles. I speak of the man. No doubt the young woman, too, gets around to the same way of thinking, — always supposing that she has felt any other way. Besides, even that kind of romanticism often defeats itself. Confined to each other's company at close quarters, without a fresh stream of outside life and ideas pouring in, they bore each other presently, — our beatific couple. They throw plates at each other's heads, and get into the divorce courts."

Ottilie seemed to be musing upon this.

"One estimates fashionable society at its proper worth, of course," continued this philosopher, sagely. "One may not care to go into it, but it is more complimentary to be asked, all the same. When you become householders you date and rank somehow from that. You make a pretense of repaying the gorgeous hospitality you may have received. If society does not come down, with its two men on the box and its supercilious eye-glass put up, to return your calls, though you may not wish to see it the least in the world, you must be offended. A proper self-respect demands it. Presently there is an irreconcilable quarrel, and that is the end of it."

This was hardly the way in which Ottilie had been most in the habit of judging. But, though arguing openly against his unfavorable way of putting the case, she was inclined to admit within herself that, for him, it might be reasonable. With the kind of bringing up he had had, he must look upon many things as indispensable which to her would not have been so at all.

There was little that escaped the range of their light discussion. *Apropos* of some feudal châtelaine or Roman contadina on the walls, they exchanged their ideas on feminine beauty and adornment. "A woman should have a certain *simple* effect in her apparel, no matter how rich the material," said Ottilie. "Angelica is an excellent instance, — none better. She should have an oval face, and a forehead from which her hair can either be brushed up, if she wishes, or worn low. It should not be too high, which is harsh and brazen, nor too low, which is unintellectual."

The speaker had a way of fixing her eye upon a distant point, and wrinkling her smooth brow by way of pursuing a line of thought the more accurately, or finding a better word or distinction. These sometimes escaped her, when she was forced to end rather lamely with a "you know."

"Could *you*, now, wear your hair brushed high?" the young man inquired, bending his mind with a certain facility to the problem.

"No; I fear it would not be at all becoming."

"Oh, yes, I think it would," he argued judicially. "I should say that you had the right sort of a forehead. You show rather more of it now, I believe, than when I first saw you. You have adopted a kind of compromise."

"You certainly *are — very observing!*" she exclaimed again, in a tantalized way.

Her thoughts flew back in alarm, and she endeavored to recall her appearance as it must have been at that first meeting. Her panoply of fascination could have been in but poor condition, after the long journey, and in her sadness of mind.

"But I cannot help it," she concluded. "And who would have supposed that men noticed things of no importance? That is to say, they are of importance, but one does not expect — at least you are not generally confronted with — so precise a recollection."

On his side, Bainbridge was of opinion that he should have been taller.

"No," Ottilie was pleased to decide critically, "you are just right."

She showed him, at his next visit, a picture of herself taken in childhood, an old-fashioned ambrotype of the kind in vogue before the photograph came in.

She took it from her pocket, saying, —

"I happened to find this among the papers in my writing-desk. You can see now what a fright I should look with my hair up."

It was a representation of a quaint little maiden at the age, say, of ten. Her hair was short and confined in a round comb. About her neck hung a conspicuous locket. Her hands, in lace " mitts," were folded in her lap. Bainbridge gazed at this little picture musingly, and returned to it a number of times. His heart seemed to warm above it and go in search of her whole past existence.

"I think I must have been a rather odd child," she said in a reflective way as, observing his interest, she contemplated it too. "I was very romantic, for one thing, and also rather dissatisfied. Once, I tried to persuade myself — having read of such things in the stories — that I might have belonged to some richer and finer family than my own and been carried off and that perhaps there would be an inquiry for me some day, and I should be restored to my ancestral rank. Yes, really, as silly as that! I used to think about it in a dreaming way, without ever looking for the evidence. I used to say, ' It might be, you know, — it *might be*.' It was not that I did not love my own family dearly. I should have counted on coming back to them in my magnificence, and sharing it with them. But somehow things seemed so commonplace in our tame little every-day life. Nothing happened; and there was so much that I wanted and could not have."

"At that time I had never seen the sea," she continued, nor even the lake at Chicago, which gives a very good idea of it. There were distant blue hills which showed at the end of the road near where we lived. I recollect trying to make believe that they were the sea, and the white dots of houses upon them sails."

The young girl's curiosity about the sea was really satisfied for the first time when she went with her uncle to the gay bathing beach of Coney Island. She did not soon lose her pleasure in it.

Bainbridge's aversion to day excursions did not now seem to hold good. He made very many of them, taking the boat at the foot of a street near his office, and had long promenades with Ottilie up and down the spacious piazzas of the hotels, and long strolls on the sands.

"I am told that this island is something like the Lido at Venice, where Byron galloped composing his poems," said Ottilie.

"I dare say that is what Mrs. Anne Arundel Clum is doing now," returned Bainbridge, remarking at the moment a mutual acquaintance of the spring. "She is riding wildly back and forth in the omnibus. She has passed three times within half an hour."

They talked of "studying the people," as they looked at them from the piazzas.

"But they will not keep still for you," complained Ottilie. "If I were a despot, I should have those who interested me stopped, and detained till I was through with them. I think I do not care for such superficial study."

"Study me, then. I will keep still as long as you like. Talk of understanding other people, I wish somebody would tell me how I am going to turn out. I should be very much obliged to anybody who would do it."

"I was spoiled and too pampered in my bringing up," he complained. "I had everything too regular and conventional. The pine-knot and cabin-floor principle is the thing."

"The pine-knot and cabin-floor principle?"

"Yes. I should have read Virgil by the flickering light of a backlog while stretched prone on the hearth. I should have learned Euclid at the gray of dawn, and in short respites from hoeing corn and chopping down the forest primeval. — Those are the fellows who come to the front. I ought to have taught school winters and taken eight years to go through college instead of four."

"Those are the fellows," he repeated, pursing his lips, and nodding with a sagacious air.

"That often results in offensive egotism and pedantry. They succeed in spite of their obstacles, not because of them, do they not?" discriminated Ottilie.

The island, which from the steamer's deck, was a more ephemeral Venice, of wood and canvas, decorated as for the carnival, was at the centre and one end a tinkling Vanity Fair of hotels, pavilions, and gay bungalows, devoted to the thousand amusements of such a time and place. Towards the other end a comparative isolation reigned. The waves broke there, little troubled by bathers, and but a few promenaders strayed along a wide beach of silvery white sand. Back from the beach were sand dunes carven into sharp curves, always shifting, and interspersed with bay shrubs and dwarf cedars.

The black rib or two of a wrecked vessel, projecting above the surface, made a convenient seat. Thither our couple betook themselves.

They watched the floods run up the sands, the foam and green translucences in the tops of the breakers, and the serene peace of the blue field beyond. An occasional fishing boat or yawl came rolling and tumbling up in the surf close by them. Sometimes the shadows of clouds crossed the field, making it black and purple where they moved. The remoter sails were lily white in the sun, and of a faint azure against it. There were always distant vessels, over by the Highlands of the Navesink, hull down, as if calmly foundering, instead of climbing up or going down the horizon, as they were.

"We are in too great haste to press on," said Bainbridge, gazing out at the prospect with half-shut eyes. "At least, I speak only for myself. We impatient ones are apt to think too much of what we cannot do and cannot have, instead of what we can do and have. We are like the Irishman hanging on under the bridge who let go to get a better hold. Now, this, — what could be more perfect? A lovely impression should be cherished as long as possible. To lie and gaze at the sea might be a career in itself."

"It makes one melancholy," Ottilie returned; "but one likes a little of that. Perhaps a touch of it is always desirable in the most perfect state of mind. When I am happy I do not feel quite well. — There, that is like one of *your* absurdities! But what I mean to say is that when things have gone exactly right, when some favorite object has been attained, and for the moment nothing more seems left to wish for, there is an over-elation and a slight sense of vacancy. I lose my appetite, I cannot sleep, and find myself presently going about with a headache, just as if it were trouble that had arrived. How strange we are!"

They noted one day near them on the sands a couple, from Ottilie's hotel, whom they knew to be engaged. This pair reclined under umbrellas, and the man was reading aloud, as they could observe, with an animated pleasure in the text. The young woman looked about her, and yawned behind her fan. But when appealed to with some question or comment she affected an interest equal to his own.

Our friends agreed that a tragedy was preparing there, in such an evident difference of tastes.

"Probably nothing in the world could be worse," exclaimed Bainbridge. "The infernal *duration* of it! To have a partner at one's side, mingled in everything, yet always remaining a stranger. She is chilly, unappreciative, plans apart for her own instead of the common weal, and finally, no doubt, seeks her ideal elsewhere. It is amusing to the newspapers and playwrights, but it is death to the participants."

"The great point, after all," he dogmatized, "is whether she will *stick* to a fellow, — whether she will pull through thick and thin with him."

"One would want to find perfect rest in marriage," he continued, enlarging on the subject in a manner for the time being at variance with that in which he was accustomed to speak of Miss Golconda Harrington and his proposed manœuvres for her fortune. "One would not want to be always on the stretch, mentally, either; he could not afford to be on a perpetual picnic. He ought to get somebody who could discount him fifty per cent., and like him even then. It should be somebody who, in consideration of knowing that he was immensely fond of her, and always meant to do what was for her happiness, even if he did not succeed, could like him even when she found that he was twice as stupid as she had supposed. There is little doubt that with the best of dispositions and the most favorable circumstances there must come some dreary times after the wedding. They come even to intimate friends, who have no bonds to hold them together, and how much more to married couples?"

"I *know* it," assented Ottilie, as if she also gave up this poor human nature of ours in despair.

"But a wife might enter more into her husband's affairs, I suppose, than some do," she went on, "that would be one resource. Then she could read the papers, and talk with him about them. — But you speak only of the man; you do not say anything of the allowances to be made on the woman's side. Of course, she would have to be discounted, too, as you call it, just as much."

"I do not admit it. She has her feminine attractions, her pretty looks, added to the count. A man is not supposed to have any particular looks, but the first duty of a woman is to be charming. A number of celebrated poets have said that, and I agree to it. The first duty of a woman is to be charming."

"Nonsense! That is the way men are always talking. Little enough they know about it. They mean, I suppose, that she ought to be as vain as possible, and devote her whole silly existence to preparing new toilettes. *I* say that she ought to cut her hair short, wear spectacles, and bloomer costume, and pay attention to nothing but the useful."

"Are there no rack and gibbet for such heresy?" cried the young man, springing to his feet.

But a part of his motive in rising was apparently to "skip" a flat stone along the tops of the waves, for he sat down again on the piece of wreck, and resumed,

"Women do not know what they are liked for —

not one of them in a thousand. That is the trouble. They had better read the poets and find out. It would largely reduce the business in the divorce courts. As an imitation man, woman is not a success. A man does not marry to have merely a rough, undelightful companion like himself. Nor is it, I should say, the undiluted ambition to have children, about whom there is no certainty that they will surpass — even if they equal — his own very moderate level. *He* has no complexion, no dimples, no dangling ear-rings that cast little shadows on his cheeks. Small pleasure too, I imagine, can be got out of his way of doing his hair, or out of the bending of his neck, or the intonations of his voice. I should really be glad to know what there is in him corresponding to all this for a woman to like!"

It might almost have been thought, as he regarded her, that it was from herself he drew the attractive details he so warmly cited.

"A woman would like *man*liness, I should say," she replied hesitatingly.

"A man of the right sort wants some one to idealize," said Bainbridge. "He wants to put her on a pedestal, and be rapturous about her. If she will do nothing on her side to keep up the illusion, what are you to expect?"

"But how about the irredeemably plain ones?"

"There are none such," he replied gallantly. "Fortunately, we do not all see with the same eyes. And if there be gradations of beauty, as we must admit, and some of it that almost approaches ugliness, by the general verdict, no doubt interior qualities are developed as a compensation. The irritation in the oyster-shell produces the pearl; the wrong side of the rug is often of a subdued richness, surpassing the right; and hyacinths give out their sweetest fragrance at night."

"But I can tell you that a woman has her notions of self-sacrifice and idealizing, too. If it be the wish of a man of the right sort to put her on a pedestal, and of a woman of the right sort to place him there, what is going to be done when they meet. What a sculpture gallery kind of a time they must have!"

"Oh, that is simple enough. They never do meet."

They paced slowly homeward from these conferences at the wreck, leaving long wavering lines of footsteps behind them. There was a heavy unrestful, erratic, larger pair, and a light clear-cut, sincere, perhaps gently-coquettish, smaller pair. Here and there they had paused. Ottilie, drew letters in the sand, or, bending lithe as a spear of the gray beach-grass, described large circles nonchalantly around her with her parasol. Or they picked up and discussed some curious bit of sea-weed or a bright pebble or shell.

"What is the name of it?" Bainbridge asked concerning one of these last, since his companion had shown a recondite acquaintance with the subject.

"You would not remember if I should tell you," was the roguish answer with which she covered her own ignorance.

Then she placed the shell against one cheek and the other, taking attitudes of mincing affectation, and cried, —

"The first duty of a woman is to be charming!"

It would have been a fitting penalty for such mockery to cover her with a thousand kisses; — but only as a friend; — surely only in the way of platonic friendship and nothing more.

XIV.

CROSS PURPOSES AT A NEWPORT VILLA.

WHEN all that was possible had been done in town, Rodman Harvey took his niece to Newport. He left her there, presently, with his family, and went away to Saratoga, to attend a convention of railway magnates.

It was thought, too, that the waters would be of benefit in his slight attacks of vertigo, to which he began to be subject with increasing frequency.

Bainbridge repaired to Newport also. Because a person has postponed his vacation a little, that is no reason why he should abandon it altogether. It is still quite warm enough at the middle of September to make a more refreshing temperature than that of the city desirable.

No definite purpose ruled his proceedings. He had nothing that he was about to do, nothing that he was about to say. He looked forward only to a continuance of his pleasant intercourse with Ottilie. Obstacles, which he had not quite foreseen, however, arose out of her new situation, the number of people with whom she was involved, and the whirl of gayeties. He found himself annoyed at first because he could not see her often enough. But later there was something even more serious.

A fortnight had elapsed when the young man came strolling along the Cliff Walk, which by courtesy of proprietors, passes, through turnstiles, along the borders of the estates. He found Ottilie with a book in a summer-house above the water. The tawny-haired Calista, amusing herself on the beach below, climbed up occasionally to take advice upon some new marine discovery.

Bainbridge explained in a matter-of-course sort of way that he had felt the need of a little change, after all, and found Newport as good a place for it as any other.

Ottilie pulled to pieces as they talked some coarse daisies, gathered for her by Calista from amid the hay which was being cut on the lawns. Afterwards she read aloud in a pleasantly murmurous voice some portions of Elaine, in the "Idyls of the King," the book she had with her. Then she rehearsed her new experiences.

"The Emperor of Brazil has been here," she said. "I have seen also an English duke, an Italian prince, with a delightfully musical name, and a Danubian princess, who is also a literary 'swell.' As to cabinet ministers, governors of States, senators, and gold-laced army and navy officers, both domestic and foreign, they are too numerous to mention."

"And you are in the midst of all this and a part of it?"

"Only a very little in the margin of the stream, not in the current. But Angelica is in the current; ah, yes, indeed. For her it is an incessant round of dinners, balls, theatricals, *fêtes-champêtres*, and archery and lawn-tennis parties at one of the beautiful villas after another. Or else she is driving on Ocean Avenue; witnessing the polo games, or the shooting or swimming matches; going to sessions of the

'Town and Country Club,' or the 'West Island Club's' bass-fishing picnics; or dancing on the yachts and men-of-war in the harbor. It almost makes one's head whirl even to be in the margin. I have been out to some of the simpler entertainments and we have a fair share of it all of course at our house. I begin to consider myself quite a connoisseur in social matters."

"And what difference do you find between fashionable society here and at your Great West? You should be able now to define our salient points, as distinguished from those of your Cincinnatis and Chicagos."

"I should say that there was more ease in entertaining here. So much of it goes on that people make a less important matter of it. Then there is the class of purely fashionable young men, who make no pretense of an occupation in life. We have very few of them as yet. But I dare say you are expecting me to make wholesale admissions of inferiority?"

"I thought perhaps you might have grown candid enough for that by this time."

"Then you will be very much mistaken. I wish I could see you try to pick out, by any difference of looks and manners, some elegant Cleveland people who were here last week. No! Our society is formed by exactly the same influences — I mean the main influences, — as yours. It reads the same things, sees the same musical and dramatic companies, — they all come to us after leaving you — has the same styles in dress, and the same trips to Europe. The boys come to the Eastern colleges, and the girls, as often as not, to the fashionable New York schools, where they are said to learn to enter a room or a carriage properly."

"Some of them afterwards have no carriages to enter," she added, " which, no doubt, results in more or less unhappiness."

Bainbridge admired the vein of excellent good sense which underlay all of her opinions.

" But now, the coming young millionaire," he said, " has he turned up yet ? "

" Not yet," she answered, laughing. " That is to say, unless we count Mr. Kingbolt, who has chosen to be really quite civil to me. Now I think of it, he is the one we selected, is he not ? Well, he has not proposed to me ; but I am sure that a number of other girls, of much more importance, must have begun to be jealous."

" Now, there is an absurd passion," — said Bainbridge presently, seizing the pretext for airing a favorite opinion. " If you like a person, you like him, for cause, for reasons good and satisfactory to yourself. It is not because you see him run after by other people. That is, supposing you to be a person of independent judgment and not a mere servile imitator. The reasons are not always easy to give, and they vary in each case, or we should all be fascinated by the same person ; but they exist all the same."

" But all the novelists use jealousy as an incentive," urged Ottilie.

" They are as wrong about that as their descriptions of the inducements to fall in love generally. They usually make it depend upon some astonishing feats, some heroic saving of life, fortune, or sacred honor, by one or both of the parties, for each other. As a matter of fact, not one match in a hundred thousand is made in that way. Lovers like to assume, of course, that they would do those things for each other, and perhaps they would; but the occasions do not offer. The couple simply walk, talk, and dance a little together, are pleased with each other's looks, study out such bits of each other's character as they can, and presently the thing is done."

Fearing, perhaps, some personal application from this, he added as an after-thought, —

"Of course, persons do not necessarily fall in love after having been through such a course as this, but they fall in love when they have not been through a blessed thing else."

The sea lay before them, blue and formal, in a wide band as it appears in the scenery of theatres. The locusts rattled in some trees near by. The heated atmosphere had a wavering motion near the ground. Tepid puffs from the lawn, mingling with the cooler breezes from the water, brought odors of the new-mown hay.

The Harvey villa crowned the long, gentle slope. It was of wood, painted in tones of Indian red and yellow ochre, and had numerous turrets, dormers, and ornamented chimney stacks. Upon the wide piazzas were willow arm-chairs with cushions. An end of bright curtain stuff floated from an upper window here and there. A tent, with tall spears and tasseled cords, like that of a Persian satrap, was pitched near the house. Portable fountains attached to rubber hose whirled their arms wildly about, like dancing dervishes, and sprayed portions of the lawn and large well-kept beds of bluish heliotrope, scarlet geraniums, and gray and purple coleus, with tall, large-leaved plants of the *Canna Indica*, rising from the midst.

Our friends ranged, in the pleasant desultory way they had, over a wide variety of topics.

Ottilie was a person of large reading. She had read everything that came in her way. Such, she confessed, had been her plan, or lack of plan. She had a fresh eager interest, which hardly excluded information of any kind from its scope. She often surprised Bainbridge by her excursions, acute as well as vivacious, into some of the graver fields of thought, into which such a person would not have been considered likely to enter.

"'Learning not vain, and wisdom not severe,'" he said, playfully, applying to her this description of what is probably quite the ideal manner of carrying off such knowledge as one possesses.

"No, I am a mere collection of smatterings," she declared, repudiating it, and began to ridicule her own pedantry.

"I shall never admit that. And besides, it is not what we know, but what we would like to know, what our interest goes out to, that makes us what we are. Do you not think so?"

"Yes, I suppose it is," said Ottilie.

They discoursed among other things on religion, as two intelligent young Americans thrown together in any degree of intimacy are soon apt to do.

"My family is thoroughly on the American plan in that respect," said Ottilie. "My father is Unitarian, my mother Presbyterian, and I Episcopalian. My brother is touched with some indefinite skeptical notions, which I do not pretend to understand. He calls himself at present an Agnostic, — whatever that may be. There is no permanent support for a Unitarian service at Lone Tree, so my illogical father goes to church occasionally with my mother or me. I was originally Presbyterian myself. It was the dignity and color of Episcopalianism, I think, that caused me to change."

"I dare say I should have to call myself Agnostic, too, if I called myself anything," returned Bainbridge. One seems to arrive at that after going the rounds, just as the union of all colors produces white, you know."

"Suppose you tell me just what an Agnostic is, now that the opportunity offers. I shall confront Paul with it."

"The Agnostic, I take it, is a person who, having shaken off the theological burdens he once carried, hardly knows any longer what he believes, or, worse yet, perhaps does not greatly care. Such a pass seems characteristic of the times. One is rather drawn into it through remarking the outrageous things that church people are constantly doing, — though we understand, of course, that it is in spite of, and not in consequence of, their system."

"Oh, I am sorry," said his companion. "It cannot be a very comfortable state of mind. I am sure that my brother is not happy. At least he will not be permanently, though just now he is so very consequential about his new opinions that he will not hear a word of opposition."

"It is not a very profitable one, at any rate, and you will find me far from consequential about it. It is a state of mind, too, that extends itself over things in general. It begets too great an impartiality. It is a soporific and not a stimulant. One course of action is apt to appear about as good as another. I think I have felt it even in those small articles for the papers. One should be something of a fanatic. How can he take on indignant airs, browbeat and scathe the opposition, when himself only half convinced? How do I know whether I am actually for free trade or protection, soft money or hard, the control of the corporations by the people, or of the people by the corporations, in the usual way, when so much is to be said on the other side?"

"Then why not get out of such a state of mind?"

"Ah, that is a very different matter."

"But you *must* have convictions. I must give you some of mine. Now let us begin. You believe in a future state?"

"What do some people want to live forever for," he returned evasively, "when they pass the life they have in such a wretched, petty way? What do they want to do beyond the stars, when they have seen nothing of what is beautiful, noble, and tender, in this world, even poor as it is?"

She argued this point with him, insisting on the possibility of development for all.

She continually said, "*I* would not do this," "*I* would not do that," with great positiveness.

"Your convictions are clear-cut enough," said Bainbridge. "You would be a sort of little Lady Macbeth of the exemplary sort. You would nerve a man up to deeds of desperate rectitude."

"Do hear me talk!" she returned. "Anybody would think I meant that I was perfection, but I am really as weak as water."

She cast away some of the daisies she had had in her hands, and brushed fragments of others from her lap with a kind of final air. There was a slight pause in the conversation.

"What pretty hands you have!" said Bainbridge, presently, as if observing them for the first time.

"I think them very ugly," and she tucked them into her belt.

"How curious it is," she reflected, "that he seems to find so many things about me pleasing."

"Come, let us see what lines of fate are written in them. Let us see what they have to say about that coming millionaire," he demanded.

This was no doubt permissible between friends. She reluctantly let him take one of her hands in his. Bainbridge began with a jargon about the "line of life," the "line of the heart," and other terms of chiromancy.

All at once he said, "Oh, here is your millionaire, sure enough. — No end of money. He will be a perfect Crœsus."

But Ottilie soon drew away her hand. It had been nervous and foolishly trembled in his from the first, though there was no reason why it should. She pretended to need it to point in an enthusiastic way an incoming sail. She had flushed a little, and offered no comment on his prophecies.

That was a charming morning, but a cloud came over it at the close. Nor did it pass like some that they saw occasionally darken along the ocean before them. It expanded, instead, till all the moral heavens, for them, were overcast with portents of the coming storm.

It began, perhaps, with an account by Ottilie of her uncle's fondness for cases of defalcation and forgery, as heretofore mentioned.

"I am quite at home in them, I assure you," she said. "There is a general similarity in all. First, there is the shock of discovery, then what the officers of the institution say, then what the neighbors and friends say, and what the pushing reporters try to make them say, when they do not wish to talk at all. Then there is the conviction that the losses are even greater than at first supposed. The criminal flies and is pursued. Perhaps he escapes to foreign shores. Or he is arrested and thrown into a common felon's cell, — or perhaps he commits suicide. All the way through there is the agony of his stricken family, possibly the insanity of one of its members, broken by the shame and grief which have come upon them."

"Pretty hard! pretty hard!" said Bainbridge, reflectively.

"Oh, why *will* they do such things?" went on the young enthusiast. "Why cannot this dreadful temptation that drags so many down be resisted? It seems the peculiar vice of our times. The fate of one does not deter others. Oh, how happy one ought to be who is even honest! It seems to me that I could see gold and diamonds around me mountains high, and never touch a thing. One can go hungry and ragged. He might feel like a soldier on the march, who has to go in the storm if need be, or when he is sick, and to sleep on the bare ground, and dines when he can. What happens then is not his own fault; he might have the comfort, at least, of saying, 'I do not deserve it.' But once succumb to dishonesty; take the bread of others, which can only be eaten in shame and bitterness; once straggle from the ranks into the hands of the guerillas and prowlers of the hostile country, — ah, what comfort is open to him then?"

"A rather odd taste in your uncle, is it not?"

"That is it," pursued Ottilie. "It sometimes puzzles me. He even expresses sympathy, which I should hardly think he would, since he is so precise in his own ideas of rectitude and his business requirements."

There was for Bainbridge an unpleasant suggestiveness in all this. The vague image of something uncanny which might have been done by Rodman Harvey seemed to follow him with a haunting pertinacity. His thoughts went back to Gammage, Jocelyn, and the palaver of old McFadd in Harvey's Terrace. He gave his companion involuntarily one of those glances betraying disquietude, in which intelligence outruns speech, as electricity outruns the mail.

It passed in an instant, however, and the bulk of his trouble was to come from another source.

The interview was now broken in upon by Kingbolt of Kingboltsville. This fortunate person, looking particularly well in a suit of white flannel, carrying one hand in a pocket of the easy jacket, came along the Cliff Walk also, and joined them. He sat down, and had evidently no intention of at once going away. Bainbridge was surprised at his intimacy with Ottilie. From a number of references it appeared that they had talked together not a little before.

Bainbridge had taken what she had said of Kingbolt as banter, of course. She had said "civil," and he had understood civility, or almost that — but this was something very different.

He went away himself in a reflective mood, leaving them together.

"It looks as though people were treating her very well," he said. "It looks as though she were having 'a good time.' Well, I am glad of that. It is as it should be."

Kingbolt, was in fact, hovering about Ottilie a good deal at this time. His motive must have been a touch of that charming, pathetic sentiment which leads the ardent lover to invest with a part of the same fond interest both the family of the beloved and everything in her vicinity. It is something even to be near those who have been near her.

Kingbolt had come back considering himself cured. But he had fallen in with Angelica again, and his infatuation was again renewed. He had made new advances, which had been repulsed, as of old. As Angelica would hardly receive him, he bethought him then of the pretext of calling upon Ottilie. Ottilie was at first puzzled quite as much as complimented. She hardly knew whether it was even permissible to decline the attentions of so magnificent a personage. But he talked to her more and more about Angelica, and at last took her into his confidence. She had by no means desired his secret, but having it, thought it no more than right to keep it intact. She had been obliged to study all her resources of non-committalism, however, in dealing with him on this subject.

"Why," he exclaimed, "did she choose Sprowle above all others? On what grounds could she bring herself to like him? If she had taken one of the first-class foreign titles, as she might very well have done, a person of distinction, of fine presence,— anybody, in short, but Sprowle," — and he dismissed his unwitting rival with an air of contempt.

Ottilie replied guardedly. "Of course Mr. Sprowle is of a very distinguished family. His connections are very influential. His mother boasts that the Sprowles were of high consideration when the Rifflards were trading coon-skins with the Indians, the Antrams trotting the Irish bogs, and the Goldstones their native German cabbage fields. As to marrying a title, I have heard my cousin express dissatisfaction with the way that kind of match often turns out. She says that she long ago decided against surrendering her own notions to those of a foreign and very different social system, and immuring herself perhaps in some old feudal castle, beyond all legitimate opportunities of resistance, should need arise."

There could have been no great amount either of new information or of comfort in what Ottilie said, but the erratic young man found a relief even in the privilege of talking freely of the cause of his pains.

When Bainbridge made his call the next day, Ottilie was really engaged in matters which prevented her seeing him. He wandered aimlessly about Newport. The next day he found her on the piazza, it is true, but Kingbolt was with her. On the next, Kingbolt came up within five minutes.

Angelica too arrived this day, on horseback, with a groom behind her. She wore her dark green riding-habit, which fitted her figure to perfection, and her silk hat shone with an exceptional lustre. She was in good spirits, and caracoled her horse in a peculiar way as she came up to the block.

"Where did you get that trick?" asked Kingbolt, affecting with her an ease he by no means felt.

"From Monsieur Meigs, my riding-master at

Paris," she explained, but more to the company than her questioner. "Twenty francs a lesson, and twenty more for the two horses. I used to ride with him in the Bois. No nonsense with M. Meigs, no staring about, no frivolity. 'Eyes between your horse's ears, mademoiselle!' Yes, M'seu Meigs, — M'seu Meigs." She straightened herself up and assumed a very stiff position in the saddle, in imitation of the bluff and centaur-like aspect of her former English riding-master.

When she had dismounted she sat and talked a while, rattling her whip on the floor of the piazza.

"They let me have a pet black and tan, at school," she said. "If you could have seen the bills for that animal! I suppose I was perfectly robbed in every way, in those times. So much for the dog's food, so much for dog's house, so much for cutting dog's ears. Poor Niniche might as well have been an elephant. Dear me, I am glad it all is over. Such extraordinary governesses as we had! There was one I remember, who kept her head tied up in a green veil. She was of such a fascinating ugliness that, positively — I happened to be looking at her one day at dinner, when she indignantly sent her plate to me by the servant, pretending that I was trying to notice how much she ate. The singing assistant at the same school had the most extraordinary mouth! I told her frankly one day that I did not wish to learn a method which disfigured people for life in that way."

Some small trait of parsimony, or shaft of cruelty which had been directed at the expense of the helpless and unfortunate, seemed to appeal most to her sense of what was important, and likely to be entertaining, in her reminiscences.

"And such husbands as they had, the mesdames who kept those schools!" she continued. "One was a mild old gentleman, who occasionally got as far with some inoffensive remark as 'I would observe, chère amie,' when his wife nearly snapped his head off with an '*est ce-que je ne sais pas ça, moi?*' Another used to turn up from South America or Africa, or somewhere, as often as his wife got a little ahead in the world, and force money from her. Once he came just before dinner, and pulled the cloth off the table, with all the dishes, in a grand smash."

"People seem to make a great fuss over a little matter like that," ventured Kingbolt. "I believe it was a favorite performance of mine when I was a child. They used to put me in a padded room afterwards, to meditate. If I kicked around there I could not hurt myself or the furniture."

Angelica paid this guest but little attention, and presently, taking her leave, swept serenely in-doors.

"It is evident that he does not come on *her* account," reflected Bainbridge.

This was the more evident when Kingbolt again out-stayed him. He seemed to have even more things in common with Ottilie than before. She wore a high color, and her manner was fluttered. Bainbridge chose to hold most of his own powers of entertaining in abeyance, and this increased the general constraint.

He went away this time with bitterness in his heart.

"Shall I warn her," he meditated, "against so undesirable a friendship? Kingbolt is one of the rashest, most dangerous men of all his fashionable set. He is gambling recklessly at this very time, losing heavy sums night after night at the Club. — Bah! a fine callow piece of business that would be, a warning. Oh, yes, to be sure!"

When he had not seen Ottilie, the day was wholly wasted. He would not have come to Newport for the pure pleasure of it. He would have taken his vacation by preference at some much less conventional place — with his gun, for instance, among the mountains. Once when he did not find her, he went, after all, to a *fête-champêtre*, from which he had intended to absent himself on her account. There was Ottilie in person, playing at lawn tennis as Kingbolt's partner. The day following, he started out, nerved with an indignant purpose. He would now at last demand an explanation. As he drew near the grounds of the villa, on the Bellevue Avenue side, Ottilie and Kingbolt emerged, seated high up in state in the dashing English tilbury of the latter. Behind them, with folded arms, as rigid as the sphinx, was Kingbolt's English groom. Ottilie held a pretty parasol above her head, and looked out sweetly from below it, her face partially screened by the lace border. Bainbridge had shortly before passed Angelica herself, driving, over the high dash of a roomy phaeton, a pair of cream-colored ponies, with Ada Trull beside her.

The two were spread out in toilettes of rainbow brightness, and he had mused to himself, "The air hath bubbles as the water hath, and these are of them." But neither, he thought, presented as elegant an effect as Ottilie. Her simplicity of style was remarked upon by others, who did not know her, and was commended as very "good form." She was spoken of as being probably a Boston girl.

There were hardly two more uncomfortable young

men, in their respective ways, in all Newport at this time than Kingbolt and Bainbridge. Newport, however, did not hold Bainbridge long. He called to take his leave of Ottilie, and in the interview threw out darkly enigmatic hints, and acted in a manner so far from friendly that she was surprised and grieved. He went away by the boat, leaving "the wretched business to go on." He understood now her fluttered manner, her embarrassment, perfidious that she was, that day when he had taken her hand and read its lines. Ah yes, perfectly well!

"Do I want to marry her, then?" he reflected, on the other hand, facing himself severely down. "Not at all. I want to marry nobody. What should I marry on, forsooth? Nothing in the situation from the money point of view has changed. She has simply done, like a cool, prudent, and business-like girl, exactly what I told her. She had my advice and consent, my express injunction. Perhaps I thought that her graces of mind and person were to be conveniently hidden from every vision but mine? But what more natural, what more precisely to be expected, than that some one of these young men of fortune should have the grain of sense necessary to see that, with but half a chance, she would make one of the most elegant young matrons in New York? Money on her side need be no object if his fancy were interested. That pair need not wait to marry, indeed."

He reflected on the enormous discrepancy in fortune between Kingbolt and himself. Then he reflected on the incredibility of the fact that he, Russell Bainbridge, should find himself involved, a second time, in a serious disturbance of the affections.

"Ah, but we are platonic friends, to be sure," he concluded with a sigh. "Friendship rests content with the calmer mental satisfactions. It desires the best good of its object, does it not? What better could I wish for her than the greatest number of millions to her fortune possible?"

He did not know, in fine, precisely what he would have had Ottilie do. How could she have known the state of his feelings, when he had not known it himself? Still she *ought* to have known. She should have given him the first chance, and pretended at least to be sorry, and taken up with her dissolute young Crœsus afterwards.

How was it now with Kingbolt, when Bainbridge had gone? As there is apt to be a perverse fate in these things, he came still to see Ottilie, but much less often. The extreme measure of his attentions had been lavished, as it happened, during the very period of Bainbridge's stay. Angelica, for her part, was pleased to consider this intimacy "very amusing." Had it been of longer duration, or perhaps had she seen more of it, she would perhaps have been led by a natural perversity to interfere. Absent so much, however, in the whirl of her amusements, she contented herself with an occasional small innuendo.

Angelica, again, fell into the way of borrowing small sums of money from Ottilie about these times, always with an easy forgetfulness of repayment. This she would do, slender as was her cousin's store, rather than change the smallest of her own banknotes. It almost seemed, as if she congratulated herself upon these acquisitions with a glee beyond their importance. Was it not "so much clear gain," since it all came in the first instance from her father's purse?

Kingbolt had finally an item of intelligence for Angelica that commended him somewhat more than usual to the favor of that young woman. He called upon her one day, and found her alone, in a cool, matting-carpeted drawing-room, whither she had retired from the glare of the heat.

"I thought you might like to know," he said, introducing his business hastily, "that 'Lady Angelica' has just come in at the head of a big field of flyers at Buffalo. Here is the dispatch."

He handed her the paper. It appeared that, earlier in their acquaintance, she had graciously permitted him to name after her a fine racing mare of his. This animal was now doing remarkable things on the Western circuit. Angelica took a certain pride in the exploits of her namesake, as somehow adding to her own importance. She listened with interest while he confined himself to this subject. But, what with the occasion, and her unusual softness of mood, he had soon strayed impetuously very far from it.

"There! It is as I feared," she said, stopping him with a gesture and a clear-eyed calmness more discouraging than anger. "You are going to make love to me, and I shall have to send you away."

He burst out at this with what he had had so long in his mind. "Oh, how is it possible," he cried, putting directly to her at last the question he had put to Ottilie, "that such a girl as you can take up with him? It is *I* who want you, *I* who love you."

Had Angelica desired she might have said truthfully, in reply to this, that she had not chosen her form of happiness to consist of expansions of affection and flutterings of the heart. She might have said, too, on the other hand, that she was an excellent judge in personal appearance, and could see very well the difference between the comeliness of this aspirant and the awkward proportions of Sprowle. Perhaps her eyes even rested upon him with a certain approval while she showed herself the most inflexible.

"But," she might have gone on to say, "I have deliberately preferred a certain ideal of distinction. You are the son of a manufacturer, who, like my father, would never have been heard of unless he had made a fortune. I shall not have as much money in marrying Sprowle as if I took you, but we shall be very comfortable. Besides, I wish to marry a man whom I can control, in order, under all circumstances hereafter, to do exactly as I please."

Really, there was something almost touching in this immolation of all the finer and warmer human impulses upon the altar of a cool calculation.

"I cannot endure it. I have never been brought up to be crossed," persisted Kingbolt in his attempt.

"It is time you began, then," exclaimed Angelica, curtly.

She had to be very peremptory with him. It was only upon his express undertaking never to annoy her again with so hopeless a suit that she would even permit him to come to the house at all. He was apologetic and subdued, thereafter and they conferred together in a milder tone.

"It is useless to consider what might have been," said the beauty, taking a philosophic air. "Fate has decreed otherwise."

Kingbolt of Kingboltsville had moods after this

which for him were little short of seraphic. The breaking-harness on the fiery, wild-eyed, young mustang, which seems preposterous beyond belief at first, has in the end its legitimate effect. The fiery, young mustang is broken, as others have been before him. Kingbolt posed now for merely a disinterested friend. His new-found amiability embraced even Sprowle. He gave out that Sprowle was not such a " muff " as he seemed. He presented him, in token of amity, with one of his fine English coaching-whips, having an extra long lash. He even spoke of getting him, in the winter, into the Capricorn, a little club within the Empire Club, a coterie of select spirits, who had the habit of dining together once a month.

Kingbolt did not lack fierce revolts, however. When moved by one of these, he rode a hurdle race, at the Aquidneck Course, which was the talk of the town. It was done on a foolish wager, against professional jockeys, and he won in a tremendous canter by three lengths. He confided to Ottilie that he had been in hopes of breaking his neck in the course of it. Again he told her, —

" Half the time it is as much as I can do to keep from sending a charge of shot into the infernal idiot," — meaning Sprowle by this pleasant description, — " at the pigeon matches."

It was not long after this latter speech that she was startled by hearing that Kingbolt had himself been shot, by Sprowle, at the Narragansett Gun Club's grounds. She was sure there must have been an affray, and in the sequel his own vindictive plan reversed. Angelica, also, had at first the idea that the shooting was due to some absurd jealousy on the part of her affianced, from whom such things were by no means to be expected. But Sprowle Onderdonk, the captain of the club, presently came to the house in person, and brought reassuring news.

"It was a mere accident," he said. "Sprowle fired low, in a hurry, at a bird which flew over the spectators' heads. He is devilish awkward about some things, you know. Kingbolt got a little of it in his face. It won't signify. He will only have a few scattering blue spots here and there; that is all. It won't injure his good looks a particle."

Ottilie was called back to town, to resume her cares for her uncle. The rest of the family were to remain until well into the autumn. The last that she saw of Kingbolt, he waved her good-by from the piazza of his hotel, where he sat with a green shade over his eyes, attended upon by a sympathizing circle, to whom the misfortunes of such a person seemed misfortunes indeed. But she had been in town only a few days when he presented himself, apparently little the worse for wear, and asked her once more to drive.

"I came back to the city to get my own doctor," he explained. "As soon as he had reduced the swelling, little trace of the damage remained, as you see."

He had a new Whitechapel cart at the door, the horses harnessed in the tandem fashion. Ottilie allowed herself to be persuaded to go with him.

As fate again would have it, Bainbridge saw the pair on their way up the Avenue. Grimly enough he recalled that Sunday when the same driver and his vehicle had been discussed by Ottilie and himself from the sidewalk. The tone of her comments would hardly have been so unfavorable now. Who could doubt that it was all settled between them? As likely as not even the wedding-day was fixed. He could almost hear the tender things they were saying to each other.

Now the tender things which the two were, in fact, saying were inquiries on Kingbolt's part — after beating about the bush — as to how Angelica had taken the news of his injury. This information had really been the object of his present courtesy.

Then, when this had been disposed of, they discussed the relative merits of side-lamps as compared with dash-lamps for a dog-cart, and whether brown-black with crimson wheels, or invisible green and canary be preferable as colors. Kingbolt showed his companion how, by an ingenious contrivance, the centre of gravity of the vehicle could be shifted, so as to be kept always over the axle, whether a groom were carried or not. He also gave her points about his horses. He called upon her, from time to time, to observe how he threaded narrow mazes and made deft turns, which to her seemed dangerous. Ottilie had acquired from her cousin Selkirk, who had taken her out once or twice, some scraps of this kind of knowledge, and now, by politeness, made the most of it.

She endeavored to infuse into her salute to Bainbridge as much warmth as possible. He chose to construe this rather into her way of gloating over him, and returned as frigid a bow as possible in return. Ottilie could by no means account for this, nor did opportunities soon offer for explanation. Bainbridge ceased to come near her. She scarcely even saw him any more.

She recalled his vagaries of speech, his professed changeableness of purpose.

"Ah, well!" she sighed gently. "I am the object of it in my turn. The friendly interest he expressed in me has no doubt come to the conclusion that was legitimately to have been expected."

XV.

IN TOWN FOR THE WINTER.

On their return to town for the winter, the Harveys began to plan their social campaign. They desired their first season in the new house, and the last of Angelica's unmarried condition to be one of peculiar brilliancy.

Something had already been done, at Newport, with the assistance of Mr. Sprowle and his cousin Sprowle Onderdonk, in the way of talking over the people who were to be invited to dinner. Those men were very powerful, socially. It was on this side that the advantage of the Sprowle connection came in. They could put your name down for almost anything, and there you were, safely chosen among the elect. Mrs. Harvey, as a Muffett, had substantial claims, of course, to consideration. But her husband had less; and what with this, and their having been abroad so much, and for some time without a house of their own, there was danger, had they been left quite to themselves, not only of making mistakes, but even of being annoyingly overlooked.

Could the actual gradations, and heart-burnings on account of them, in the upper class, be discerned by those below, they might serve as a motive, almost equal to that of Christian resignation, for a more contented state of mind. The stars are all a long way off, and all shine; but ah, the enormous gaps there are between them!

Conferences, for drawing up the programme, were held in the comfortable sitting-room of Mrs. Harvey. Ottilie was present as amanuensis. She had many readjustments to make in her notes before all was complete.

Sprowle had taken advantage of his opportunities to find out what people of note were going to do, and carefully brought word.

"The Corlaers will give two balls," he reported: "probably one at Delmonico's, and one at their house. The Bourdons will give private theatricals, and that sort of thing; the Antrams a set of Germans. There will be an unusual crop of 'coming-out' parties early in the season, — Mrs. Schinko's, for her second daughter, leading off about the middle of November. The Vanderlyns will give only dinners, as usual."

"Those Vanderlyns have reduced it to an exact science," Angelica interrupted. "Their dinners are their year's work. They make their preparations one year for the next. They send their invitations never less than three weeks in advance, so that there can be no interference from 'previous engagements.' Two months of the winter they dine people, three times a week. Then they stop short and devote themselves to accepting the hospitalities offered in return."

"They have a stunning good cook, you know," said Sprowle.

"Yes, they have a superb *chef*, but I know very well it is only for the time being. Vanderlyn has a way of letting you know that everything they have is got up in the house. They depend upon no vulgar outside assistance, — no, indeed. 'How can such a person — aw — come into your kitchen or your dining-room, and do anything, ye know?' he says. 'Why, he can't find a blessed pot or a kettle, ye know,'" and Angelica pretended to twist up the end of an imaginary moustache.

"You must look out for the Mondays of the Family Circle Dancing Class," resumed Sprowle. "There are to be three during the winter, and one after Lent. The 'Patriarchs' will give three balls, as usual, on Mondays, too, beginning early in December. The young swells, the 'Bachelors,' take Thursdays, and are to have two. Here is a partial list of the dates; I will let you have the rest as soon as possible. Yes, all that will go on just as usual. Of course some new things will be started, also."

"The trouble is that as soon as a thing gets well agoing in New York," said Angelica, "it begins to run down."

"That is so," said Sprowle. "All sorts of common persons elbow their way in. You cannot tell how they do it, but the first thing you know there they are. The only resource then for the top swells is to leave it, and start something else. There is one novelty on the carpet already, in the shape of a 'Ladies' Ball,' to be under the patronage of a committee of dowagers."

"Ah, yes," said Mrs. Rodman Harvey with interest, "the Ladies' Ball."

"Judging by the row they are having over the invitations, and the way black-balling is going on, I should say it was to be *the* exclusive affair of the season," continued Sprowle. "Mamma was a member of the original group, of course, and *you* are all right. That has been looked out for. — By the way, when your name first came up, to be added to the list of managers, that young Mrs. Bergen Ap-Zoom — a flighty creature, you know, who has just got back from somewhere, I could not tell you where — had the impudence to ask, 'Who is Mrs. Rodman Harvey? I don't believe I ever heard of her.' 'You may not have heard of her,' mamma replied, — pretty sharply, I can tell you, — 'but I would have you to know that her daughter is shortly to marry my son.'"

The speaker finished with a laugh, and seemed to look upon the anecdote as very amusing.

"Well, I must say!" exclaimed Mrs. Harvey, flushing with anger.

"You use quite your customary tact in telling us that, Austin dear," said Angelica, with far from an admiring expression.

She marked Mrs. Bergen Ap-Zoom for future consideration, as a Seminole might have cut a notch on a stick. But it was exactly in order to be placed forever beyond the reach of such slights as this that the match with Sprowle was being engineered. Sprowle did not quite understand his offense, and continued in a rather mystified way with his information.

"I had better bring up Van Boskirk from the Club, to see if there is anything I have omitted. Van has it all at his fingers' ends. — And you had better have in Scatterthwaite, you know," he concluded, "and just glance over his records so as not to send out invitations to people who have been dead several years, and that sort of thing."

When the necessary emendations had been made, Ottilie read out, with the proper date affixed to each item, a list comprising two balls, three four o'clock teas, and two "ladies' luncheons" on a large scale.

There were also to be dinners, of from twelve to twenty covers, every Thursday, from December up to Lent. This was the more formal hospitality, that of an intimate sort to be sandwiched between. Their general "day at home" was to be Tuesday, after three.

Scatterthwaite was afterwards summoned in. He was a person who united with the functions of a church sexton a discreet supervision of the machinery of society. No wedding, funeral, or reception of the first class was complete without his fostering care, if it were only in distributing the invitations, or watching the descent of the guests from the carriages. By means of confidential communications made him he was sometimes able to forestall, if he would, an awkward duplication of dates, or a too great similarity of programmes. These can by no means be wholly avoided, however, since the days of the season are so few, the range of possible entertainments so limited, and those who desire to avail themselves of it so numerous.

Scatterthwaite found it useful to keep such a record of the movements of society as could hardly be done by simple individuals actually involved in its whirl. He could supply the proper addresses, prevent the extending of invitations to persons long since deceased, as Sprowle had said, and others fallen into poverty or hopeless disgrace; and he knew what families had young sons and daughters coming up, and now about of an age to be formally noticed.

Then Clocheville, the new caterer, who was making his way to favor, Haricot, spoiled by prosperity, having grown so reprehensibly negligent of late, was brought before the conclave. After him came Spang, the florist. These were contracted with to furnish services and the supplies necessary at the proper dates, and carefully noted all in their little books. Clocheville was only for the grander occasions, Conrad and the resources of the house being sufficient in themselves for the lesser.

The bulk of Ottilie's labors resolved itself into the putting in order of her aunt's book of addresses, — which contained in all probably a thousand names, — and in sending out the invitations from it as occasion demanded.

"Aunt Alida" had no talent for resigning any considerable part of the burdens of management. Her active-minded, amiable niece was thus left with much of leisure on her hands. She occupied herself in keeping up her studies or practiced her music. She associated herself in some charitable enterprises, in which she became interested through some of the quieter new acquaintances she had made. One of these was a society for sending out poor children to homes in the West, and she managed to secure places for a number of the *protégés* in and about Lone Tree. Another made substantial garments for the poor; and another was a "flower mission," which brightened the bedsides of the sick in the hospitals.

She found Rodman Harvey inclined to respond freely, at this time, to demands upon him for such purposes. "The old man is going it pretty strong on the charity lay, just now," said his clerk, McKinley, at the store. "You hardly pick up a paper but you find him presenting a stand of colors, or a barrel of flour, or a silver pitcher, or a set of furniture, to some armory or church fair, or something that way."

"Well, his head is level. He could n't play a better card for election purposes no way," a comrade returned.

Ottilie's charitable tendencies were not shared by Angelica.

"She will bring small-pox or some other dreadful calamity into the house," she complained. "She ought to be stopped, if only for Calista's sake."

Such concern in Calista's welfare was the more remarkable since her usual attention to the child was no more than to criticise the sharpness of her elbows and shoulder-blades, and push her out of the way. This was a programme she was hardly likely ever to vary from unless Calista should become a beauty.

"One would think that the rich had nothing to do but give, give," Angelica proceeded. "They are as poor as the rest of the world, if you look at the demands upon them. I suppose papa will be begged out of house and home yet. I expect to live to see the day. What poor family, for instance, has to keep up an establishment like this, — eight horses, an opera box, give dinners and dress? I believe there is too much luxury already among lower orders. I am half inclined to subscribe to the theory that it is a mistake to do so much for the weak and suffering. It is better that they should die out. There would be fewer people, but those remaining would be good for something. All criminals ought to be shot, to save the expense of their keep; and the pauper sick exposed on islands, as in the good old days of the Romans."

Ottilie had heard the self-same doctrines from Bainbridge, told in his exaggerated way, and had paid no great heed.

"Oh, he likes to hear himself talk," she said.

"He is like the son in the Scriptures, who said he would not go into the vineyard, but really went, and was so much better than the other one who said he would, but did n't."

But in her cousin's mouth, though she used a bantering tone, the words had a different ring, — almost the air of cold conviction. The same trait appeared in Angelica's line of comment on any case of magnanimous effort or self-sacrifice, incidentally reported. Such unbusiness-like proceedings appeared to excite in her less admiration than contempt.

"That is all very well for those who like it," she would say, "but you will not find *me* doing it."

She seemed to value herself upon her superior good sense in this. She prided herself, too, upon her incapacity "to be taken in." This was much to her credit, no doubt, and a quality to be recommended to others.

Still, considering that she never had been taken in, nor suffered any of those disappointments which often sow the seed of suspicion in natures originally warm and confiding, a little more of the candor and trust natural to ingenuous youth might have been pardoned in her case.

As to simple pleasures, to contrast her with Ottilie, she hated them. She understood only those of the complex and costly sort, confining her interest as it might be said, to that part of life which is grown under glass.

She continued her borrowing of small sums of Ottilie. The child Calista, observant of this, for all her quiet way, took it upon herself to impart the information to her mother. Mrs. Harvey insisted thereupon on repaying the loans from her own pocket, against the protest of Ottilie. Angelica made no offers of restitution even now. She received her mother's mention of the subject, on the contrary, with an indignant air, made as if Ottilie had brought the complaint herself, and took occasion to show her resentment quite offensively.

An open little tiff occurred between the two for the first time. Ottilie worsted her aggressor with a gallant intrepidity, accompanied by a charmingly dignified air. She broke down, however, immediately after, and went sobbing to her room.

"I do think it a pity you two cannot agree," said her aunt, as if the blame had been equal.

At this Ottilie redoubled her tears, and was almost ready to leave the house. But the next moment Mrs. Harvey came to her, dried her tears affectionately, and assured her that justice should be done. The matter came to the ears of the merchant prince, also, and he sternly bade his daughter apologize.

"I told you how it would be, mamma!" cried Angelica, passionately, to her mother, when she had withdrawn from his presence. "You cannot *have* that kind of people, and their dreadful feelings." She apologized to Ottilie, nevertheless, as she had been told, making her peace with a certain haughty grace. She said that she had been unconscious of giving offense.

Rodman Harvey passed much of his time in the house, in a plainly furnished office, opening from the library. He had a safe there and some atlases and statistical works, which he used in preparing his addresses for the Board of Trade or the Civic Reform Association; and there was a writing table, covered with green leather, at which he signed his checks.

He retired early, as a rule, and only went out to gayeties where his interest or his dignity were likely to be much enhanced.

If not in this office, or den, of an evening, he was often to be found in his billiard room. His cronies, Hackley and Hastings, joined him there; or his elder son, Selkirk, took part with him in a quiet game. His younger son, Rodman, Jr., whose appeals for a latch-key still continued unavailing, was sometimes invited down also, as a wholesome respite from his studies. This youth secretly scoffed at his father's game, without daring display too openly his own superior prowess, lest he be questioned as to how he acquired it. He repined at the necessity of frittering away so much valuable time in slow fashion with "the governor," when the pleasures he knew of outside were going on without him. In this discontented frame of mind, he proved so severe a critic and made so many disputes over the most innocent shots, that he was far from being an agreeable companion.

Hackley and Hastings were the guests when Ottilie was sent down, rather late one evening, with a message to her uncle. "Ask him, please, for the memorandum I gave him for the upholsterer," said Mrs. Harvey. "I wish to add something. Oh, and just say quietly, that one of the guests for our Redway dinner to-morrow has disappointed us, and I wish him to find some eligible person to fill the vacancy. Tell him to fix it in his mind! I shall depend upon him."

The billiard-players extended a warm welcome to the young girl as she came down among them. Hackley gallantly insisted upon her making a shot for him. She did this with no great willingness, showing in the process the unconscious grace of her slender figure.

Mr. Hackley was short, well-fed, and bald. At fifty he still gave himself the airs of a merry bachelor. In the street he walked with a dignified bearing, carrying his head a little on one side, and one hand open behind him, with the palm outwards.

He assumed with Harvey a brusque air, as one who spoke his mind without fear or favor. But it might have been noticed that his sayings were generally of a complimentary and not an offensive sort. His way was to affect to give to gross flattery a certain air of abuse.

Ottilie, with a quick intuition, distrusted the sincerity of his professions, and she did not like too well the near proximity of his large bald head, and large mouth and teeth.

She did not find that her uncle chose his intimates with too great discrimination. Perhaps this was the truth. In natures of a certain cold kind, self-centred, without "magnetism," as the saying is, to whom companionship is not an absolute necessity, there is a degree of simplicity in these matters. Their friends often choose themselves, instead of being chosen, and fasten themselves on. To both these friends Harvey had done many favors, chiefly of a financial sort.

Hastings was tall, large-bearded, taciturn, and non-committal. There was nothing in particular for him, except, in Ottilie's eyes, his engaging wife, with whom her friendship still continued. On the other hand, also, he had nothing against him. He was as taciturn as Hackley was talkative, attended to his game of billiards in a business-like way, and nodded intelligent acceptance of remarks rather than commented upon them verbally.

Ottilie, obliged to wait a little for the opportunity to speak to her uncle apart, then to wait longer while a servant was sent to find the required memorandum on his writing-table, sat down on a luxurious cushioned bench affixed to the wall.

She heard the gentlemen talking about the mansion, which was still too new a subject to be exhausted.

"Come!" said Hackley, giving the air of an impertinence to what was really an opening for its owner to indulge a little self-glorification, "the whole thing cost you a good quarter of a million dollars."

"Worse yet," replied the merchant prince, smiling. "A quarter of a million went for the house and ground alone. Say two hundred thousand more for the decoration, furnishing, and pictures. You shall have it as it stands for half a million dollars. That leaves but a bare living profit on the transaction."

"I don't just happen to have the sum about me," returned Hackley, creating some amusement by pretending to feel for it in his pocket-book. "In fact, there are often times now when I don't have a little amount like that about me. What with speculating, manufacturing, and so forth, in these late years, sometimes making, sometimes losing, I have seen the time, more than once, when a cashier's salary at the Antarctic Bank, regularly paid, as of yore, would have again looked to me like a very comfortable thing. Perhaps none of us ever bettered ourselves greatly by leaving the bank. Here am I, as you see. Burlington, the president, got himself made a general in the civil wars, and minister to a foreign court; but glory and languages will not do to bring up a family of daughters on. He has been unsettled in his affairs ever since. Then there was old Gammage, the note-teller, you know, who went to the devil with drink."

"It astonishes me, sometimes, to find such a roof over my head, after all the old house of Harvey & Co. has been through," said the merchant, following this with a piece of retrospect of his own. "You recollect some of its tough times, Hackley, yourself."

"Yes, I recollect." Hackley's countenance wore an evasive expression, and his comments led away from rather than up to the subject.

"When I think of it I could not tell you how we escaped. I could not, really," persisted Harvey.

Was it imagination on Ottilie's part, or did Mr. Hackley look at his patron in a singular way, from half-veiled eyes, and then as if in upon himself, introspectively? It would have been strange, indeed, had Hackley known any means by which the house had escaped, when Harvey did not know it himself.

"There was, then, an Antarctic Bank," reflected Ottilie, nervously. "There was a General Burlington, and a Gammage, and this is the Hackley, as specified by the vagrant McFadd, that day in Harvey's Terrace, when the prisoners escaped."

"Pshaw!" she broke out. "What folly! To imagine that if there had been anything, and so many people cognizant of it, it could have possibly waited till now!"

The following afternoon Bainbridge happened in at Rodman Harvey's store, to report upon some collections of a dubious character, which had been put into his hands.

"By the way," said Harvey, as he was taking his leave, "have you anything to do this evening?"

"No," returned Bainbridge promptly, supposing some further offer of employment at hand.

"Well, then, I wish you would excuse the informality of the invitation, and come up and dine with us at seven. We are to have the Hon. Lyman S. Redway. He is in town for but a few days, and we had to catch him when we could."

Harvey had neglected till now to carry out the instructions sent him by his wife to fill the vacant place. This was a presentable young man, who would do for a guest as well as another, and save the trouble of further search.

"With great pleasure," said Bainbridge.

He cursed his hasty admission that he was not engaged, but could not now withdraw it. After all, perhaps Ottilie would not appear at dinner. As to the Hon. Lyman S. Redway, a distinguished political economist, for whose character and attainments he had the highest respect, he was a man well worth seeing. At the worst he could devote his attention very much to him.

XVI.

THE MERCHANT PRINCE DINES A POLITICAL ECONOMIST.

Rodman Harvey dined now a brother merchant, now a magnate of the stock exchange or the railroads; again, a military or naval officer of distinction, or a high functionary of state. Or again, it was one of his dignified foreign correspondents, or perhaps some scion of nobility who brought letters from these to facilitate his tour through America.

Once he gave a dinner to the great fortunes, in which were some of those amassed with such fabulous rapidity of late in California.

The capitalist Goldstone said on that occasion, to a lady at his right, "I suppose you will have no eyes at all for me, with my poor little million."

Bainbridge entered the Harveys' drawing-room as nearly as might be at the appointed hour of seven. The hostess received him affably, asking, —

"Where have you been?"

Having thus recognized the fact of his previous existence, she turned again in her bustling way to other guests. She was dressed to-night in precisely that toilette of maroon satin and diamonds which we have seen in her portrait, by Huntington, as exhibited at the Academy of Design.

Small groups were sitting or standing about, and the rooms were full of that gently murmurous, expectant conversation characteristic of the twenty minutes before going in to dinner.

Angelica's pug Marmion, his neck ornamented with a wide silk bow, to match his mistress' dinner dress, trotted sedately about. Bainbridge stooped to pat him. The favorite avoided the caress with a wearied air, seeming to say, "Oh, no. That may do very well, from strangers, for dogs in general; but in my case there is no necessity of anything of the kind."

It was rather late when Ottilie appeared and the curiosity of Bainbridge was satisfied. He looked around next for Kingbolt, but Kingbolt was not there. The younger portion of the company consisted of Sprowle, his cousin Sprowle Onderdonk, Ada Trull, Daisy Goldstone, and a Miss Farley, daughter of an ex-secretary of the navy, who was here with her father and mother. There were also Selkirk Harvey and a Miss Van Voorst of Albany, lately brought to visit in the house for his especial benefit.

It began to be feared that a general indifference to the female sex, in the son and heir, might extend to the degree of not marrying at all, thus defeating the ambitious hopes to be accomplished through him. To contend against this, his mother was in the habit of artfully throwing in his way young women of the desirable sort and personal attractions, with the purpose of stirring at length his sluggish fancy.

When Bainbridge had identified all, he found, besides those above, the dowager Mrs. Sprowle; the mayor of the city; the governor of a neighboring State; Dr. Miltimore, the polished divine; Dr. Wyburd, who could be depended upon to give a certain animation even to the most abstruse topics; Mr. Hackley; Blithewood Gwin, the well-known journalist; and Baron Au, the Pomeranian consul-general.

The eminent political economist was long in coming. Pending his arrival, a party was organized, under the host's guidance, to explore the cellars and similar appurtenances of the house below stairs.

"All that," said Rodman Harvey, "is the department upon which I especially pride myself. I claim much of it as of my especial invention and contrivance."

It was thought at first that ladies could not go; but the ex-secretary's daughter, picking up her skirts in a dainty way, set the example, and others, with Ottilie among them, followed. Bainbridge remained behind.

These lower regions were found to be of a spaciousness and elegant neatness hardly surpassed by those above. The party, on their return, displayed much enthusiasm about them. The ex-secretary's daughter, gesticulating with a pair of small, nervous white hands, might have been heard explaining the plan to Sprowle Onderdonk.

"The contrivances for hygiene and comfort," she said, "are simply wonderful. The heater has a self-acting gauge and regulator, so that the temperature can never possibly rise above or fall below seventy Fahrenheit. The air is filtered through cotton-wool, the water through something or other which I forget. There is an electric battery, so that the gas lights itself, and no matches are necessary. And a hydraulic elevator takes you up-stairs, if you like, without the trouble of climbing."

"I should be afraid it would all blow up, you know," said her listener with a bluff facetiousness.

The Hon. Lyman Redway now arrived. His title was derived from service as a member of Congress. He was a man of fine presence. He offered apologies in a courteous way for having kept the company waiting, showing that the delay had been unavoidable. A number of the guests had met him before, a few having heard his discourse of that very day on the tariff question, before the Chamber of Commerce. Those who had not already made his acquaintance were now presented, and all went in to dinner.

Bainbridge had been speculating, with vague anxiety, as to who his partner was to be. Mrs. Harvey resolved it all at once by saying, —

"I am going to ask you, Mr. Bainbridge, to take in my niece, Miss Ottilie Harvey."

He offered his arm to Ottilie. Exchanging a conventional word or two, they moved onward with the procession. Both, having made up their minds to appear particularly at ease, found themselves, on the contrary, particularly uncomfortable.

The table, around which the guests proceeded to take their places, in the high-backed tapestry-covered chairs, was a spot of genial brightness in the semi-obscurity of the dining-room. It was lighted by waxen tapers shaded with colored silks. The illumination of these fell softly upon a multitude of utensils of gold, silver, fine porcelain, and Venice glass, and cloth of snowy whiteness, open-worked along the edges and showing a ruby velvet mat below. In the centre, an antique galley of silver, laden with fruits and flowers, rested upon a lake formed of a mirror, and having banks of flowers. The walls around were gravely and richly decorated with old tapestry, upon the ground of which hung some paintings, chiefly portrait and figure subjects in prevailing dark tones.

William Skiff, assisted by Alphonse, moved in and out discreetly, serving the viands from behind a tall screen. An orchestra of stringed instruments played softly in an adjoining room. Its music, instead of conflicting with the talk, seemed like a low accompaniment to recitative, to bind all its fragments into a certain unity and rhythm.

Ottilie and Bainbridge talked but little. The young man's manner was distinctly frigid, and the young girl had not the faintest idea of the cause. The intervals of silence between them lengthened. They gazed at the table and listened to the conversation of the other guests. The "governor of a neighboring State," at Ottilie's right, developed a taste for her society, and also a certain bantering way that might not have been quite expected from one of his station.

Baron Au, whose deficiencies in the English language by no means sufficed to check his tendency to be a very effusive person, was heard setting forth his daily practice from the point of view of hygiene to Miss Ada Trull.

"I haf learn your American prov*erb :* 'Times is money.' I rise myself each morning at seven of clock, take cold bat-z-th, so cold what I can, and walk myself one hour in z-the streets."

"I should think you would rather speak French, Baron," commented Ada Trull.

She was much too captivating to be quarreled with for impertinence, and knew it very well. Her blonde hair, "banged" over her forehead, was more like a cap of polished gold this evening than ever.

Hackley, at Bainbridge's left, was discussing with a neighbor the fruitful theme of stocks. Something of what they said oddly fixed itself in his memory and had its consequences afterwards.

"I confidently expect," Hackley declared, "to see Devious Air-Line at one hundred and fifty before the winter is over. Harvey is president, you know, and everything he touches turns to money. It is in the high-priced stocks, after all, and not the low, that money is made. If I had funds, I should hold Devious Air-Line for a big rise."

Whether Miss Van Voorst, who faced our couple, was aware or not of the altar upon which she was designed to be sacrificed, she could be seen paying an amiable deference to the apathetic Selkirk at her side. She had a dimple in one cheek of which it seemed that an impressible person might have made a great deal more account.

"Do you think her pretty?" Ottilie asked, for an appearance of civility, at least, should be kept up.

"Rather," Bainbridge answered. "Hardly equal to your cousin, or Ada Trull."

The peculiarity about Miss Van Voorst was that the lids of her almond-shaped eyes did not seem to open quite wide enough for the full orbs of vision, which gave a quaint, near-sighted look, not at all unbecoming.

"It is strange that glasses, and the near-sighted air should impress us, is it not?" said Ottilie. "Not to be able to see very well is rather distinguished; but if a person cannot quite hear, or taste, or smell, or has lost an arm or leg, no merit whatever attaches to those infirmities."

The exploring party who had been to the cellars continued to compliment the merchant prince upon his mansion. He received their praises modestly. He even made a pretense that it was but a poor affair at best.

"They turned us out of Union Square," he said. "We found we could not afford to live on property worth four thousand dollars a foot. So we crept in to a shelter from the weather as best we could."

"I understand that I am found fault with, in some quarters," he continued, "for not having built in a more correct taste. I am aware of the existence of certain fashionable new styles, — 'Queen Anne,' 'Queen Elizabeth,' and the like. But this is to be borne in mind; if you ever wish to dispose of a house of the regular pattern you always have a customer for it, while if it be out of the common you must wait for somebody to come along who is educated up to it. We are in such a transition state, too, through the growth of the city, that it is but a question of time — and of a short one at best — when any and all of our houses will be torn down for stores, or readjusted as they stand."

"If I had the caricaturist's faculty," said the Hon. Lyman Redway, "I should represent private life in New York in the guise of a brown stone mansion, tearing up Fifth Avenue, with a rag, tag, and bobtail of shop-fronts in full cry behind it. The chase began at the Battery, continued all the way up Broadway, and is now nearing the Central Park."

"Better pull them down before they tumble down and crumble down of themselves, as they seem inclined to do, with this soft brown sandstone so much in use," pronounced the journalist Blithewood Gwin. "Perhaps you have seen," — to Redway, — "and if you have not you should, — a curious antediluvian bird-track that has lately appeared, on the corner-stone of this mansion. For my part, I never look about me but I see surfaces flaked, corners gone, and even stout balusters eaten away to a good half of their substance."

"Mineral substances are contained in the stone," began Dr. Wyburd. "Or the grains are imperfectly consolidated, which admits of the absorption of water, and freezing and thawing. I hold, however, so far as that is concerned, that the bird-track in question" —

"Bird-tracks, — that is always such a bad sign," interrupted Mrs. Harvey, half absently. She appealed with a little anxious nod to the ex-secretary's wife, who returned the nod in a confidential way.

"Bother signs! Why are there never any good ones?" exclaimed Angelica.

"Where, then, is private life, being so harassed and pursued, going to?" asked Redway.

"Up in the air, with the French flats," suggested Blithewood Gwin. "That is its only refuge, since space is so scant on this narrow little island. I expect to see, in time, flats higher than Cologne Cathedral. Why not, with that beneficent invention, the elevator? Why cannot an elevator be made to run up a quarter of a mile?"

"Well, it would suit me if private life would seek that refuge at once, and let my place at Fort Washington alone," grumbled Sprowle Onderdonk. "In a general chaos going on there, they are cutting a boulevard directly through the centre of it. The worst of it is, it takes the old house in its course. I am to give a garden party there shortly, the day before they begin to ·pull it down. It will be quite a historic sort of an occasion. Dr. Wyburd has agreed to give us a poem. I should be glad " — to the guest of the evening — " if you would come. Will you allow me to send you a card?"

"Such a charming old mansion!" Mrs. Sprowle took upon herself to explain. "It is the Sprowle country-seat, though now in possession of the Onderdonk branch. It was built by colonial Governor Sprowle. Almost everybody of note, both in the old times and later, has been entertained there."

"It is probably in that high, rocky part of the town, overlooking the river, that the great residences of the future will be built, before the up-in-the-air period of which we are told begins," said the mayor. "They will probably be on a scale of magnificence beyond anything yet reached."

"Are we to think, then, that it can ever be safe to greatly increase the present style of display?" Dr. Miltimore inquired. "An alarming spirit of socialistic revolt has already appeared, and who shall say to what lengths it may reach? Communism in a republic, with all our safety-valves, our opportunities for expansion and legal redress, our equal rights, which should obviate the need of it, is a more dangerous symptom perhaps than under monarchical governments, where it has a certain excuse for existence."

"I have every confidence in the people," announced Rodman Harvey.

"So have I. That is what we say when we are running for office," said the governor. "Our friend Gwin can put it in his paper. But, between ourselves, we recollect what we have seen in some of the railroad strikes, for instance. Militia regiments loan their muskets to the rioters, and timid officials fail to take even such steps for repression as are open to them; though, to be sure, very little is open. Abroad there are the standing armies to put down disturbances. But suppose a really serious fight breaks out here between capital and labor, or between wealth and poverty, — suppose a mob take it into their heads, for instance, to be enraged at the superior dwelling our host here lives in ; what is to prevent their bringing it clattering down about his ears ?"

"You must let us get a crack at them with the Narragansett Gun Club first," suggested Sprowle Onderdonk.

"The side that can pay is all right," maintained Hackley. "Your communists would rather take two dollars a day, any time, to defend property, than pull it down on speculation."

"Our government, perhaps our whole system, may yet need changing," observed the ex-secretary. "I am not one of those who believe that the last word has been said, or perfection reached, republic though we are. There is a great deal of clap-trap on that subject. A government should be simply the most efficient police and central business agency for the public ; that is all. In itself it is entitled to no reverence whatever."

"I confess, for my part, that I do not easily conceive a more perfect luxury than this," resumed Dr. Miltimore, gazing about him admiringly. "Perhaps we do not sufficiently understand the point to which we have already attained. If my good friend, our host, will allow me to speak of him thus, I dare say that in personal state as well as actual power and scope of affairs he far surpasses many or most of those great merchants of the Low Countries and Venice and Tyre and Sidon, over whom history makes such a stir."

"Hear! hear!" cried several guests, clinking spoons against their glasses in polite accord.

This should have been a rather proud moment for Rodman Harvey, to be thus described and acclaimed by such competent judges. Is there no one at hand, in the fashion of the old classic triumphs, to whisper in his ear, "After all, man is but mortal"? Perhaps it is to the sage-looking William Skiff, bending forward now for an instant towards his master, that this duty has been confided. No, he but receives an omitted direction concerning the wines.

The illumination at the table was peculiarly favorable to Mrs. Rodman Harvey. By day her complexion began to have a parched look, and show deep little furrows, which had once been soft and mobile lines, at the corners of nose and mouth, as if Father Time had been so well pleased with them that he had never stopped till he had graven them in. By night there was still a good deal of it left. She now went back a little upon the last subject, and turned it her own way.

"Governments? yes, I think so, too," she said. "They ought to be changed. I am sure ours is very far from perfect. If something could be done now to establish by law the positions of the best people! I used to reflect upon it in Europe. There were my children, brought up with every luxury and refinement. Why were they not just as worthy of titles as many I saw enjoying them, without half their advantages? Under the Empire, now — Of course I was not in favor of the Empire; so much was said in the newspapers — Still, it was very pleasant. The Emperor used to ride in the Bois every day, and he quite got to know the children at the school where my daughter Angelica was — You remember, dear — He used to smile as he passed, when the pupils were walking, and make the little Prince Imperial bow, too, and kiss his hand. It was very charming. Do you not think," to Redway, "something should be done to give family its just rights? Do you not think a great deal more ought to be made with us of the aristocratic quality?"

"I should have to rule myself out so completely that I dare not agree with you," returned the Hon. Lyman Redway. "I find myself almost sharing certain prejudices based upon the feeling you speak of; but possibly you do not remember that I began life as a shoemaker. I am, as it were, my own ancestor."

He spoke, as his habit was, in a full manly voice, and at entire ease, as if making the most agreeable statement in the world.

"How delightful!" exclaimed Mrs. Harvey, feigning, with difficulty, a polite enthusiasm.

"He is a bold one to beard the lions in their den," said Bainbridge, allowing himself to find a certain amusement in the circumstance. "Look at Mrs. Sprowle! Have you ever seen her wear a more supremely Roman-nosed, uncompromising expression of disdain? She believes in the refinement and perfection of types from generation to generation by careful abstinence from any part in the useful work of the world."

"How! You abet scoffing at family, — you who are yourself so 'swell?'" returned Ottilie. "I have it both from Miss Emily Rawson and Mrs. Ambler."

She held up two fingers of each hand curved inwards in a way she had of putting an objectionable word in quotation marks. It seemed as if the constraint between them were going to thaw out, and the sun to appear.

"Our basis for such distinctions is so weak," said Bainbridge. "We descend from our little lawyers, doctors, and store-keepers. They have had to count their pennies, have kept but a beggarly servant or two, and had the plow or the mechanic's bench but a short remove behind them at best. The large, grand way of living of the great families abroad, on the other hand, might seem to beget correspondingly large and noble ideas, though we see as matter of fact that even that does not do it. Still if we had our duke, now, with his two palaces, his three castles, his four or five 'halls,' and hunting lodges *ad infinitum;* and a line of ancestors who had led armies and fleets, swayed Parliaments, and been as magnificent as himself for five or six hundred years, — that would be something like."

"This setting up to be better one than another," said Ottilie, "seems universal, in some form, and confined to no class."

"Of course it is. The butcher gives himself airs over the baker and the candlestick maker, at one extreme of society; and no doubt there are emperors who look down upon vulgar, pushing little, upstart kings, at the other. It is useless to rail at the trait. We are to go on torturing one another with it, I suppose, till the end of time."

"Would you have no distinctions at all, — no social aspiration?"

"A legitimate desire, I should think, would be to wish to be as good as the best, but not any better. Even that would do away with many a heart-burning. I should say that an aristocrat, nowadays, should have a good mind, good intentions, and be presentably dressed, and healthy, if possible. He should be courageous — wedded to whatever is refined and beautiful, but not enervated, not afraid to march and leave it at the word of command given by a higher duty. Redway here seems to have most of what is needed just at present."

They were getting on with a certain animation in this matter, when Miss Ada Trull chose to lean towards Ottilie, from the other side of the table, with a pose and beaming smile which might have been pure friendliness, or only intended for effect upon some masculine admirer, and say, —

"We are talking about Mr. Onderdonk's *fête*. The Baron and I are going up on Mr. Kingbolt's drag. I hear that you also are to be of our party?"

"Yes," returned Ottilie. "Mr. Kingbolt has asked me."

Bainbridge cut short a speech he had under way, and withdrew into himself. Ottilie felt the change. Something had distorted their old relations, as they saw themselves distorted in the convexities of the silver utensils before them.

The recent Bloomfield case came up for discussion, among other topics. It was an old story. Bloomfield, a once reputable person and high financial authority, had embezzled trust funds and lost them in Wall Street. A number of society people, among others the ingenious Mrs. Eglantine, had suffered cruelly by him.

"It is the strangest thing," declared Mrs. Harvey. "I would have trusted that man with untold millions."

"To be sure you would, madam," commented Dr.

Wyburd. "That is precisely the sort of person who can do those things. Without our confidence, how could he secure the necessary opportunities?"

"He admitted, when captured, that it was an inconceivable relief to him after the whole thing was out," said the ex-secretary. "He declared that no punishment could equal the torment he had endured for months, in the vain endeavor to conceal his frauds and redeem himself from the vortex of speculation."

"It shows the amount of comfort there is in such courses," said Dr. Miltimore. "And the truth of the saying, 'Stone walls do not a prison make, nor iron bars a cage.' He carried around with him, a cage of his own making more secure than triple steel. No doubt every instance in which he saw others exposed, while he still escaped,— for the papers abound with these cases every day,— filled him with dread and remorse, and served as a part of his punishment."

The guest Hackley fidgeted in his chair, and cast furtive glances towards their host.

"Considering the opportunities afforded by the unlimited necessity for confidence that exists, and the way we are all more or less cheated in smaller matters," said the governor in a confidential tone to Ottilie, "it may be that there is much more of this Bloomfield business going on than is usually supposed. Possibly, even, it is only the few who come to grief, while the majority tide over their infractions of the law, their perils and difficulties, the chances turning in their favor, and are never discovered. Come! that is a rather good idea. Your uncle, with his large experience of life, should know. Let us ask him. Ask him," he said, with a pretense of egging her on, in a mischievous way, "whether commercial life is really teeming with dishonesty, temporarily hidden: whether all of his business associates, if the truth were known, are as bad as Bloomfield, or worse."

"No indeed; I shall do nothing of the kind," replied Ottilie.

But her neighbor appeared to find this way of putting his question by proxy too facetious an idea to be abandoned.

"Your niece was asking" — he began; but his voice was overpowered by other conversation.

"Your niece was asking," he persisted, this time securing the attention of Rodman Harvey, "whether there is an immense amount of Bloomfieldism in business life, successfully consummated and never heard of? I think I shall have to refer her to you. What is your opinion? The point is, whether all of you Chamber of Commerce men, to whom our friend Redway has been expounding on the tariff, are merely first-class peculators, embezzlers, and forgers in disguise, only waiting to be found out."

"You know I did not ask that, uncle Rodman," protested Ottilie, in confusion.

She fancied she caught the eye of Bainbridge fixed upon her with a peculiar scrutiny. Might not her protest be construed into an indication that there were reasons why she should not have asked the question, if she had wished? Pshaw! What misunderstandings! What an agitation over a nonsensical bit of pleasantry!

Hackley at the question had dropped his dessert-spoon with a clatter. It fell upon his plate of Dresden china with perforated border, and thence to the floor. He stooped hastily for it, not waiting for the servant, and came up with a flushed face, which he mopped with a handkerchief.

But the merchant prince himself, entirely unfluttered, answered with a deliberative calmness. The glance of Hackley might now have been thought to have an admiring character, as who should say, —

"Well, if you are not a cool hand, I know little about it, — that is all."

Rodman Harvey's smile was faint, it is true; but then his smiles were never broad.

"I am inclined to think," he replied, "that the greater part of the dishonesty that exists comes to light. The community has a certain safeguard, in my opinion, in that the persons who engage in such courses soon lose their heads under the stress of the burdens and anxieties, and cannot long maintain the coolness and sagacity needed for success to save them from exposure."

The ladies rose and withdrew, rustling their silken robes over the floor. The gentlemen remained a while, to smoke some choice cigars made to Rodman Harvey's special order. Though he himself touched tobacco in no form, he thought it in keeping with his dignity to give his guests the best. Presently they joined the ladies again, in a music-room hung in red damask, where coffee was served, with cordials in little cups of crystal in Russian gold filigree. A trio of excellent professional voices entertained the company with singing.

In the freedom of the first breaking up, Baron Au, showing in a stretching way his relief after the long sitting, approached Daisy Goldstone.

"If you did hear me z-the horn to blow when I pass your house on z-the coach, about ten of clock last night?" he inquired.

"Oh, was that you? I thought it was Mr. Rowley, or Mr. Kingbolt. They often do it when they come by late."

Dr. Wyburd, moving easily about with his hands behind him, caught the name last spoken.

"There is a fortunate person, young Kingbolt," he said. "I should just like to have his income a few months, that's all."

"Is it really so very large?" Angelica inquired, with interest.

"The Eureka Tool Works is on an enormous scale, and, I hear, doing particularly well. I had especial facilities for knowing a good deal about the whole thing at one time, but that was years ago. Old Colonel Kingbolt died, as you might say, in my arms. A curious thing, — I happened to be at Bridgehaven at the time, and the family were good enough to think that my services might possibly be of avail. It was a trifle that killed him. He allowed himself to be agitated over it in such a way that it proved the immediate cause of his death. He was a particularly excitable man."

"Ah, indeed?" said Angelica.

"Somebody had used his name in the way of forgery," went on the speaker, who needed but slight encouragement to be discursive. "He got news of it from some bank here in New York. It was rather hushed up. There was something mysterious about it. The bank officials would not give him names or particulars, after they heard that the paper they held was not made by him. Their refusal drove him wild.

I never heard that there was any particular loss to anybody by the transaction. It might have been an error, a misunderstanding. At any rate, I never learned more. This is one of the cases where a favorite idea of mine, that if you hear the first part of a good story you are likely in time to hear the last, has not been borne out."

"But you may hear yet, doctor."

"Oh, I dare say. But it is of no consequence. Only I sometimes think of it in seeing the son, and remarking a certain resemblance between him and his father. The circumstance I have mentioned took place in the last days just preceding the outbreak of the war. It came upon the top of the excitements of that eventful time. Kingbolt imagined plots to undermine the great enterprise he had built up. He had the gloomiest forebodings, too, of the state of the country. He feared that the rebellion was to be its disintegration and ruin. It came also upon the top of a period of excesses, ending in something like an attack of apoplexy, which had confined him to his bed. Between ourselves, he was not a man of the most exemplary habits. He was a hard drinker, not regularly but by fits and starts. No constitution less robust could have stood it so long. A fine animal: handsome, full blooded, with curling hair, a thick neck, a muscular arm, and a temper like a Berserker's. A remarkable person in many ways was old Colonel Kingbolt. Not so old, either, since he was cut off at forty-seven, in the prime of his days. He had made his own way up from the bottom, — the regular American history."

"One gets so tired of the regular American history," said Angelica.

"He had a remarkable inventive faculty and a naturally fine mind, that would have commanded respect anywhere. He had the good taste to marry an amiable and refined lady, who no doubt kept him somewhat in check. Now, to show you what he accomplished entirely by his own exertions"—

The doctor proceeded to give some details about the Kingbolt manufacturing property.

Bainbridge observing Ottilie among the listeners, chose, with that time-honored fatuity in virtue of which lovers drag difficulties into their own way and plant them obstinately there with both hands, to represent her as drinking in eagerly the enumeration of her lover's riches. He seized an early opportunity to take his leave, and departed.

He walked a long way up the Avenue in the dark, then down, and turned into the more cheerful brightness of Broadway. The audiences were now coming out from the theatres. He saw young husbands, with young wives who clung to their arms, and looked up contentedly in their faces, as they trudged away homeward, engaged in pleasant comments on the play.

He entered a horse-car, and there was a charming young couple with a large sleepy child. They had come, he judged, from the few words of talk they exchanged, from spending a day in the country. They said they were very glad to get home. The child, a girl, lovable in the *abandon* of her sleepiness, with long legs in floss-embroidered stockings, which dangled to the floor, sat between them and held a hand of each.

How sweet it was, that ideal of domestic happiness! "Am I a pariah, then," he said, "that it is never for me?"

He sat late in his chamber, trying to read, but giving way further to the bitterness of his thoughts.

Opening his window, in the still small hours of the morning, he observed a great fire in progress at a distance. Serpent-like flames were licking up from a looming mass of dark buildings to the coppery sky. He thought it might be the furniture factory of Hackley & Valentine, and so the next day it proved. The distance was too remote for any of the uproar of the conflagration to be heard. It burned a while as if in silence, and quite uninterfered with. The interior of the block before him took a strong ruddy glow. Every least object came out with a vivid distinctness, down to the clothes on the lines.

Then the flames began to abate. Deluging streams were being poured in upon them. The interior of the block retired again into its wonted obscurity. Then, upon the darkness of the night arose showers of glittering sparks, scourged from the embers by the water, and began to drift gently along the sky. It was as if the destroyed property were transmuted into a value a million times greater in some kind of celestial coinage.

Or again it was like the pretty classic fable of Jupiter searching for Danaë, in the form of a rain of gold. The assumed mercenariness of woman has been a favorite complaint with lovers from the beginning of time.

"That is right," cried Bainbridge, humoring this last conceit; "that is right. To the northward! To the corner of West Blank Street and the Avenue! She is there. Danaë is there."

XVII.

THE PAST OF KINGBOLT OF KINGBOLTSVILLE.

The despised passion of jealousy had, after all, done its work with Bainbridge. It had shown him that he was violently in love. Forced to contemplate Ottilie as the wife of another, he knew the desperate pain it would cost him to lose her.

"Piece of my life," he cried aloud, "how shall I tear you out of it? What can I do without you?"

It did not answer to recall the days of Madeline Scarrett, and to charge himself fiercely with being of a weakly susceptible disposition. Some obstinate interior voice kept repeating of Ottilie, in spite of his assumed belief in her unworthiness, —

"She *is* what you only fancied the other to be."

The former experience, however, had made him intensely skeptical, and added to his natural fund of stoical reserve. He knew that it was possible to conquer and forget.

Such enforced conquests sometimes eat out the vitals of a warm and generous nature, and leave it like a forest tree through which a flame of fire has run.

The brain of the young man seethed with a hundred contradictory plans. Before he had time to carry any of them into execution, something occurred to put a very different aspect on the case.

Meantime he had suffered himself to be drawn

back, one evening, for distraction, to Miss Emily Rawson's. That affable acquaintance affected at first to take him for a stranger, who, by some mistake, had got into the wrong house. She refused his hand, but presently took it with a warm and friendly pressure. She was embroidering a table cover, seated by an astral lamp, which stood upon a small table, and cast around a becoming light. She had taken a new interest of late in decorative art, a society where its principles were advocated, and a wareroom where articles made in accordance with them were offered for sale.

"My design is something out of the common," she said, holding the work up to inspection. "How do you like it? It was drawn expressly for me by Mr. Lloyd, the architect. I met him at Bridgehaven, where I spent a few days last summer. Bridgehaven is not at all a bad summer resort. The air there is very good. Mr. Lloyd and I were at the same hotel. We spoke of you among others. He told me you were classmates at college."

"Yes, we were classmates. We used to call him simply 'G.' I recollect him better by that than by his name. There was another Lloyd, known as 'A. B.' It was necessary to distinguish them."

"That college life must have been so pleasant. By the way, we were near the large property of another classmate of yours, — Mr. Kingbolt."

Bainbridge heard this name with astonishment. He had come here for some small aid in escaping the memory of it, and it was the very first thing to be forced upon his attention.

"Yes," the fair embroiderer went on, "there was a glimpse from my window of Kingboltsville, — the factories, a private race-track, and the large stuccoed mansion where the family resides. The conservatory is immense. I was told that the original Kingbolt bought all the land thereabouts for a song, and redeemed it. The best of it is among the most desirable residence property in the city, of which it now forms a part. I saw the fortunate heir's mother and sisters, but he himself was not at home. I was not interested in him, however, at that time, but just now I am. I want you to tell me about him."

"I don't know that I recollect anything in particular. I am afraid I cannot help you."

"What was he like in college?"

"We were not intimate friends. — Bridgehaven struck you, then, as a passable summer resort? For my part, I find those interior Connecticut cities too warm."

"Did he graduate with a high rank? Was he a hard student?" the questioner persisted.

"He was dismissed for some informality, I believe, before arriving as far as that," said Bainbridge, with a kind of final air.

"And is that all?"

"Yes — no — I believe that is all."

"Well, that is not enough for me. Ah, here is Mr. Lloyd. I shall ask him. Perhaps he has condescended to burden his mind with a little more detail."

Mr. Lloyd, who was in the habit of calling occasionally, entered now in fact to pay his respects.

"I want a description of Kingbolt of Kingboltsville, whose place we saw last summer," said Miss Rawson. "Mr. Bainbridge won't tell me anything. I have reasons for wanting to know."

"I cannot be expected to say much good of him,

you know," returned Lloyd. "Well, I was in his set both in college and for some time afterwards, and I dare say I understand him about as well as anybody. He left the alma mater considerably earlier than the rest of us, owing to circumstances, as the saying is, over which he had no control. He dashed his money freely, and lived in great luxury, for that primitive time and place. It used to be said that he never wore a suit of clothes a second time. That is a period, you know, when fellows are very particular about their clothes. Among other doings, he erected a hall at his own expense for his secret society. Bless me, how much we once thought of that nonsense! There was no secret at all, you know, but we pretended that there was; had a meeting place which from the outside looked like a charnel-house, though we did nothing but play cards, and drink claret punches within; and we went around with the mysterious air of murderers. The hall cost Kingbolt forty thousand dollars. He got his mother to persuade his trustees to let him have the money. They thought that perhaps he would be more contented, take an interest in his studies, if they humored him. It did not work so, however. The faculty, after a good deal of forbearance, had to send him off. He was really too much. They could not have maintained discipline, if they had n't."

"He invited a number of us up to his place afterwards to celebrate his coming of age," Lloyd went on, showing a certain zest in these reminiscences. "When we got there we found him turned quite serious. His trustees had talked to him, after he was expelled, and made some impression. They described to him how his father had built up a great business, which had come to be known pretty much the world over; how he had been honored by foreign governments; how he had been mayor and governor, and might have been ambassador, if he chose. They said that the son ought not to throw away, and discredit the memory of all that had gone before. They said that if he did not now wish to take a profession he ought to go into the works and become competent to manage them himself. To this Kingbolt finally consented. When he had arrived at this decision, nothing would do him but to wear a blue shirt and jack-boots and carry a tin dinner-pail, like an ordinary hand, and begin by oiling up the machinery. He never does, or at least never begins, anything by halves. It was in this costume that he showed his visitors through the works, — fashionable girls and all, — when they went to the birthday celebration. The festivities lasted three days, quite on the English plan. It was an idea of his sisters, who had been abroad a good deal. As for his mother, she was a person who consented to almost anything. She was lady-like and well-meaning, but weak. One could easily see that. The fact is, Kingbolt had no particular bringing up. He was never controlled. I was told that his father — as long as he lived, for he died early — treated everything the boy did as a huge joke. He used to say that he had not made a success enough of it in his own case to lay down rules for the government of others.

"'Let him fight it out on his own account,' his father would say. 'He must have some good traits from his mother, and may be one or two that are not so bad from me. Let him fight it out! No doubt, in the long run, the good will prevail over the bad.'

"So if the boy got black in the face with temper, and smashed the crockery, they simply put him in a padded room. If he kicked the governess with his new boots till she cried, they comforted her with liberal presents. His mother took everything in the tearful, prayerful style, and wondered at him."

"They allowed him to kick his governess? A cheerful beginning, I must say," commented Miss Rawson.

Bainbridge, who had been about to withdraw, found himself listening in a kind of dazed way to this review of his rival's career.

"Well, at his coming of age," G. Lloyd went on, "there were dancing, and illuminations, and distributions of presents, and driving gayly through the streets of Bridgehaven in all the conveyances the stables could turn out. Kingbolt was again 'one of the boys,' and joined in the proceedings with a will. If I had been parent or guardian of his, I should have dreaded the effect of such a break in his newly established routine. Whether it was in fact an entering wedge, within the year he tired of being a horny-handed son of toil, and came down and joined us in New York.

"We had taken our sheepskins by that time, and a group of choice spirits was assembled in the different professional schools. You recollect about it, Bainbridge? You were one of us occasionally, before you went into your manufacturing, orange-planting, and what not."

"Yes, I remember," said Bainbridge, gravely.

"Kingbolt came down at first on a visit," pursued Lloyd, "and the boys urged him to stay."

"'If I do, what shall I do about my trustees?' he

asked us. 'Old Judge Bryan is continually harping at me about the glories of the past. He would consider me hopelessly lost.'

"'Hang your trustees!' I recollect Anthropoid Walker replying. 'The old Judge will be only too glad not to have anybody to overhaul his accounts. Let him alone to embezzle your property in comfort. You 've got a soul above axle grease. Come into the law school with us! Look at me! I ascribe my future greatness entirely to that noblest of professions, the law.'

"Let me see! Anthropoid Walker and Zeus Baldwin — we kept up the old nicknames — were in the law school in Lafayette Place. Sprowle Onderdonk was another of the legal aspirants. He was older than the rest, and we had not known him so well in college, owing to his having been in an upper class. But with his leisurely way of taking things he had arrived at this point only at the same time. He had a good mind, that man, and with a greater pressure upon him to use it, might have done something really worth while. He still sticks to the law in a desultory way, I believe, and keeps an office. You recall him as a man of ability, do you not, Bainbridge?"

"I recollect a sledge-hammer style of argument he had sometimes in the debates in Linonia," replied Bainbridge. "We used to think he might succeed in politics."

"I was a Brother in Unity, not a Linonian, myself. — Our college societies," — to Miss Rawson, in explanation of these names. "De Longbow Rowley was studying medicine. That fellow was always telling the most preposterous yarns, and keeps up the habit yet. Whitehead Finch was in business.

His family had got him a place in a broker's office, allowed him two thousand dollars a year to keep off the pangs of absolute starvation, and left him to shift for himself. Gus Ramsdell also professed a purpose of becoming a shining light in commerce. He had begun by entering the store of Rodman Harvey, at three dollars a week, but found that this interfered too much with his society engagements, and left. They 'did not know how to treat a gentleman,' he said. He had not yet found another opening to his taste, but represented himself as in search of one. We used to charge him with looking for a place, and hoping he wouldn't get it. Sprowle Onderdonk used to say that Ramsdell had told him, to quote the exact words, —

" '*I* am not going to work as long as I have my health.'

" For my part," still went on the narrator, " I was young and foolish then. I was in an architect's office, paying the firm for the privilege of learning the business. They had to catch me to make me do it, though. I often went down to the office at two or three in the afternoon, and left at four. If the principals were out, even this brief space was spent, as likely as not, in fencing with a fellow-draughtsman, with the T-squares.

" Well, this was the general character of the interesting circle to which Kingbolt now joined himself. He set up handsome bachelor apartments, which soon became a rallying point. More than once, after an evening of lively adventures elsewhere, we all spread ourselves out on his furniture, and passed the night there. He gave small suppers, at which one of the amusements was to shoot the necks off the champagne bottles instead of uncorking them. Such rackets as we had! Ah, yes, indeed! With little English hats on their heads, with sticks and eyeglasses, their hands in the pockets of their English clothes, and quips and cranks innumerable at the ends of their tongues, the group tore about from one pleasure to another incessantly. I dare say we were a sort of terror. We took boxes at the spectacular dramas. We knew where the best beer was to be had, the best Welsh rarebit, or anchovy sandwich. We patronized the Tyrolean warblers at the Bowery Garden, Herman's on Fourth Avenue, where leading artists were to be seen, and Schwalbach's on Fourteenth Street, where actors resorted after the play. I remember how the joints of beef, piles of oysters, the green salads, and vivid scarlet of the lobsters, arranged in ornamental pyramids on Schwalbach's counter, impressed me the first time I saw them. We were 'seeing life'; that was what we were after."

"You describe to me not only Kingbolt, but a whole state of society," said Miss Rawson. "That is more than I expected, — but of course you do not suppose that I approve of you."

"Oh, we reformed. I, at least, since I had my living to make. They are all club men now, those fellows, and great swells; I have little or nothing to do with them, except when I go and bore one of them, unblushingly, for his influence in some building contract. Athletic sports were a part of the programme. Not that we took any great part in them, but it was the thing to be posted, and to be present on all eventful occasions. The base-ball and cricket games, the dog shows, the shooting and rowing matches, — those were the important things in life.

A good running high jump would draw the coterie away from their ostensible occupations, to Hoboken, for a day. The long purses — and Kingbolt's was the longest — attended religiously regattas at Saratoga, or base-ball matches at Chicago or Baltimore. If the university nine or boat's crew of our college chanced to be passing through town, or the glee club gave a concert, you may be sure that a patriotic effort was made to give them as hilarious a time as possible."

"And fashionable society? I suppose you were great breakers of feminine hearts, for instance?"

"As a rule, society was rather looked down upon. Still, we condescended to an occasional party. We trained around in company, taking a sardonic view of things and calling the *débutantes* 'young gushers.' When it was over we bounded up-stairs, two at a time, drawing cigarettes from our pockets as we went, bustled into our ulsters, got the loudest explosion out of our crush hats they were capable of, and so — not yet being club men — off to Delmonico's, Schwalbach's, or other of the chosen resorts. — I remember we entertained a kind of reverential awe of the older class of club men we saw heading the important movements in society and on the turf. Some of them were bald, corpulent, weather-beaten, and with large whiskers, — the kind of men I for instance had been used to seeing only as officers of banks and companies, deacons perhaps of churches. Occasionally, one of them took his racing-stable abroad, and contested all the great events of the European turf. An existence which could keep a continuous interest in life for persons of that age must mean pleasure indeed."

"But thus you do not separate yourself from Kingbolt," interrupted Emily Rawson. "Were you all exactly alike? You do not show how he differed from the rest of you."

"He was more whimsical, — that is all. He separated himself from the rest of us mainly by that. He lets nothing stand in the way of a whim. He pursues it to the bitter end."

"Ah, indeed!" said Emily Rawson.

And "Ah, indeed!" mentally echoed Bainbridge, in a dull way. This trait in Kingbolt was the knell of his lingering hopes.

"He ran out to Colorado, now and then, for a hunt," continued Lloyd. "He was not greatly given to reading, and not a person of a romantic fancy, I should say; and for a time Europe seemed without attraction for him. At length, however, he went across with Gus Ramsdell. He proposed only a brief stay, but it extended to several years, and left his law course entirely in the lurch. The pair traveled, at first, rather on the comic plan, modeled themselves after the personages in a class of literature then a good deal in vogue. They were locked up, for instance, at Cologne, for beating a *commissionaire*, — I am sure he deserved it. Ramsdell came back, but Kingbolt remained. The dignified side of things gradually took hold of him. He picked up languages, and titled acquaintances, and began to conduct himself *en grand seigneur*. He registered as Kingbolt of Kingboltsville. In those places — comprising the greater part of Europe — where all the Americas, their languages and peoples, are confounded as one, and a corresponding ignorance prevails of their social system, he was taken to be, in his own country, the chief of a clan, or the lord of a barony at least. An

African potentate who had bought machinery of the Eureka Tool Works, and conferred a decoration on the young man's father in old times, gave a hunt in his honor. A splendidly caparisoned steed led by slaves was sent out to meet him as he approached, — quite like the Arabian Nights. He killed a wild boar, the tusks of which still ornament his rooms, with other trophies. At least Kingbolt relates all this. I dare say it is so. He was never particularly given to stretching the point, like Rowley.'

"Not particularly," assented Bainbridge, being appealed to.

"He returned from Europe with new airs and graces and plenty of new ideas about spending money. He was elected now to all the clubs, and in close relations with the older men he had been used to revere. It was at this time that he distinctly went in for a society career, and set up for a 'glass of fashion and the mould of form,' in town and country. Then he went off again, briefly, on an earnest tack. I doubt if it was anything more than a paragraph in a newspaper that set him a going, — a paragraph suggesting to rich men to do something to improve the condition of their tenantry. He ran across me again, turned sober by this time, I assure you. I had my living to get, and was able to follow that idle group only about as far as you could throw an elephant by the tail. Well, he ran across me again, as I say, and took me to Europe with him to perfect plans for an industrial museum and model cottages. I was to have — well, he promised everything; and he meant it, I dare say. But he proved an insufferable task-master. Our old intimacy went for nothing. We quarreled violently, and he turned me adrift; that was the way of it. It was devilish awkward at first, I recollect, — out of money, away from home, and my time and labors gone for nothing; but now I can look back at it more coolly. No doubt I was somewhat to blame myself. He had fallen in before this with a certain St. Hill, who attached himself to him as a parasite, and probably had something to do with inducing him to abandon the philanthropic project. He brought back St. Hill instead of myself. That man could give you points enough about Kingbolt, I dare say. And that is the extent of my information."

The architect drew a long breath, as if after having talked interminably.

"Sure?" queried Miss Rawson.

"Positive."

"Well, we are very much obliged to you. Concerning his more public career, I knew more or less already."

Lloyd and Bainbridge exchanged some casual remarks concerning an art club, where, it seemed, they were in the habit of meeting occasionally, and Bainbridge rose to go.

As he was passing out he met the Rev. Edwin Swan coming in. This was the assistant at one of the minor Episcopal churches, a deserving, quiet, plain person of most respectable position naturally, who was thought to be looking for a wife. Their fair entertainer seemed fluttered at the encounter in her parlors of so many desirable men. Each would comprehend, she hoped, in particular the recreant Bainbridge, that, though she were not in demand by him, she was by others.

"But I have not told you the reason of my interest in Kingbolt of Kingboltsville," she said confidentially, at the threshold, to the departing guest.

"No," said Bainbridge.

"Well, I have seen him driving out our friend Ottilie Harvey. I hear also that he paid her great attention at Newport. I have my informants, you see. 'Such things *have* been, said Private James.' She would be an enterprising little minx if given but half a chance. I am sure of it. Do you not think so?"

"Very likely," said Bainbridge.

XVIII.

AT THE EMPIRE CLUB AND AROUND TOWN.

ONE morning, at this time, Arthur Kingbolt of Kingboltsville awoke at nine o'clock, and rang the bell for his body servant. Ten or eleven was his more usual hour, and the services of Greenway, besides, were generally in requisition to rouse him from his heavy slumbers. He had found the well-trained Greenway in the employ of one of the smaller London clubs, and brought him over for his own service.

"Get to work now, Greenway," he said. "I am going to get up."

The discreet Greenway first handed in the morning draught of a "brandy cocktail" which his master was accustomed to demand, as best adapted to his peculiar constitutional needs, then proceeded deftly to shave him, while he still reclined under his rich Persian hangings. He next laid out a velvet jacket, braided and faced with silk. While Kingbolt exchanged for this the night-gown of China silk in which he had slept, and rose, and lounged in an easy-chair, with a cigarette and a morning paper, the servant brought the articles of dress for the day's wear. There might have been seen a store of clothing, hats, boots, shoes, and walking-sticks, in an adjoining apartment, sufficient to equip a company.

The luxury of these chambers could hardly have jarred even upon a feminine taste. The masculine element was shown in pictures of types of female loveliness — photographs of actresses and the like — of a rather free sort, and in weapons, and trophies of the chase. There were the wild boar tusks from the hunt with the potentate of Barbary; there was the head of a red deer, shot, with a Scotch lord, in the highlands; the head of a " big-horn " of Montana, and another of a fallow deer of the Adirondacks.

"Get me a breakfast here, will you, Greenway?" directed the master, in a petulant tone. "It does n't make any difference what. I'll stand that villainous club cooking no longer. No, on the whole, I'll go to Delmonico's. Don't forget," he added, in a parting direction, "to take back that beastly driving-coat to Millerick. What does he take me for?"

When in the street, however, he changed his mind again, and went to the Empire Club, after all. Greenway thought he had rarely seen his master in a more capricious and irritable frame of mind than at present.

Kingbolt was hailed in the lobby of the club by some men who affected to take his appearance at that time of day as a remarkable phenomenon.

"Turning over a new leaf, — out to see the sun rise, — early dewdrop, and that sort of thing, eh?" said Whitehead Finch.

"I'm not turning over anything. I suppose a man has a right to get up, if he likes," the new-comer rejoined, not too amiably.

"Well, you can't keep the London style going a great while here," said Ramsdell. "Lord, I've tried it! I used to sleep till four in the afternoon, regularly. Over there in the fog, it makes no difference when you burn your gas; one part of the twenty-four hours is as good as another. But here it is a different matter. If a fellow does n't show himself in season, the programme is made up without him, and he is likely to get left."

"Your friend St. Hill is posted again — quite a stiff little sum," said De Longbow Rowley, nodding towards the bulletin board, where various matters of interest were officially brought to the attention of the club.

Kingbolt walked over to it, and read the notice of the extent of St. Hill's arrears. Such a delinquency subjected the offender to embarrassment of this kind, and after a certain time, if still unsatisfied, to loss of membership in the club. On going to his letter-box, he found a note from the same person which proved to be an appeal to take down the announcement and liquidate the writer's small indebtedness, as "a temporary accommodation," for which he would remain forever grateful.

"There is getting to be too much of this sort of thing. I am sick of it," he muttered, stuffing the note into his pocket.

But when the rest made the bulletin the text for an abusive discussion of St. Hill, it suited his perverse humor to stand by the man. The Empire Club was rather a noted place for gossip. The characters of both men and women were often handled there in a style hardly to have been surpassed by tea-drinking spinsters of the old school. This, however, rarely precluded the extending of the usual pleasant civilities to the victim, though fallen in with but the very next moment.

"What sort of a company has the fellow got? What keeps him a-going, any way?" inquired Gus

Ramsdell, who had long since come into property, by inheritance, which placed him beyond the need of aspirations, commercial or otherwise, connected with the problem of self-support.

"It's a swindle, as sure as a gun. That's my opinion," said Mr. Rowley. "I should not be surprised to hear of his being shown up and dropped out of decent society, any day."

They are not dropping people for those things now," said the elderly Watervliet. "The Texas style is more in vogue. In Texas they don't consider a man out of society till he is hanged."

Watervliet's own means of support were not always of the most ostensible. A friendly hand, now and then, stopped a gap in his exchequer. He varied his sitting in the club window with an occasional long voyage to the tropics in somebody's yacht, in the winter. In summer, he had been known to admit deprecatingly, in a rare moment of weakness, that his livelihood cost him little more than his railroad fares. He passed from one hospitable country house to another, in a continual round of visits.

"Look at the way he took in that gudgeon of a Stillsby," said Northfleet, continuing on the subject of St. Hill. "He pretended to make a venture for him in stocks, and sent him word presently that his money was doubled. He did not pay the money over, though; you may be sure of that. He advised now that it be put into another deal, which promised even better than the first. Stillsby, of course, was delighted and advanced more funds. The upshot was that he never got a cent. When the sum was big enough St. Hill gobbled it. He regretted to say that an unfortunate turn of the market etc., etc. Still, he felt that if favored with a new opportunity he could at once redeem the previous losses and return a handsome profit on the whole investment. It's a very old dodge,— that is. I say, that is what St. Hill did to you, isn't it, Stillsby?" the speaker called to Stillsby, who had just come down the stairs.

"Yes, sir, that's what he did. I put up— He, he, I"— Stillsby stuttered, in his eagerness to tell the story.

"Bah! Wall Street is Wall Street," said Kingbolt contemptuously, setting foot in the elevator to go up to his breakfast in the restaurant above. "What do people expect?"

"Yes, that is so, too," assented Stillsby, who had the habit of agreeing with whoever spoke with authority.

When Kingbolt had breakfasted he found the same men, with others, sitting in the conversation room, by the large windows giving upon the Avenue. A few who were reading newspapers offered laconic remarks, from time to time, on subjects enlisting their interest.

"I see there's another duke, a great swell, coming in by the French steamer," said Northfleet. "I suppose that pushing Mrs. Poyntz will go to his hotel, grab him by the hair of the head, and have him on exhibition before he knows where he is. Poor duffers! They can't help it at first, I suppose."

"I see old Elphinstone Swan has dropped off," said Ramsdell. "That must be what the club's flag is half-masted for to-day."

"I thought that old buffer was dead ages ago," commented De Longbow Rowley, yawning.

"Not at all; far from it," returned Finch. "I have had my eye on his prospective widow. Madeline Scarrett has made rather a good speculation of it. Here she is, about as young and handsome as ever, with all the old man's money to do as she likes with."

After this, silence for a while.

Mr. Watervliet broke it with a low whistle, expressive of keen emotion. "I see Canterbury Boy is gone," he said.

"What! — No! — It can't be! — When? — Where? — How did it happen?"

There was a general letting fall of papers, and a rapt manifestation of concern.

"At the Fashion Course, Long Island, yesterday, at five in the afternoon," read out Watervliet, in a melancholy tone. "Taken with bleeding of the lungs at three o'clock, and expired at five. Only in the seventh year of his age. By Jove, that's hard! it's hard."

This striking instance of the brevity of life, and the vanity of all things mortal, cast a deep temporary gloom over the company. Such members of it as had won money in times past on Canterbury Boy were moved almost to tears; and even those who had lost ignored the fact in the sudden shock of his taking off. Anecdotes of his past began to be exchanged then others of a kindred sort, all pervaded by the same pensive air. Finch recalled pathetically a horse-owner who decked a pet mare, after her victories, with collar and pendants of diamonds. Rowley related the case of a veteran jockey who had desired to be buried on the race-track at the three-quarter pole, in order to hear the inspiring rattle of the hoofs above his head.

This gloom lifted by degrees. Upon some chance reference, the prospects of Rodman Harvey in the coming election were spoken of. Harvey had distanced General Burlington in the convention, and secured the regular nomination of his party, and banners, duly weighted and pierced, and adorned with execrable portraits of himself in the usual way, had long been hanging for him across the streets. His rival at the polls was to be Michael Brannagan, of Tammany Hall. Bets for and against Harvey were being freely offered, when Sprowle Onderdonk entered.

"Hang your bets!" he cried. "Stir yourselves for once, and come out and vote for him! He is the Sprowle candidate, you know. We want him elected. His daughter marries into the family. See?"

Kingbolt got up at this, and moved restlessly about the floor.

"Well, count on me for one," returned Northfleet. "By the vay, that's another pretty girl they have up there at the Harveys', — the one they rather keep in the background, the cousin — what's her name? Ottilie. You get a glimpse of her now and then, you know. What is she like?"

"Kingbolt can give you the points. Ask him! They were as thick as Siamese twins last summer, — sly dog!" replied Onderdonk.

"What is she like, Kingbolt old boy, — the demure Miss Harvey number two, the gem of purest ray serene, the dark, unfathomed caves of ocean, etc.?" pursued the inquirer.

"On the intellectual lay, I believe. Wants to be quoted to, and that sort of thing. Don't trouble yourself to pitch in; you'll never get ahead."

The not over-bright Stillsby, on hearing this, crept up to the library, and was soon buried deep in a literature of large volumes of poetical quotations.

Kingbolt, leaving the club, passed Sprowle with a surly "How are you?" treatment at which that person appeared surprised, having been accustomed to a much more friendly manner of late.

Gus Ramsdell came out into the hall after him, to say, "Don't forget the Capricorn dinner to-night!" Then, "Whither away? I'll join you. What do you say to a game at the Racquet Club? Or will you put on the gloves a while? I spent most of yesterday over the ticker, watching a little turn I am making in Wall Street, and to-day I want exercise."

"I have got to go and see my tailor," said Kingbolt.

"Who, Millerick? By the way, so have I. Perhaps after that you will come up town with me to a stable. Rickardson, with whom I used to have dealings, has opened a new place, and I have promised him to drop in. I am on the lookout, in a general way, for a new off-wheeler for my four-in-hand. I think I ought to have something rather better in that place. The chestnut isn't quite what he should be of late."

When the pair entered Millerick's place, — one of the select shops on the Avenue, ornamented both without and within in the new style of decoration, — the fashionable tailor came forward to meet them, affably rubbing his hands. He was a tall, spare man, with large side-whiskers. He wore a long frock coat, of a spotless, technical sort of elegance. Kingbolt raised his voice in complaint almost from the door.

"I have come to overhaul you about that driving-coat. Don't you know I could n't show myself in a thing like that? Where is it? Yes, now, here! Could n't any human being understand that I would n't be seen with such shoulders on me as those? You have Eastlaked your place all over, you know, Millerick, with your pictures, your gilding, and stiff-jointed traps; but you can't Eastlake me. I won't have it. Well, it's of no use; I shall have to get my things over from London, again, as before."

Millerick met this attack with an excellent grace. "You are perfectly right, Mr. Kingbolt," he said, tossing the garment aside, with a large air. "It is not a proper coat for you. The fact is, we were changing cutters. But you shall have another right away. You will naturally want it for Mr. Onderdonk's garden party, the day after to-morrow. It will be quick work, but it shall be ready, and this time without fault, I guarantee."

"Oh, well, Millerick, if you are going to take it that way," said the young Crœsus, not to be outdone in magnanimity, — and it is desirable, after all, to stand well with one's tailor, — "you put it in the bill, all the same! I suppose it only wants a touch here and there. Mistakes will happen, you know. At any rate, let me have some kind of a coat by to-morrow night. Do you understand?"

"Millerick is the only man in town who will do that," he said, somewhat mollified by this exhibition of his power, as he departed with his companion.

"He won't do it for me," said Ramsdell. "He would see me in Jericho first. How do you manage it?"

Ramsdell's acquaintance Rickardson was found in a large, new brick stable, presiding over an auction of horses. He was posted up at a little desk at one side, above a track on which the paces of the animals were shown off. Spectators, for the most part livery-stable keepers and others connected with the equine interest in a small way, crowded thickly on the track, with catalogues in their hands. They made way reluctantly as each horse was sped around, and filled in immediately after, as if such a thing as danger to life and limb from iron-shod hoofs had never been heard of.

"Anything in our line, Rick?" called Ramsdell up to the auctioneer where he stood at his desk.

"I should n't wonder if the next lot but one would be worth your while a lookin' at, Mr. Ramsdell," replied Rickardson.

The "lot" just then before the house was quickly disposed of. The next was brought out and run around the ring by a stable-boy. The onlookers scattered to escape maiming for life, and closed up imperturbably, as before. This lot was a young filly of excellent stock, but marred by some blemish, which allowed her to go for a song.

"She's a young un, and a good un!" cried the auctioneer. "Look wot you're a gittin'. This magnificent two-year-old filly *at* seventy dollars' bid!"

The inexperienced filly tossed up her head against the restraining halter, and stared in a wild-eyed way at the crowd.

"This here magnificent filly at seventy dollars' bid! Eighty, do I hear? At eighty dollars! Eighty! Eighty dollars! Last call! *At* eighty dollars! — Sanders," with a sudden fall in his voice.

The "next lot but one" now followed, the stable-boy this time on his back. This candidate for favor was described in the printed catalogues as "the chestnut gelding Rob Roy, coming seven years old next March: greatly admired at Long Branch last season; the property of a gentleman going to Europe, and got to be sold at any sacrifice."

Kingbolt gave a start at his appearance, and began to study his points with keen attention.

"Ah — ha — a!" cried Rickardson with a gusto. "Here's the stock you're all a-waitin' for. Splendid, fine, high knee action. Beautiful combined saddler and driver. Send him along, there!"

The stable-boy struck the animal with his whip, and rode down the crowd, which escaped annihilation by another in the usual series of miracles.

"There he is, — all in a nutshell!" continued the sanguine auctioneer. "Let 'em see him walk! *There's a beauty!* Game, beautiful-gaited, without doubt the most beautiful-styled young horse in New York! — best-styled and most promising young horse in North America to-day!"

But before any offer could be made for all these attractions, Kingbolt, who had scrutinized every motion of the so-called Rob Roy with a painful intentness, pressed forward to the auctioneer's desk, and throwing up one hand, cried out excitedly, "You can't sell that horse! There is no Rob Roy about him. He's my horse Jim. You just wait till you hear from me! Do you understand?"

To Ramsdell, who in much astonishment had endeavored to follow him, he said, "That's *Jim*, as sure as we are alive! I let St. Hill have him to keep for the summer, and here he is selling him out on me. He has changed him, but I would know the horse in a million."

Rickardson was disposed at first to put down this unseemly interruption. "Beauty!" he continued to the audience, by way of keeping the sale still in motion, while the pros and cons were being discussed.

Influenced, however, by the representations of Mr. Ramsdell, he withdrew the chestnut gelding Rob Roy from auction. He explained to the public that a mistake had arisen among gentlemen, which would no doubt be settled " fair and satisfactory" to all concerned.

"Was there ever a more stupendous piece of cheek?" said Kingbolt, in a towering rage. "St. Hill told me that the horse had gone a trifle lame, and been left at pasture. He would have told me after a while, I suppose, that he was dead, and I should have taken his word for it. And to think of what I have done for that man! Well, this ends it. By the way, oblige me, will you, Ramsdell, by not saying anything to the other fellows, just now! I was rather crowded into defending him this morning."

Kingbolt was actively on the lookout for his knavish *protégé* for the rest of the day. Up to the hour of the Capricorn dinner, at seven o'clock, however, he had not fallen in with him.

The culinary department of the Empire Club was enlisted to do its best for these little Capricorn dinners. The terrapin was to-day, accordingly, of a flavor not to have been surpassed out of Maryland; the canvas-back done to a turn. The Château Latour was comfortably warm, the Steinberg Cabinet iced to the finest touch of perfection. The dishes called out considerable discussion of a gastronomical order. It was good form to be to a certain extent *gourmet*. De Longbow Rowley laid down the axiom —

"You can tell who a man is better by his style of ordering a dinner than in any other way."

Anthropoid Walker, who had taken to politics, and become a member of the legislature, had abandoned on that account but few of the attributes of swelldom. His accomplishments as a good fellow, also, seemed to have stood him in good stead, in his new career. He described a dinner he had given, from motives of policy, to his brother legislators at Albany. He boasted also of having been able to distinguish from one another, by the taste alone, seven different kinds of wine of a kindred sort, with his eyes blindfolded.

"We have seen you when you could n't tell champagne from water, and you know it," said Sprowle Onderdonk.

Walker admitted this, but claimed that the experiment referred to was made at an earlier stage in the evening.

The ages at which various wines are at their best, and phenomena attending their decline, were touched upon.

De Longbow Rowley declared that he had seen port so old that it had turned snow-white. He forgot precisely where or when, but would swear to the fact, though the rest pooh-poohed it.

"All I know is," said Zeus Baldwin, who had abandoned the law, and was now a doctor of medicine, "that they sell you, at one of the German cities, a wine which they say dates back to the year 1600 or so. It costs three or four dollars a thimbleful. It has become a mere thick syrup."

"Oh, they fill it up, you know," objected Northfleet.

"Not at all!" said Sprowle Onderdonk. "It would n't be so beastly if they did."

Society scandals, sporting matters, and narratives of personal adventure followed. De Longbow Rowley was at the front, in accordance with his reputation, with the most marvelous experience. It had been met with, he said, in his second-but-one-before-the-last expedition in the wilds of Crim Tartary.

Whitehead Finch thought good to parody this, to the delight of the company, with an egregious invention of prowess and desperate doings on a Mississippi steamboat.

"I was the only peaceable person on board," he said, "and beset by a gang of bullies and cut-throats. Alone and unarmed against such numbers, what could I do? The captain and crew were in league with them, also. It was as much as my life was worth even to show resentment. But they little knew the sleeping lion they were arousing. They crowded the mourner too far. Unable at last to control myself, I rushed to a red-hot stove in the cabin, and bit a piece out of it, just to show what I could do. For an instant those burly ruffians stood paralyzed. Before they could recover I had flown wildly to the deck and leaped over the bow. I took the precaution to spring as far out as possible. It must have been some two hundred feet. The desperadoes thought I had suicided, and I could hear their shouts of demoniac glee rending the air behind me. But far from it. I calmly waited till that ill-fated boat came by, and seized her cut-water in my teeth, — our family are known, I may say, for their excellent teeth. With a few ferocious yanks I tore the whole front out of her, and she went to the bottom like a shot. Not a soul but myself was left to tell the tale. I rarely mention it. I, sometimes, almost regret having used such extreme severity. Still, in a pinch like that, a man cannot always be expected to act with the coolness that might be most judicious."

Rowley was accustomed through long practice to take rebuffs of this kind with much good-nature.

"I wonder if this new French duke will be wanting to marry an American girl, like the rest," he asked, branching out in a new direction.

"American girls have got to marry somebody," said Gus Ramsdell, "since they can't have us."

"Why don't we go over and take their titled women in return?" inquired Northfleet. "Come! I have a notion to go and propose to a Lady Georgiana or Hon. Miss Percy something or other, for a change."

"By the way, speaking of marriages," said Sprowle Onderdonk, "I may as well give you a bit of news. The day for the wedding of my cousin Sprowle with Miss Harvey has been set, and the cards are ordered. As I shall not have another chance of the same sort, I intend to call my garden party of Thursday partly a celebration in their honor. I have asked Dr. Wyburd to add a few lines of an appropriate hymeneal sort to his poem. You must all come up in your drags, and give the occasion as distinguished a look as possible."

Kingbolt who had shown no great interest in the gayeties of the feast, up to this point, lost now even the little he possessed. His lack of appetite was so glaring as to be openly commented on by the others.

"Has Dr. Zeus Baldwin been talking to you, Kingbolt?" cried Northfleet. "Your theory, doctor,

I believe, requires that nothing be taken into the stomach for twenty-four hours before going to bed."

"Forty-eight," promptly replied Dr. Zeus Baldwin.

The violent indignation Kingbolt had proposed to visit upon St. Hill had in a measure evaporated before he finally met with him, later the same night. The offense had become of a lesser consequence, in the new stir of emotion aroused by the announcement of Angelica's wedding-day. The time fixed, and near at hand, for her final loss? As long as this was not actually complete he must always have entertained some lingering, unreasonable hope.

St. Hill was lounging in the reading-room, with for him a downcast air, when Kingbolt came out from the Capricorn dinner; and this Lucifer-like spirit then rather attracted than repelled him. Something irregular and desperate was most in consonance with his own mood.

The *protégé* was at first startled and confused at being suddenly taxed with his fraud. He pleaded embarrassment in business, losses and delays in the collection of his debts. Then, growing bolder, on finding that the reproaches addressed him were after all but of a half-hearted sort, he held that the attempt to sell the horse must have been some piece of stupidity on Rickardson's part, and had not been done by his, St. Hill's, order.

"How can a man half tell what he is doing, in such a fix?" he said. "Things like that staring him in the face, for instance!" He pointed to the bulletin board. "I can't even decently show myself here except at this time of night. I was in hopes you would have taken that down."

He spoke in a melancholy way, more in sorrow than in anger, at the neglect of a friend, which touched him in a very tender place.

"You are *always* in a fix, man, and I am sick and tired of it!" cried Kingbolt. "Why don't you economize? Why don't you do something for your*self*? You have the best of everything. You eat better dinners and wear better clothes than anybody else. You *look* as if you were worth about forty millions."

"I have to, old fellow," argued St. Hill. "When a man is down on his luck, that is the time he has to look his best. If he is really prosperous, it doesn't make much difference. Besides, *you* cut off one promising source of revenue I had. You recollect how you prevented my giving Rodman Harvey a twist."

"Twist the whole lot of them now, if you like, and be hanged to them!"

St. Hill did not disclose the fact that he had already made this attempt and failed. He was astonished anew, however, at finding his patron's infatuation over, just as he had begun to act upon the belief that it was confirmed, and this source of profit lost to him for good. He had sold the horse in truth with the purpose of reaping all the benefit possible from the last stages of this connection. He cursed his folly for having done so; but Kingbolt's present demeanor encouraged him to hope that he might reinstate himself in favor, in spite of it.

Kingbolt was for a night of wild dissipation, and the parasite readily fell in with his humor. They joined to themselves finally a couple of kindred spirits, met with among resorts the bare existence of which — important as is the part they often play in the lives of ornaments of polite society — it is the custom of society to ignore.

The quartette repaired to a gaming establishment, provided with every convenience and luxury and very discreetly kept. Before daylight the heir of the Eureka Tool Works of Kingboltsville had squandered a sum which increased his reputation for prodigality even with those to whom large figures were no novelty.

He awoke in his apartment that day, not at nine in the morning, but four in the afternoon. There came to him almost at once, the unwelcome reminder of an engagement he had made to drive a coach-load of friends to Sprowle Onderdonk's garden party on the morrow. He devoted some reflection to the best means of getting out of it, but none occurred to him as very feasible.

"No," he decided finally. "I will appear before Angelica at the *fête*, given to celebrate her coming nuptials though it be, with a proud and contemptuous demeanor. It shall be made plain to her that she is by no means the cause of agitation in my breast she may choose to imagine."

XIX.

A GARDEN PARTY ON THE HUDSON, AND ITS SEQUEL.

WHATEVER scruples or misgivings Ottilie Harvey may have had in taking her seat on Mr. Kingbolt's coach, on the day set for Sprowle Onderdonk's garden party, they were dispelled, for the time being at least, by the novel pleasure of the ride.

The eyes of all pedestrians turned admiringly towards the imposing vehicle, as it rolled up the Avenue. The fresh-faced young English guard stood up in his place, in the bold attitude of one of the angels on the Church of the Heavenly Rest, and woke the echoes with his horn.

Ottilie thought the great city more delightful than ever. It was bathed at this season in an atmosphere of liquid amber. The scarlet and yellow leaves had begun to drift idly down in the squares from the rich masses of foliage to which they belonged. The pretty women, back from the country, promenaded in dresses of darker and warmer stuffs, premonitory of the coming winter. Strangers crowded into town, and the streets were filled to their utmost. If the bronze Washington at Union Square indeed supervise the cohorts debouching before him he had need of all his strategy now. Along Fourteenth and Twenty-third streets, small dealers had spread out their merchandise of blue china, oriental fans and boxes on the sidewalk itself. On some of these days there were parades of militia regiments, and the young girl looked out of her window upon swaying bayonets as far as the eye could reach, as if the surface itself were in motion. At evening the profiles down all the western cross-streets were thrown out black against skies of smoky orange and crimson, — full chords of the color-harmonies of which the falling leaves were but wandering notes.

"If Europe can be brighter, more picturesque than all this," said Ottilie, "it must be lovely indeed."

She exchanged now but little talk, and that of a conventional kind, with the persons about her. Her acquaintance with most of them was but of a formal sort, and Kingbolt was engrossed with his horses.

A number of the drags forming a junction constituted a small procession. A somewhat circuitous route was chosen, that the rendezvous might not be reached too soon. They passed through the copses of Central Park, then the transitional region above, which was neither city nor country. There were bowlders, shanties, and goats; isolated blocks of new houses, like sections of plum-cake sliced sharply off; and paved and sidewalked streets, forming causeways across low grounds, utilized by thrifty Germans for market gardens. The Elevated Railroad, that spider's-web trestle with little stations high in the air, like habitations of lake-dwellers, or *chalets* from the land of dreams, which now traverses the region, was still in the future. The parallelograms of crops in the market gardens, fresh yet as in early spring, were thrown down beside one another, like a series of rugs in the royal Ottoman greens.

Farther on, the expedition threaded the embowering lanes of an area of handsome villas. Some were of stone, ivy-clad, and all shaded with fine trees. Now and then a policeman of the mounted force was encountered slowly pacing his charger, or trying the fastenings of a lodge gate, to see that all was well. In the freedom of these secluded places the gayer spirits began to give free rein to their several devices. Baron Au instructed Daisy Goldstone in the approved method of winding a coaching-horn. Ada Trull drew off her long *mousquetaire* gloves, and essayed an accomplishment, which she fancied she possessed, of producing shrill whistles through her joined hands.

In fine the merry-makers turned back a little, and came down to the Sprowle manor, on the Hudson, in the last day of its existence. It was garlanded as if for the sacrifice. The tall columns of the portico, in the old-fashioned classic style, were hung with wreaths and festoons. Large bunches of flowers were set out in the old-fashioned wainscoted rooms, deprived now of the greater part of their furniture, and swept and garnished for dancing. On the morrow, at daylight, the minions of improvement would begin to throw down the shingles with a clatter from the roof and tear the sheathing from the stout old frame.

The coaches were unlimbered and let stand upon the lawn, where their canary, blue, and scarlet sparkled as vivid spots of color throughout the afternoon. Luncheon was to be served under a tent at two o'clock, and this followed by Dr. Wyburd's poem. Archery and lawn-tennis were provided for such as cared for these sports. Others walked in a neglected old garden, full of box, yew-trees, hollyhocks, and dahlias, or strolled away beyond the limits of the grounds.

Baron Au organized a round game, rather worrying people into it, on the plea of a chill in the air. He had seen it given with success, he said, at lake parties at Saratoga, and elsewhere, and the Italian and Turkish ministers had taken part in it, which proved that it must be dignified enough for anybody.

Kingbolt simulated indifference well, as he had proposed. He took part gayly in the round game, danced with Ada Trull, and escorted Ottilie about a great deal on his arm.

Angelica thought he must be contemptuous indeed to console himself with such a rival as the last. She would rather have seen him, too, with a certain air of depression and gloom — though, to be sure, what difference did it make?

Dr. Wyburd's poem proved to be a record of names and doings, more or less authenticated, about the Sprowle family given in a poor doggerel. Poetry, perhaps literature in general, was not the doctor's strong point, although he dabbled in it much to his own satisfaction. A sufficient idea of the character of his performance may be had from some such couplets as these : —

"Colonels Corlear and Robert, those men of strong will,
And Verplanck D. Sprowle, who built the first mill;
Governor Cyrus, Chancellor Garrett, — also first judge of court, —
And Rufus, the patriot, whom no British gold bought."

The approaching union of Sprowle and Angelica was mentioned in its turn. A clumsily turned compliment had been inserted in praise of the paragon of youth and beauty who was both to confer and receive honor by consenting to unite herself to the illustrious Sprowle lineage. This was received with applause, and the health of the pair was proposed in a eulogis, tic toast. Sprowle rose to reply, but acquitted himself in a manner little to the satisfaction of his critical betrothed.

It might have been supposed that Miss Angelica Harvey would be especially content in her choice, on such a day of glorification of the family importance, which had been her principal object in making it. This, however, was hardly the case. Whether it were that inopportune discontent which is said to always hang about the culmination of human wishes, or a regretful drawing of contrasts now at the last moment, or merely a pique at the indifference of Kingbolt, she was much out of sorts.

Kingbolt's indifference proved so well simulated in the beginning and so poorly in the sequel, as to provide New York society with something like a nine days' wonder, and radically change the fortunes of a number of our characters.

The company scattered at random after the delivery of the poem. Ottilie interested herself in the antiquity of the place and the series of attractive views. From the high colonnaded porch there were vistas of the river framed in the foliage of the great trees. Now a white steamboat forged across them; now a becalmed sloop drifted into them; or a puffing tug passed with interminable slowness, by reason of a long train of canal-boats in its tow. The hazy atmosphere dropped a bluish veil between the foreground and the distance. Over among the cliffs of the farther shore patches of the autumn foliage seemed as if dimly burning. A row-boat, moving across the deep shadow and reflection of that farther shore, drew a long line of silver behind it.

There was talk, on the porch, of remains of revolutionary earthworks still existing in the vicinity. Stillsby pressed himself upon Ottilie as an escort to go in search of them. Not greatly versed in polite arts for escaping boredom, she amiably accepted him. This youth had primed himself to-day — having heard an inkling of Ottilie's taste — with a liberal stock of poetical quotations, and was looking for an opportunity to put them to their intended use.

Kingbolt offered Angelica flippant "congratulations" of the usual sort, which secretly exasperated her. Somewhat later, they two were left together, removed from the rest, near the gate of the old-fashioned garden. With the situation thus, Angelica could not forbear opening her mind a little.

She was looking particularly well to-day, Kingbolt thought. He could see it with half an eye, though affecting not to attend, and though he was in the habit of finding each successive toilette the most fascinating. She wore her gray corduroy coaching dress, with a wide-brimmed hat and feather to match; and around her waist a silver belt with a long chain depending from it nearly to the ground, holding a multitude of pretty trinkets, as vinaigrettes, tablets, dog-whistles, and betting-books, which clinked as she walked.

"I would rather you would not be angry with me, if you are," she began. "If there is anything in which you think I have been wrong, — under the circumstances, — I am sure — I am very sorry. I trust that we shall part as friends."

She was very enticing thus, but Kingbolt thought good to make little reply. He refused to be drawn out of a reserved and gloomy air he now assumed, and which the young lady thought much more becoming to him than the other. By little and little, as if unconsciously, they had ventured into the garden, and were pacing the principal alley. This alley led to a retired bower on the crest of a well-wooded slope which declined to the river. The bower was of lattice-work, in the Dutch style, with a roof painted red, and finished with a weather-cock. Persons within were invisible from the side of the house. Here the two, having strolled to it, presently sat down.

Meanwhile Ottilie and her eccentric escort had found the historic earthworks of which they had gone in quest, and were retracing their steps by a pleasant path up the wooded slope. Stillsby, proceeding by gradual stages, had now launched fairly into his stock of intellectual lore, and was looking for consequences from the onslaught. He had quoted from "My name is Norval;" "Farewell, farewell to thee, Araby's daughter;" the "Maid of Athens;" and the "Seminole's Reply." The mystified Ottilie was beginning to arrive at an amused conception of his object.

The interview in the bower had proceeded but a little way, when Kingbolt burst out into a torrent of reproaches and entreaties, as of old. Angelica had reason now to repent her ill-advised course in allowing the subject to be reopened in any degree whatever. She rose, in alarm, and would have gone away, but Kingbolt detained her. She seemed obliged to argue with him somewhat further, now that she had once begun.

"How utterly without reason you are!" she said. "You talk the wildest nonsense. Just imagine for one moment what a stir there would be, what an upheaval in society, if the engagement of anybody of consequence — I do not say mine, but anybody's

— should be broken after having gone as far as this."

"What is a hubbub of a few days, or a few weeks, — or a few months, for that matter, — compared with the happiness of a life-time? I know you do not care for Sprowle. How can you? — you, so beautiful and superior. Yet you have got to go on with him not merely for a little while, but all your life-time. Remember that! Oh, break with him, Angelica! It is not too late. Oh, break with him!"

He caught her hand, but she drew it quickly away, saying, —

"Let me go! I cannot let you talk so about him. I am going back to the house."

"He is a milksop, a molly-coddle, a fool. I consider him but little better than Stillsby," pursued her companion excitedly. "All the men know it. The idea of his being able to appreciate a girl like you! And as to morality, — if you come to that, he is not a straw better than the rest of us."

As the young woman had not selected her future husband chiefly on grounds of his superior wisdom or morality, this argument was not as effective as some other perchance might have been.

"No! Impossible!" she reiterated. "Do not detain me against my will! Let us go back at once!"

"Well, then, I cannot bear it, do you understand?" cried the lover, throwing out his arms in a wild way. "It suffocates me! It tears me to pieces! There are fellows who talk about suicide. Plenty of them would not do it, you know; it is all talk; but I believe I am one of the kind who would. You will hear nothing more of me till kingdom come, after you are married to him. I cannot *live*, I tell you. I *will* not live."

The blood rushed to his face and stalwart neck, swelling out the veins. He contorted his body in a writhing way upon the hips, and threw his arms aloft, in the attitude of the young Orestes pursued by the Furies. It must have been a spasm, now in mature life, like those of his childish days, when he had been shut up in his padded room. His fine figure was displayed in these unconscious movements to excellent advantage.

Angelica, approaching, laid a hand persuasively on his arm. "Let us talk reasonably," she said.

"Reasonably? There is no reason but in your being mine, and mine alone."

He turned quickly. His handsome eyes blazed into her own. What an adulation was this, compared with the sluggish way of Sprowle! She delayed an instant too long in this dangerous proximity. Kingbolt took her in his arms, and kissed her passionately. She did not resist.

Ottilie, with her sentimental companion, was at this moment emerging from the wood.

"Longfellow, now, is a nice poet," Stillsby was saying. "You take his — now — that 'Excelsior.' I call that A 1."

"Yes," rejoined the long-suffering Ottilie.

The embrace in the bower flashed full upon the view of both.

"Hi!" ejaculated Stillsby, his eyes starting from his head in uncontrolled surprise.

But Ottilie managed to draw him back into the covert of the foliage before they were themselves perceived, and they returned by another way. When they had gone some little distance in silence, Ottilie offered as a deprecating suggestion : —

"It seems to me it would be better not to make any mention of what we have seen."

"Oh, certainly not! *certainly* not!" her cavalier hastened to protest, with alacrity, "if *you* wish it."

The warmer and more human impulses had prevailed, after all, over calm calculation, and the engagement of Angelica was definitely broken. She was not less capable of acting upon impulse than Kingbolt, it seemed, and she had the most obstinate of wills to sustain any course upon which she might enter.

The pair set to discussing the difficult problem of their future. Mrs. Harvey would consent to the reversal of her favorite plan only with extreme difficulty; that was certain. The calmer and sterner opposition of Rodman Harvey to the unbusiness-like step was to be dreaded even more. Then Sprowle was to be got rid of, and there was the presumable rage of his mother and all the Sprowle connection, though of these Angelica affected to make light.

She was very affectionate with her new lover, petted and soothed him, but repudiated his suggestions, which were more notable for a vehement contempt of the obstacles than for tact.

"Leave it all to me," she said, finally. "Nothing must be said or done just now. We must appear for a while mere ordinary acquaintances, as before."

She began with her betrothed a course of alienating tactics, on the very journey back to town. The next day, for he was fond of her, and came often, she would not see him. The next, when he brought her some present, she ridiculed it in an exasperating way, saying, "You dear, good, stupid thing, do take it away! You have no more taste than Marmion." At a subsequent meeting she gave out that she had *heard* something against him, — against his moral character. Being pressed, she would not tell what this was; then said it was of no consequence, though having still every appearance of retaining a prejudice. She was absent-minded; asked him repeatedly, "What did you say?" and paid no attention to his answers. In short, she crowded into the briefest space of time the greatest number of annoyances. A saint would have been unsettled with less. When at last Sprowle resented this conduct in a fairly vigorous way, for him, she became hysterical.

"Go!" she said, in the true spirit of the meek wolf with the ferocious lamb. "All is over between us. Nothing that I can do any longer is right. It was not so once." She pressed her handkerchief to her eyes, and went sobbing from the room.

She granted him another meeting, however. In this, although her ultimatum of the day before was not at first adhered to, she managed to make the situation in the end more acrimonious than ever. After this she wrote to Sprowle that she could now see that they had never been congenial, though they may have thought so. It would have been folly for them to marry. She hereby canceled her engagement with him. It was to be considered absolutely and finally at an end.

She hurried back to him his ring and other presents. Efforts on his part to see her, repeated expostulations by letter, were in vain. He offered humble apologies, — though he knew not for what. He offered to have the wedding put off; to wait for her indefinitely. No, all was useless.

Through chagrin, he did not at once make known to his mother what had happened, but went out of town for a few days. Never in all his career as secretary of legation, his lounging in club windows, participation in the observances of polite society and athletic sports, had he met with or heard of such an experience before.

The situation as between Angelica and her mother settled itself only after such a violent contest as might have been foreseen. It ended in the triumph of the stronger will, as could also have been foreseen. The girl declared her purpose to marry Kingbolt irrevocably fixed, and that no power under heaven should shake it. The defeated mother then went reluctantly over to her side. They planned together that the cause of the dismissal of Sprowle should not be disclosed, not to Rodman Harvey more than others. It was to be attributed to uncongeniality, a caprice, a quarrel, — anything but the substitution of a new lover. If Kingbolt should appear afterwards, — as what more natural than that there should be other suitors? — and be accepted, no necesssary connection need be found between the two events.

This arrangement was foiled, however, by the indiscretion of so apparently unimportant a person as Stillsby. The manners of Stillsby at the Empire Club for the first few days after the scene he had witnessed at the garden party were a marvel to all who knew him.

"What the devil is the matter with the fellow," asked Whitehead Finch, — "smirking, and glowering, and snooping about like that? He seems to get lighter in the upper story every day. He was well enough when he first joined the club. I recollect when he had almost as much sense as the average."

"Calibre of his associates. Dropped to the level of the rest of you," said Watervliet, using the freedom of a privileged character and an old bird.

To forbear from adding to his own importance by disclosing what he knew, especially when the news of the broken engagement came out, and it was spoken of as something mysterious and unaccountable, was more than Stillsby, after heroic effort, was capable of. He confided his secret to one and then another, and the club was soon buzzing with it. It came in this way to the ears of Sprowle Onderdonk, with others.

It was the afternoon of Election Day, as it happened, when the political fortunes of Rodman Harvey were being weighed in the balance. Sprowle Onderdonk hastened to Stillsby, had the story out of him, and was soon after closeted with his aunt, and his cousin Sprowle, now returned to town.

The dowager Mrs. Sprowle ordered her carriage, and drove to the Harvey mansion. She made her way up to Mrs. Harvey's boudoir, where she had so often been before on more agreeable errands. Her black and vindictive aspect told the cause of her coming, even before she had opened her lips. Ottilie, who was in attendance, trembled at her violent reproaches.

If "My dear Mrs. Sprowles" and "My dear madams," uttered in the most deprecating way by Mrs. Rodman Harvey, could have saved the day, it would have been done. But it could not. Angelica, however, hearing in her chamber above some rumor of what was in progress, came down, in a semi-invalid condition, pale, disheveled, in a charming wrapper of lace and knots of ribbon. She lent her assistance, engaged the enemy intrepidly, and, moved, perhaps, by the consciousness of being wholly in the wrong, had soon thrown all attempt at conciliation to the winds. There was a vixenish quality in her anger when at white heat which a lover of the amiable in woman would not have cared to see. Mrs. Sprowle retired down the staircase, breathing threatenings and slaughter.

"The brazen, brazen girl!" she muttered. "That ever I should have taken up with such people! . . . Oh, if I had but known this before!" as she pulled together the door of her carriage with a trembling hand.

And again she said, at a conclave of the Sprowle interest summoned to meet at her house that evening, "Oh, if I had but known this before!"

If she meant that she might, in that event, have done something to impede Rodman Harvey's election, and strike at the women of the family through him, it was now too late. At sunset Michael Brannagan, nominee of Tammany Hall, was beaten, and Harvey duly elected next representative in Congress from the most important district in New York. Baleful glances might be shot across the street from the darkened residence of the Sprowles, but these could not prevent that of the merchant prince from being brightly illuminated, nor the coming of troops of admiring friends to offer congratulations on his victory.

Towards eleven o'clock, when the returns were verified, and there could be no dispute about the result, the henchmen who had borne the heat and burden of the day arrived with a brass band to tender a serenade. In the cheering concourse were many of the merchant's clerks. They did not reside in his district, and had not been able to vote for him, but had felt the excitement at the store, where it had relaxed the usual discipline for a day or two. They had chaffed and offered wagers there with a zest that would not have misbecome the Empire Club, and they now came to hear "the old man" speak.

He stood forth, his head bare, on the broad steps. The noises about him were suddenly hushed. At the Sprowle mansion, as elsewhere, was audible his opening phrase, "Fellow citizens." Then followed such fragments as "the proud satisfaction,— the momentous issues,— one whose interests are identical with your own,— this great New York,— this imperial city of ours,— washed on three sides by rivers, with a bay capable of holding the commercial navies of the world.— Men of all nations and climes, — the enterprise, wealth, and skill of our people. Thanking you once more for your kind attention, he concluded, "I will bid you good-night!"

There were more shrill cheers; the band struck up briskly; there was a bustle of hand-shaking on the steps; some of the leaders were invited into the house; refreshments were passed around outside. Then came more music by the band. It marched away, its notes sounding fainter and fainter in the distance, and the merchant prince was left to repose upon his new honors.

Rodman Harvey made much less of the news of the substitution of Kingbolt for Sprowle, when it was broken to him, than his family had dreaded. Whether it was that he was occupied with his own affairs, and did not fully appreciate its bearing upon himself, or for other reasons, he appeared, after a decorous amount of advice, to regard the choice of Kingbolt with genuine favor.

"He has so much more money, you know, papa," urged Angelica, anxious to make the case the most secure possible.

"Yes, I know," he replied. "The Eureka Tool Works, and its founder, Colonel Kingbolt, are like household words."

"The matter chiefly concerns you," he said to the two women. "You made the first match for reasons good and sufficient to yourselves, and now that you are pleased to change your views I do not know that I am called upon to interfere. Only do not let it happen again. It is most unbusiness-like and reprehensible. I trust that you have done everything, as far as possible, to reconcile the Sprowles. They are a strong clan, and their ill-will is a matter of consequence."

The women suppressed some of the aggravated circumstances of the affair, and did not tell him that it was war to the knife already with the Sprowles.

The news had its various effects in many quarters. It came to Mr. Fletcher St. Hill upon the heels of his fancied recovery of control over Kingbolt, and caused in that financier a profound revulsion of feeling. Now, indeed, was his patron lost to him, and it was time for him to make to himself new friends in the mammon of iniquity. He moved his Prudential Land and Loan Company two flights higher up in the Magoon Building. He took himself, after a while, with his grudge against Harvey, to the Sprowles. They received him with open arms. He was to aid them in working up a campaign. On the strength of this Sprowle Onderdonk advanced him money. St. Hill imparted, gradually, and under strict pledge of confidence, his secret, and showed Harvey's treasonable correspondence in his possession. "My business relations are too delicate," he explained, "and my situation here as a Southerner too critical, to allow me to engage in a contest with so powerful an adversary. There is no telling what calumnies he might invent, and even give a certain currency, too, in return, through his recognized standing."

"These are good, but not enough," groaned Mrs. Sprowle over the letters. "They would have injured him politically, but more is wanted."

"She would have liked to convict Rodman Harvey of arsons, assassinations, — the most heinous of crimes."

The news came to Bainbridge by the mouth of G. Lloyd, the architect, the day after Harvey's election. It was a dismal, wet November day, one of those that herald, in peculiarly disagreeable fashion, the advent of winter. The rain beat like small shot against his office windows, and scourged the ferry-boats and wandering sails before it like guilty things, down on the wide yellow river. In the squares it tore off the leaves by the handful, and endeavored to beat them into the ground with a superfluity of malice.

The two met in the damp hall of the Magoon Building, at noon, and their umbrellas ran little pools upon the tile pavement while they talked.

"By the way, another lively exploit of our friend Kingbolt," said Lloyd. "We were talking about him, the other evening, you remember. Heard?"

"No," said Bainbridge.

"He has cut out Sprowle with Harvey's handsome daughter, and got her for himself. Fact!"

"Heavens — No! But is n't it pretty sudden?"

"They say he has been dangling around her this ever so long. I got it from some club men. People saw them hugging each other at a garden-party up the Hudson. That's what brought on the crisis."

Bainbridge walked about in the blustering weather in a rapture. Perhaps he hardly noted that it rained. For him it had suddenly become the most genial of days. The sun was shining at but the slightest remove behind the enshrouding vapors.

Ottilie not another's at all? and still open to him? He knew very well what he meant to do at the first practicable moment for getting up town. He called himself a million idiots for having so mistaken the true state of affairs. What must she have thought of him? And he a lawyer, and presumably in the habit of attaching something like its real value to evidence! He entered a florist's, and sent Ottilie some flowers, accompanied by a note.

Ottilie, in her room, looking out of her window at the dismal prospect, received, that afternoon, a pasteboard box full of Jacqueminot roses. They were cut with long stems, and laid in a protection of cotton-wool. Their dewiness and perfume were still upon them, as if fresh from the conservatory. The young girl had never had a more delightful compliment. The inclement season trebled its charm. What did it all mean? She read the following lines: —

DEAR MISS OTTILIE, — I seem to have been laboring under some stupid delusion. Happily, it is past. I wonder if you will be at home this evening. I shall give myself the pleasure of trying to find you.
Sincerely yours,
RUSSELL BAINBRIDGE.

Delusion? What delusion? What was she to understand? Here was testimony enough, if more were needed, that in Bainbridge one was dealing with no ordinary person. She sat in an attitude of pensive reflection, burying her face from time to time in the lovely roses. She was greatly puzzled. At any rate, he was coming to see her again, and of that she was very glad. Suddenly she started up, seized her pen, rang for a district telegraph messenger, and wrote: —

DEAR MR. BAINBRIDGE, — Thank you so much for the flowers you have been kind enough to send me. What a bit of tropical beauty and fragrance on this blustering day! I am sorry to say, however, that I cannot be at home this evening. I am not wholly mistress of my own motions, as you know, and my aunt has made some arrangement for me which will keep me away both this evening and to-morrow. I consider it very unfortunate. But will you not come very soon after that? Your "delusion" is a great mystery. What can it be? I think I have had reason to fear some such delusion on your part as that you had fancied you cared a little for yours truly, but found you did not. With sincere regards,
OTTILIE HARVEY.

Could Bainbridge have found Ottilie in the first flush of his enthusiasm, she would have heard from him an ardent declaration of his state of mind, whatever effect we may suppose it to have had upon her. But this was not to be for some time longer. He had a night and a day of enforced reflection. Even after that he did not at once find her alone. Nothing, in fact, had changed in their circumstances, from the point of view of marriage. Were they not as poor as ever? It is only in the story-books, when true-lovers take each other for better or worse, throwing prudential considerations to the winds, that everything else is immediately added unto them. "Rodman Harvey would look at a proposal for his niece's hand as an attempt upon his purse-strings, and would close them tighter than ever. And who wishes him to open them on my account, since he will not on hers?" said Bainbridge. "No, let us wait a little." He had an indefinite sense that something must turn up to aid them. The immediate danger was over. He would study out a solution of their difficulties at leisure. Their former relations were resumed. Why hurry, in fine, a situation which was so charming in itself?

He began to walk much in Wall Street in his noon outings. He studied the backs of the capitalists who had achieved notable success there, then crossed over and met them face to face, and endeavored to divine their secret. Some were of very ordinary aspect, — shamble-gaited, and of pinched and mean little physiognomies. They did not look happy, with all their money, and plenty of well-authenticated stories showed that they were not. But that was not to the purpose; so much the worse luck theirs. If he, Bainbridge, had it, he could be happy.

The dark mass of Trinity Church rose at the head of the narrow, opulent street, its quiet old churchyard in such contrast to the eager human life rushing by, as if death and graves were the most improbable of myths. Down the street jutted out the temple-like porticoes of the sub-treasury and the custom-house. The multitudinous needs of commerce had spun a cobweb of telegraph wires across the sky. At places they ruled it into squares like those of the ledgers below, and again converged in bundles like ships' cordage. Trays of gold pieces shone in the windows of the basement offices, as if here, indeed, Jupiters had rained themselves down, having come, by mistake, to the wrong part of town. The brokers waited in the dark interiors for customers to take the glittering bait.

Bainbridge gathered up one day all his resources, including a moderate loan from the Hudson Hendricks, and went into Wall Street.

An idea had taken possession of him. Speculation was not an ideal means of redeeming one's fortunes, and no doubt he should be ashamed of it afterwards. But it was a means, a possible means, and there seemed no other. There was talk, just at present, of unusual opportunities for gain. The market was actively "booming." He determined to regard his venture as an augury. To win Ottilie, if he succeeded; to give her up to a better custody than his, if he failed! Surely fate would be propitious to so deserving a cause.

There was a plan of buying on a "margin," or percentage, by which one secured control of a number of shares vastly out of proportion to his small capital. In this way, in the event of a rise a large profit was reaped; though of course, in the event of a considerable decline, on the other hand, the capital one put in was wholly wiped out. Bainbridge bought shares of Devious Air-Line, on a margin. There seemed a certain fitness in connecting himself with the fortunes of Rodman Harvey.

Devious Air-Line remained stationary for a long time. Then it dropped off a point or two.

XX.

"LALAGE, SWEETLY SMILING, SWEETLY SPEAKING."

CONVENTIONAL lovers in the conventional stories are always aware of the precise extent of the regard they have for each other. It is generally a frenzy amounting to madness. They take the earliest (and every subsequent) opportunity of declaring it, and thereafter it is of no will their own, but only the most insuperable of physical obstacles, that keep them apart.

But who shall picture all the fluctuations of feeling, the misgivings, the blowing hot and cold, of lovers in real life, where there are so many affairs besides those of the heart demanding attention; so much marrying and giving in marriage, indeed, with hardly a pretense of affection at all? Balked in his first intent, Bainbridge did not renew it. His imagination hovered over Ottilie with an all-embracing tenderness, but he did not make her any set speeches of affection.

When they had met a number of times, and he had not referred in any way to his note, Ottilie said to him, —

"Perhaps you do not remember that you have not told me what your 'stupid delusion' was. I am dying to know."

Taken by surprise, he was hardly able to vary from the truth with great ingenuity at so short notice.

He had hoped that as the matter had not been alluded to so far, it would remain uninvestigated. He gave to his admission, however, a flippant air, as if it were of but the most trifling consequence.

"Oh, — that? Oh, yes!" he said. "That was a misunderstanding about Kingbolt, you know. I was over-worked, or absent-minded, or something. I often get things wrong. I fancied that it was you to whom Kingbolt was paying court instead of Angelica."

Ottilie did not reply on the instant. She looked at him with a gaze at once bewildered, reflective, amused. What a compliment he paid her! He had been seriously considering her, then, an eligible partner for Kingbolt; she, who considered herself so little eligible for anybody. Why, the plain implication was, too, that he, Bainbridge, had been jealous of her. She dared not trust this hypothesis; it was too wild. But in the instant of making it her heart beat quicker, and it remained warmer towards Bainbridge ever after.

"Oh, you thought it was I?" she said. "That is very interesting. If you could only have known how he was boring me with his talk about my cousin all the while, you would not have thought so. I hardly knew what to do. I could not betray his confidence, and yet I did not want it. I never supposed his persistence would have any result. So that accounts for your — So you thought" —

She nibbled her lip with her even white teeth in the effort to repress her smiles. But her smiles were rather of keen delight, which she feared might betray itself, than derision.

"The circumstances fitted into one another so perversely. Your riding with him so much, you know, and all that," said Bainbridge.

"And so you stayed away?" She broke into a merry laugh.

"Well, yes. I did seem to stay away."

"Do you not think you are of a rather peculiar disposition?"

"I advised you, you know," said Bainbridge, waiving an answer to this question. "A companion of that kind, if I had been right, would naturally have taken my place. I thought I ought to furnish a clear field."

"And no favor."

"Well, no; not very much favor."

"You do me great honor, I am sure. Perhaps the advice is good yet, in principle."

This was a critical passage for Bainbridge. The tone and look of banter he assumed were likely to give place at any instant to a blazing avowal of passion. "I am well over it," he thought.

"Your cousin's new engagement is openly announced, I hear," he said, changing the subject.

"Yes; as the murder was out, boldness was the best policy. I think they are doing a number of things on that basis, still. It is a continual round of dinners and theatre parties for Angelica. Mr. Kingbolt gets his friends to give them, or gives them himself, sometimes at Delmonico's, sometimes at his own apartments, where he has suitable chaperons to preside. I have seen some of the *menus* of these dinners. One is embroidered on satin, another is on a silver tablet. Lovely presents are given the guests: fans, sashes to match the ladies' dresses, gold pins and butterflies for their hair, and satin bags of confectionery.

It is one rain of gifts for Angelica, besides: parcels from the jeweler, the florist, and confectioner all day long. Do you want to hear about her engagement ring?"

"Certainly I do. What is it?"

"A diamond of five carats, in a plain setting. Oh, how it glitters! She has another ring, also a present, with a pink pearl and two diamonds. It came in a porcelain jewel case, in the shape of an egg, a little jewel itself. This was inclosed in a teak-wood box, elaborately carved, and this in a silk bag, drawn with a cord. You would have screamed."

"I am almost tempted to now, at your feeling description."

"Angelica has given him in return a lock of her hair, a photograph for his dressing-table, a cat's-eye ring, and a sofa pillow partly embroidered by herself."

"You seem to take a certain interest in such matters."

"I dote on them. I have my epicurean tastes, too. Poor old Lone Tree! I fear I am forever spoiled by the leaven of luxury."

"I dare say she is very fond of him?" suggested Bainbridge.

"She must be. She adjures him affectionately to be careful of his hands, for her sake. She thinks he is ruining them by driving his coach, and other sports. But, seriously, you see how she has offended and defied the influential Sprowle family. If you could have seen that old woman's face, the day she came to reproach my aunt about it! I was frightened to death. What do you think she will do? What *is* done in this fashionable life, when people bitterly hate each other, and want revenge?"

"That is one of the problems. Well, they have their opinion of one another, and when they get sympathetic listeners they state it. Good old-fashioned vengeance, in fact, appears to be dying out. It is not a modern luxury. Few facilities are afforded now for its indulgence. Mortal enemies do not usually invite each other to dinner, and discriminating hosts do not put them next each other, if they chance to meet."

"Could the Sprowles attack my uncle in any way?" added Ottilie, with anxiety. "They might think it best to strike at my aunt and cousin through him. Probably no other means would be so effective. I am sure I should feel nothing more keenly than any taint of disgrace that might attach to him."

"Nonsense!" said Bainbridge. "They may annoy him in some trifling way; but if your uncle really had any points open to attack, it is not likely that he would be as stiff and uncompromising as he is with everybody."

"Well, I shall feel easier in mind when my cousin's wedding is over."

The merchant prince went off to Washington in December, and took his seat in the House of Representatives.

Kingbolt and Angelica, having impressed their new situation upon society to the extent they thought needful, went away to pay a visit to the family of Kingbolt at Kingboltsville. The young heir was considerably overdue there. It was long since he had conferred with his trustees, and they, having the management of things so very much in their own hands, began to look upon him almost as an interloper. He owed it to his mother and sisters, also, to introduce his betrothed to them.

His enthusiasm, which under ordinary circumstances might have cooled somewhat, was kept aglow by the opposition he met with. He squared himself defiantly against it. It was a wonder he did not come to blows with Sprowle Onderdonk. It was probably due to the forbearance of the latter that an outbreak did not take place. The two passed each other in the lobby of the Empire Club for a while with a haughty aggressiveness of mien.

"Still," said Onderdonk, "it would be stretching a point for me to take it up in that way. It is my cousin Sprowle's affair, the idiot! If he can afford to let it alone, I suppose I can. Besides, this fool of a Kingbolt is not the culprit. It is the Harvey people. We must make them feel it, root and branch. Perhaps we shall show them in time that slights are not to be put on a family like ours with impunity."

Mrs. Sprowle spoke of Kingbolt in much the same way. He was, according to her, "a poor dupe," "the rich young plebeian whom those designing women had got into their clutches," and who was more to be pitied than blamed, even bad as his private character was.

At Kingboltsville the heir went with Angelica to take a glimpse of the great Works. "Would you believe," he inquired, "that I used to come here myself, with blue shirt and dinner-pail, like one of the ordinary hands, and grease up the machinery?"

"Fancy!" his sweetheart replied, with supreme contempt.

It was a source of wonderment now to the young man himself that, with his superior opportunities for enjoyment in the world, he could ever have allowed himself to be deluded by such absurd notions of duty.

An evening party was given, and provincial society came out to do Angelica honor. The young woman professed surprise to see how very well some of these persons looked. She preserved with all of them a chilly demeanor. Nor did she get on better with the family itself. She privately termed the two widowed sisters "frumps." They spent a humdrum existence, ample as their resources were, looking after small cases of charity, founding a church or a school, or patronizing some mediocre artist who came up from New York to establish classes in "decorative art." They dressed in black, though their bereavements were many years remote; and when they descended from a carriage you had a glimpse of rusty gaiter and stocking.

Kingbolt's mother ventured an injudicious comment, in her timorous way, on his future bride. "We all admire her so much, Arthur," she said. "She is so brilliant in looks, so accomplished. I hope and pray that she will make you happy. But if you could only have chosen one a little less — a little more — not quite so worldly-minded, perhaps, dear."

The son, resenting, in quite his youthful way, any impugnment of the wisdom of whatever he might choose to do, returned some brusque, impatient answer. His sisters said, "You should not speak so to your mother, Arthur." Upon this, he flung himself out of the room, agreeing with Angelica, that they were hostile to her, as she said. The pair presently left so unappreciative a society, and departed to visit at Washington.

There Angelica went about on her lover's or her father's arm. The great New York merchant had been from the first put on important committees, and taken a prominent place in Congress. His beautiful daughter was something of a new sensation. She gave statesmen from the interior such a lesson in feminine elegance as they had not before enjoyed. The newspaper correspondents, taxed to the utmost though they are, sought fuller resources of word-painting to describe her. Ottilie read some of their glowing accounts of her cousin's appearance at the afternoon receptions, the ball of the British minister, the General of the army, Admiral this, and Senator that. Angelica assisted, too, the "ladies of the White House," — who were glad of her, and somewhat abashed by her; and she dined more than once in company with her father, at the President's table.

Angelica's opinion of the whole, in return, was not favorable. "It is a perfect menagerie," she said. "If it were not for the legation people, it would be quite intolerable. No exclusiveness, no fixity, no traditions! Everybody goes everywhere. What does a society based upon a little brief office-holding amount to? These furbelowed daughters, neices, and cousins of the good *bourgeois* legislators, no doubt think it heaven. Probably it is to them, who have never seen anything else."

It was thus she stigmatized the multitude of pretty girls flocking from all parts of the country to the gayeties of the place. She made herself as elegantly severe in attire as possible, by contrast. Murray Hill looked down disdainfully on Capitol Hill and all its affiliations.

Kingbolt coincided, as a newly engaged lover

should, in most opinions that she chose to express.
He amused himself, during his expatriation, with an
incidental run to Baltimore, where he knew some
pleasant fellows of the Maryland Jockey Club. He
picked up from a needy inventor hanging about the
Patent Office some ingenious new device in telegraphic communication, which he set about having
put in operation between his house and stock-farm
at Kingboltsville. He proposed to Angelica that his
yacht should be brought around for a trip to Bermu-
da; but to this she did not accede. We may leave
them here for a little, and return to New York.

The Christmas season went by. Owing to the
change in affairs, there was not the amount of gayety at the Harvey mansion as proposed at the beginning of the season. Mrs. Harvey took Ottilie about
with her more or less into society. She wished her
companionship, but never quite let her lose a sense
of her peculiar situation. Bainbridge took to going
out, also, to places where there was a likelihood that
he should meet with Ottilie. There were by no
means the same unconstrained opportunities for seeing her at the house as before. He was still wheeling round the circle of obstacles by which he seemed
beset without finding in it any loophole of escape.
Devious Air-Line recovered the point or two it had
lost, but did not rise above the purchase price.

Sometimes Bainbridge said to himself, "I will not
marry her, for my own sake." That was his selfish
mood, and meant that he desired to take upon himself no further burdens.

Again he said, "I will not marry her, for *her* sake.
Why should I pull her down? Have I not well
tested my capacity and prospects? Without me she

stands an excellent chance to be prosperous and happy."

But still again he exclaimed passionately, "I will marry her, in spite of everything!"

He set off more than once to act upon this impulse, but either did not find Ottilie when he would, or in her presence recovered his equanimity.

Once he dropped in of a morning, at a "Shakespearean reading" at Chickering Hall, and saw her in the audience, following carefully with a text in her hand. She was reaping now some of those "advantages" of the metropolis, of which she had had so exalted an idea. He knew of her going also to lectures at the Academy of Design, to old Dr. John Jones's sonorous discourses on Reformers and Men of Letters, and to the Rev. Wayland Howland on the Cathedrals of Europe, illustrated by the stereopticon.

Bainbridge contemplated her awhile, at the Shakespearean reading, from a vantage-ground in the rear, and went away without having made his presence known. How attractive it was in her to sink her personal comeliness, — which many others would have depended upon as a career in itself, — and endeavor so ambitiously to fill her pretty head with mental furniture! It *was* a pretty head. The hair, except a tendril or two which escaped, was drawn upward from the delicate nape of her neck. One smooth cheek was muffled by the bows of her bonnet. The other, with long, dark eyelashes projecting from it, showed its rounded profile, now more, now less, as she turned.

The next meeting of the pair was at an afternoon reception, or four-o'clock tea. They were at the corner of a door-way and each held and tasted in a dilettante way a cup of the beverage which gave the entertainment its name. Bainbridge managed at the same time to keep his hat and stick under his arm. The rooms were full of a chattering audience, chiefly ladies, in elegant street toilettes. These drove from one to another of a number of similar receptions, in progress at the same time, with card-cases in their hands, and remained but a few moments at each.

"I saw you at Chickering Hall," said Bainbridge. "you are always giving yourself infinite pains about some learned thing or other. You know more now than any dozen other New York girls put together."

"Oh! oh!" exclaimed Ottilie, scandalized. "Very well; if you call it learned to go to a panorama, or an innocent little Shakespearean reading, what will you say if I begin to talk Herbert Spencer and Mill, and Tait's researches into the original atoms of matter?"

"I shall say, don't do it!"

"They are in the shape of rings, always in motion, as if contending with one another," she went on archly.

"The researches, or the atoms? Well," in response to a frown, "let primordial atoms delight to bark and bite, if 't is their nature to; but that is no reason why we should."

"At any rate, persons who have everything to gain and nothing to lose ought to be ambitious, and learn all they can, do you not think so?" Ottilie insisted. "Besides, I shall never know enough to hurt me. I sometimes think I should like to be a professor,—always learning something important, and arousing an interest in it in others."

"You take a roseate view of professors. There

are a good many of a different sort. They are too
often chosen from the class of learners by rote, who
never have known what a genuine enthusiasm for
scholarship is. That kind but stifle the germs of it
in those confided to their care."

"A professor, after all," he concluded, "is a part
of the machinery. One would rather be a finished
specimen of the product."

It happened that this particular four-o'clock tea
was of a more elaborate sort than usual. The people
by whom it was given were spoken of as in an upper
grade of "strugglers." They still thought it desirable to commend themselves to favor by a lavish expenditure of money, which would not be necessary later.
The display was commented upon with an admiration
thinly veiling contempt, by those who would not have
imitated it. Flowers adorned the banisters from top
to bottom, and were set about in forms of tea-kettles,
temples, swans, and ships, on the piano and other
furniture. Pretty children, costumed as flower-girls,
presented each guest at his entrance a choice nosegay.
A flower-wreathed silver fountain sprayed into the air,
instead of water, a delicate perfumery.

"Do you know that this is not orthodox talk for a
four-o'clock tea?" said Ottilie. "You distract one
from looking about. You should tell me how very
difficult it is for men to attend affairs of this kind,
and how surprised you are at finding yourself here.
You should say that men have not the gift of small
talk, you know; and, if inclined to be humorous,
that it is really very dreadful to find one's self in such
a minority among the fair sex. I should remark that
it is said to make a fatal difference in a cup of tea
whether the milk or the sugar be put in first. 'Yes,'

you should reply; and state further that if a cup of tea be not perfect at the first mixing, no alteration can make it so. Meanwhile, we should both be staring about the room, thinking whom we would like to join, or have join us, next."

"So you are spoiled by luxury?" Bainbridge inquired, going back.

"I suppose I am. Still, I don't know. I want to see a specimen of everything; then I shall decide which I like best. It may not be this fashionable life, after all. It *is* a decadence, I fear. These stories of the flirtations of married men with young girls, and men with other men's wives,— I do not believe them, of course; but it shows something wrong that they get the currency they do."

But this was a line of subjects to be more freely discussed with Mrs. Clef, for instance.

"What I should really like to see," Ottilie went on, her face brightening, "is literary society. I should like to meet the people whose names you see in the papers, authors, artists, who discuss things really worth while, and come to some conclusion about them. The bright ones in this fashionable society say sparkling, audacious, amusing things, but that is all. Nothing is advanced, nothing settled."

"They would be glad to have a niece of Rodman Harvey at the places where the people you speak of assemble. I can drop Mr. Stoneglass a hint, down town. I know his wife will be pleased to send you an invitation, when her receptions begin."

"Really? Oh, I thought it would be very difficult. I supposed that my aunt, not being literary, was not eligible. I had never dared to aspire to it."

"You will meet people whose names you see in

the papers, but you will find very little settled, my poor child, even there. This is not a world, in fact, where much is settled. Then there are writers from whom one had expected a great deal, who are found to have told in their books all they know, and perhaps even more. You get nothing further from them. Still, having entertained us in print, it may be their privilege to be as dull as they please out of it."

"But what will they think of *me?*" said Ottilie, shrinking diffidently from the idea now that it was unexpectedly found feasible.

"The chief condition of comfort is to consider what you think of people, not what they think of you. I dare say, however, you will not be frightened. They let me in. To tell the truth, literary lions of the first magnitude do not abound in New York. The best of them do not always turn out either, and when they do they roar but gently. The field is left a good deal to the minor lights. I fear you will be disappointed."

"Oh, no, I shall not. Anything in the shape of a live author! I recollect making a pilgrimage, once, to get the autograph of a lady writer in our neighborhood, about as good as Mrs. Anne Arundel Clum. We high-school girls at fifteen used to think she was wonderful. If she had been Sappho, or Madame de Staël, she could not have received us with greater dignity."

"Yes, Mrs. Stoneglass, on the whole, will be the best for you," said Bainbridge, as if having reflected on the several places available. "Stoneglass has dined with your uncle, you say, and that will make it pleasanter. He edits the "Meteor," and his wife writes the bright Fanny Copperplate letters. She is better known than he, though his work is so much more substantial. When his rivals wish to be malicious, they speak of him as Mr. Fanny Copperplate Stoneglass. The entertainers are usually persons who themselves dabble, in a minor way, in letters. The right one to hold a *salon* of the traditional sort has hardly yet arisen. She should be appreciative and intelligent, of easy and friendly manners, and surrounded by a certain degree of luxury. She should not bore people with a small literary vanity of her own, nor have axes to grind."

" When will Mrs. Stoneglass' receptions begin ? "

"Some little time from now. I will let you know. They will probably be held Sunday nights, as usual."

" Oh ! Sunday nights? We-ll " — said Ottilie, hesitatingly.

" Yes ; another of our imported customs. Sunday afternoons and evenings are coming into favor for a great deal of quiet sociability. Actors are free on Sunday evening, for one thing. You may see some leading actors at Mrs. Stoneglass'."

Ottilie fell to reviewing the fitness of her mental equipment for meeting this formidable company.

" I read so little now, compared with what I used," she said; " I do not keep up at all. I am quite ashamed of myself."

" I, too, read almost nothing of late. It may be that as life becomes more interesting, books grow less so," said Bainbridge. " Perhaps we shall read again later on, to contrast our own experiences with those of fiction. I have had the last new novel of Blank's lying in my room for a fortnight, and not yet touched it. I hear it has a legal plot. I wish I knew what it was without the trouble of perusing it."

"Send it around to me; I will read it for you," volunteered Ottilie.

"Take care! It is too tempting an offer. I may hold you to it."

"I am not at all afraid."

He sent it around to her, in fact. At another meeting, not long after, she gave him a concise account of the story in a way which would hardly have done discredit to the best narrative powers of Angelica, or Madame Batignolles-Clichy herself.

"Do you know it was very nice of you to do that," said Bainbridge, holding her hand a moment longer than seemed necessary, as she gave it to him for good-by.

"Was it? Well, I am glad you appreciate it."

She looked brightly up at him; but somehow her face flushed under his glance, and her eyes fell. He hesitated over her hand, but dropped it without saying anything further.

Ottilie permitted herself reveries and speculations on the basis of the jealousy to which Bainbridge had confessed. It was the wildest of suppositions, of course. It would have meant that their association had not been purely platonic, after all, and nothing was more firmly established. But supposing now, as a mere hypothesis, that he really could like her in another way, he was the *kind* of person one would be rather glad to marry. His looks pleased her; she admitted it. He was manly-looking, of a certain distinguished air; people would be apt to notice him in a crowd.

"They say very nice things of him, too, in contradiction of his own account of himself," she went on. "Judge Chippendale praises his legal acquirements, and his personal courage in the affair with the shanty tenants. You never get a word out of *him*, though, on the subject. He is more serious than he used to be, too, — almost reasonable enough sometimes for anybody. I knew that he never believed his own wild theories. It was only his way of talking. How well we have got on together! How sympathetic and appreciative he is with me, when sympathy has been by no means common! We have not seemed to tire each other; at least I hope I have not tired him. Whether we agree or disagree, our discussions are equally grateful."

She would have liked to do something very warm and affectionate for him, — as for a dear brother. Once when she had sat down to write letters home, she scribbled almost inadvertently on the paper, —

Mr. R. Bainbridge. . . . *Mrs. Russell.* . . . *Mr. and Mrs. Bainbridge.* . . . *Mrs. Ottilie Bain* —

But at this point she exclaimed, " Ridiculous! " tore up the paper hastily, and looked over her shoulder in blushing alarm, lest by any chance she might have been observed.

"He to marry a poor girl," she went on, " with his tastes, his needs, his ambitions! If such a one had any conscience she would refuse to become a burden upon him, even if he were so foolish as to ask her. He should have the best wife in the world. He must have one who will be an advantage to him, — aid him to rise, not draw him back."

These were possibly far-fetched scruples, but such as they were, they were those of Ottilie Harvey.

Ottilie was sometimes taken to her aunt's box at the opera. Bainbridge, whose relaxation was music, went also, in a more modest way. He could see that the same class of fashionable men fluttered about the Harvey box, probably by force of habit, as when Angelica had been there. One night, of a number, he sat with his eyes fixed upon Ottilie's slight figure, at a distance. The love passages on the stage were of unusual tenderness. He heard in the melodies, the supplication, and pathos, an echo of his own affection. He went to pay his respects in her box. The opera-going men of unexceptionable good form were there. Mrs. Rodman Harvey was saying to one of them, in a languid tone, —

"We have no more voices. Grisi and Malibran were the last of the giants. The light style of singing is destroying our music."

Bainbridge found Mr. Northfleet, of the Empire Club, bending over Ottilie. "The German music is more bracing and tonic," he overheard him say, with an elaborate, languishing air, — a manner that had won him success with the fair sex before now, — "the Italian sweeter, cloying, if you will. But give me the sensuous Italian music, after all! There are times when it draws you out of yourself; fills you with vague, ineffable longings."

"Like going through Tiffany's in the holiday season," returned Ottilie, with her luminous smile. "Yes, I have felt that way, too."

Thus she parried the sentimentality of these persons, and seemed to stand less in awe of them than formerly. But there were too many of them. Although no aspirant so flagrant as he had taken Kingbolt to be appeared in the field, Bainbridge no longer knew whom not to dread, whom not be jealous of.

One memorable afternoon he was passing through the street in which the Hastings family resided. It abutted at the Avenue upon the massive Egyptian reservoir. The shadows had already begun to climb the opposite row of houses. He walked on the shaded side, but was presently sensible of a light flashed in his eyes from across the way. Looking over, he saw that it was the mischievous little Hastings children who were playing him this trick with a mirror from an upper window. They replied to an admonitory shake of his forefinger with laughing shrieks. Ottilie Harvey appeared in some confusion behind them.

"I have been looking after them for an hour or two," she explained to Bainbridge, holding parley down to him from the window, "while my friend Mrs. Hastings has gone after a new nursemaid. You will not think much of my discipline."

At the instant Mrs. Hastings herself rolled up. "Are you planning an elopement, or is it only a serenade?" she asked gayly, alighting from her coupé. "Well, come in! I will help you. Perhaps we have a rope-ladder in the house. You must stay to dinner," she insisted hospitably. "We need somebody to carve. Mr. Hastings is detained down town, and will not be at home."

Bainbridge, not unwillingly entered the house with her. Ottilie brought the children down to the parlor, and made many apologies for their bad behavior. They were a boy and a girl, charming in their dainty attire; a little over-boisterous and spoiled, but lovely to the height of the ideal.

At the dinner-table, Bainbridge, in Mr. Hastings' place, had quite the air of a man of family. A parrot, kept on a stand at one side of the room, was loosed from a large tin cage, at dessert, and practiced the feat of eating a grape and a bit of sugar from his mistress' hand. He vouchsafed, with his cold air, to come also to Ottilie. She had for this pet, as for other others, an abundant stock of affectionate murmurings and cooings. There was some talk on matters of cookery between her and the hostess; not of the epicure's sort, but such as good housewives indulge in who have masculine tastes to look after, and feel a due sense of the responsibility. Mysterious formulas of "two of flour, one of saleratus, and one of sugar," were mentioned. Ottilie said, —

"I always make my salad dressings with cream as well as oil."

Mrs. Hastings was busy, it appeared, with inducting the new nursemaid into the duties of her office, for a considerable time after dinner, and our two young people were left alone. Ottilie sat down at the piano, and played a little, ever and anon turning back to talk.

"I have been this morning to Harvey's Terrace," she said, among other things, "and have heard of a case which distresses me. The elderly school-teacher, Miss Finley, who went away to live with the pretty one, her friend, married from there, has come back in a pitiable condition. It seems that she let Mr. Cutler, the man her friend married, have her money — her savings of years — to invest, and cannot get it back. Neither can she get any interest. The young man has put it in as a special deposit in some company where he is employed, and probably lost it. The poor girl cannot eat nor sleep. She may lose her place in school also; for of course a person so distracted is not fit to teach."

"A sad case, indeed," commented Bainbridge. He thought, however, quite as much of the good heart and charitable energy of her who recited it as of the case itself.

"I want my uncle to do something. I shall mention it to him the next time he comes on from Washington. The young man was formerly in his store. Perhaps he can force him or his employer, in some way, to restitution."

The traits of the Hastings infants, in another turn of the conversation, became the starting-point for an exchange of sagacious views on education. Bainbridge alleged that the method of training of most people, his own at any rate, was wholly indefensible.

"What is wanted," he said, "is a scheme of education based upon the scheme of an international exhibition. First, the primary materials; then the forces of nature; then the forces as utilized by machinery; then the products of machinery; then man in his history, manners and customs, governments, and fine arts. The chimera of study for the mere sake of mental discipline should be discarded; something of real interest should be learned at the same time. The elements of the various branches of human knowledge should be reduced to their lowest terms, and given to the child at a very early age. In infancy one thing is as easy as another. At that flexible time of life everything is possible. The child should be put in possession of all his physical powers, too. He should make the most of his arms, legs, eyes, and voice. Indistinctness of speech should not be tolerated; neither should awkwardness of carriage. With proper management, the eye might be trained so that drawing would be as easy as writing. It should be a mere matter of choice whether a memorandum were made with a picture or a paragraph."

"Oh, indeed?" said Ottilie.

"Yes," the theorist went on; "the child should learn geology, botany, and natural history, and get an idea of the artistic beauty in common forms and lights and shadows. With this, he would have something to amuse his walks abroad. He would be kept from the mischief traditionally waiting for idle hands and vacant minds."

"But with all that," said Ottilie, "you would hurry your infant into an early grave. Good health is of much more importance."

"But I *say* good health," protested the young man. "I *say* physical exercise, the more the better. And only the broad, simple features of the sciences to be given."

"That is all very well for Julius Cæsars and Napoleons and Admirable Crichtons, who can do fifty different things at once, but you will kill the child," insisted Ottilie perversely.

There was a certain penetrating feeling of domesticity in their situation. By a little stretch of the imagination it might have been they who were at home, and Mrs. Hastings their guest. They commented with favor on the small house, abounding with evidences of a refined taste.

"But I thought you cared for nothing on so modest a scale," said Ottilie; "though an establishment like this is expensive enough, goodness knows. I recollect your scoffing at the idea of any residence smaller than the Custom House, or Saint Peter's at Rome."

But nothing was more to Bainbridge's taste at this time than details of economy, accounts of cheap rents, of making much of slender incomes, and the like.

"I suppose persons might do with less if they really loved each other," he said.

"If they really loved each other," said Ottilie, in a dreamy voice, and with half-averted head, "perhaps they would think very little of their circumstances. Nothing that they could do, no surrounding of their lives, could seem tame or commonplace."

Bainbridge was standing by her at the piano, ostensibly for the purpose of turning the music. His heart throbbed so, upon this, that he thought she could hear it. "I must speak. I will," he said to himself. He walked to a small table near the centre of the room, perhaps to collect his ideas. The evening paper, carelessly thrown there, lay before him. His eye fell upon a line of it which stood out with a startling distinctness.

There had been a flurry in Wall Street, and Devious Air-Line had fallen five per cent. He took his hat, and left the house.

The next day the flurry in Wall Street continued. The omen for which he had been waiting declared itself. His poor "margin" was wiped out, and he was left, besides, a debtor for the sum he had borrowed.

"Better luck next time!" his broker cried to him, cheerfully, as he hurried away from the conclusion of the transaction with a face of deep despair. It was so marked that Judge Chippendale, meeting him, noticed it, and had the story from him, in the first unguarded moments of his agitation. "Nothing wonderful about that," said the judge, with but a scant sympathy. "It is out of just such persons as you that Wall Street lives. Better have the experience now, while you are young, than later. It will be money in your pocket, in the end. If you had succeeded, you would have come to the same result later in life, when you could not have stood it as well."

So they could afford to talk to him, they who had not lost, they who knew nothing of his hopes, nothing of the disappointments of his past life. He rushed up to his office to be alone. Ah, yes, he was young. He set to work to eradicate this idle passion of love from his heart. As a philosopher and man of experience, he knew that it could be done. He knew that its growth was a matter of proximity, habit, repetition of charming impressions, and that it could be diminished, and made to disappear, by abstinence from the food on which it had fed. No doubt the requisite period of time could be definitely calculated. He had early acquired a dreary kind of knowledge. He knew that men may survive in a calloused way, the keenest of agitations, till these pass away, and become as a dream; and that happiness is not necessarily put down in the programmes of all of us, desperately though we may strive and agonize for it.

He determined to go a journey. As he was shutting up his office, Mr. Fletcher St. Hill, who had moved nearer to his vicinity of late, accosted him.

"Oh, by the way," said St. Hill, "I dare say you can tell me where to find a person by the name of Gammage; a respectable old gentleman, you know, who formerly did some light work for me. If I knew of his whereabouts I could give him a job of copying."

"He is not in the city. He is up in the country somewhere."

"I should not mind paying his expenses to town, if I could find him," said the inquirer, with an eagerness not wholly suppressed.

"I really cannot help you. I do not know where he is," responded Bainbridge, coldly.

This was, in fact, true. The person with whom Gammage had last lodged, among the farmers of Westchester, had brought Bainbridge an account of the old clerk's doings there, and reported that he had taken a small agency of some kind, and disappeared from view. He had gone back into the remote interior, this informant said, to a considerable remove from the lines of railroad, and not returned.

Some little time after, on his return from his journey, our young attorney saw Gammage advertised for in a "personal," over the office address, and apparently the initials, of Sprowle Onderdonk. As neither St. Hill nor Onderdonk would be likely to want the broken-down teller of the Antarctic Bank for his own merits, Bainbridge could but suspect some purpose to annoy Rodman Harvey by means of him. They were moving, then, in that matter? He was very sorry, not for Harvey's sake, but Ottilie's, though he was trying so hard to forget her. Nothing was to be done, however. He only trusted that Gammage had retired so far as to be permanently beyond their reach.

Bainbridge's journey was into Central Pennsylvania, where he took in person some collections confided to his care. On his way back he fell in with Emily Rawson, on the same train, and they traveled a part of the way together. This led to a renewal of their intimacy. He wanted distraction. As well take such as she could furnish, he said, as any other!

He was not likely, at any rate, to meet Ottilie there. His steps almost drew him perforce, when he set out on his walks, in the direction of poor Ottilie, now again cruelly neglected, but he resisted the impulse.

The sympathy of Emily Rawson, although she could have at present but a dim idea of what she was sympathizing with, was grateful. She had him "smoke to her" again, and play his violin in accompaniment to her piano. How they philosophized now, more than ever, on the elusiveness of happiness, the unsatisfactoriness of life! Why could he not like her? he asked himself. She was made to be liked. She was womanly, accomplished, tender, restful. Her experience gave her an added charm. He could find no fault in her but that, perhaps, of liking him a little too well.

One evening at the piano, without any ostensible cause, she let her head fall upon her hands, and wept. Bainbridge tried to soothe her. He asked, solicitously, "Oh, why? What does it mean?" She replied that it was but a nervous mood, and meant nothing.

Weakened, unstrung, by a purely physical impulse, he had well-nigh offered himself to her, — though not for one moment forgetting Ottilie, — and added this new feature to his complications.

XXI.

BY FAR LESS FAVORABLE TO THE PLATONIC THEORY.

WHEN Bainbridge had not appeared for some time, Ottilie grew vaguely restless.

After the events last narrated she indulged in an unusual amount of day-dreaming about him. How warmly he had bent over her that evening at Mrs. Hastings'! How the charming domesticity of that occasion had appeared to take hold upon him also! What had he been intending to say to her? What had he had in mind to say, too, that other evening after she had read the book for him, and he had stammered over her hand, in thanking her for it? She was almost afraid of the next meeting. The idea of it made her heart throb faster.

Ah, if he *might* care for her! If it might come about, in some improbable way, she knew not how, that they could always remain together! In the gravity of her twenty-one years, she endeavored to lift the veil of the future. Without Bainbridge in the foreground it all wore a very chilly look. She had before her a useful career, duties to many and to herself; she had not the slightest right to count upon him, and there are so many other matters than those of sentiment for a well-regulated person, such as she desired to be, to think of.

Still, a natural bias towards romance, strong within her, was yet unsubdued. She dreamed what young girls, and at some time all good women, dream — of a strong protecting arm to shield her from the hardships of the world; a person to whom she could look up with reverence, and yet whom she knew that on occasion she could twist about the smallest of her fingers. He should be so misguided as to think her an adorable person, even if few others did. He was to go in and out about his affairs every day from a home and fireside which she was to regulate at her own sweet will, like her doll's house in childhood. All this moved in a fluttering way through her fancy. She could conceive of but one figure that fitted into her pictures of domestic happiness.

He did not come, however. She missed him greatly. It could not be that he was engrossed with more important affairs, for she heard of him elsewhere. She knew of his going to Miss Rawson's, from the information of that lady herself, who came to call on her. Miss Rawson spoke of the Hasbrouck girls, and renewed in Ottilie something like a pang of self-reproach, as if it had been treachery on her part that she had not been able to do anything for them.

Then the visitor chattered about Bainbridge. She dwelt upon his charming qualities. "I see him now constantly," she said, watching the effect upon Ottilie, "though he at one time almost gave me up."

She took out programmes of some private theatricals, in which his name was prominently set down. They were to be given at her house. She begged that Ottilie would come.

"Girls love to have the man in whom they invest their vanities admired," says the tranquil Coventry Patmore.

Probably nothing is truer, but it is not in this way,

with these dangerous airs of proprietorship. Ottilie tortured herself with the idea that it might be Emily Rawson who was the cause of her troubles. She cried over it after the visitor had gone, but then resolutely put the feeling down: "I *will not* be so silly," she declared to herself.

Recollecting what had happened before, she wrote to Bainbridge, making some pretext for him to come; but he declined. Still, his reasons for doing so were plausible, and had not the air of being trumped up.

Then, one day, Bainbridge left a formal card at the door without inquiring for her. She was really at home, and he had not tried to find her. It seemed terribly significant. She thought herself definitely abandoned.

Shortly after, they met at one of Mrs. Clef's musicales, to which Ottilie was asked for the first time. Emily Rawson was there and played selections, as on a former occasion. Bainbridge paid her much attention. It was done with a purpose, though, we may confess for him, it almost broke his heart. He was in the midst of his manful effort to put his passion down, and deal with himself on philosophic principles.

He conducted himself towards Ottilie with an elaborate courtesy.

"This New York of ours is such an enormous place," he said, "that it defeats itself. One deprives himself of great pleasure, and is in danger of losing valued acquaintances, through the sheer impossibility of getting about."

"I thought perhaps it might be another — misconception," said Ottilie, bravely, — "something that might need to be explained."

She made this essay from a sense of duty, with a timid little air of uttering a pleasantry. Bearing in mind the needlessness of their former misunderstanding, she did not think it right that this opportunity should be allowed to pass, even if the overture must come from herself.

She saw an agitated expression overspread the countenance of the young man, and felt that he but left her the quicker for the attempted explanation.

Presently Miss Rawson said to her, "Do you know, this is the very place where I first heard of you? Mr. Bainbridge gave me such an entertaining account, the evening of the day he met you at your uncle's store. We sympathized at your peculiar situation."

They had sympathized over her together, then! She had afforded them entertainment! They had had this good understanding, then, long before she was ever heard of! Ah, what a poor, inconsequential person she was!

With bitter pangs of jealousy she persuaded herself that this was the key to the enigma, this the fatal rivalry in which the destruction of her own happiness was involved.

"In Emily Rawson are united," she said, "most of the traits of which he is in search. Her accomplishments, her fortune, her knowledge of the world, her interest in purely mundane things, her sprightliness and intelligence, would all attract him. As likely as not there was something between them before I came. Perhaps I was but a stop-gap, a light distraction during some interval, some lover's quarrel."

She made herself miserable with this notion, though trying all the while to repudiate it. "If he *has* used me as a pastime, oh, it was cruel, it was unworthy," she said, bristling with a certain fierceness, "and I ought to hate him!"

Then she recalled, to do him justice, that he had addressed her no word of love, further than might be contained in his slight pretense of jealousy of Kingbolt. On the contrary, he had advised and enjoined her to marry on the same mercenary basis that he professed himself.

The days passed, and still he did not come. The young girl grew paler and thinner. Her aunt ascribed the deterioration to the languor of the spring, which was now again at hand. Mrs. Rodman Harvey had little time, however, for close observation of persons of minor importance. Her hands were full of the wedding of her daughter, for which the date had been set and the preparations were actively in progress.

Ottilie had fits of weeping. At times the sense of loss gave her intolerable pain. She could not conceive the possibility that any other person could ever fill the place of Bainbridge, or her feeling towards him abate.

She had a wild impulse to write to him and pour out her affection in unmeasured terms. Could women never rise to that? Was there nothing better than cold convention and usage? Perhaps if he only knew how much, how much, she loved him, it might awaken in him — it might palliate the unheard-of effrontery. Was there no sacrifice, no heroic evidence of her affection that she could devise? Only to let him know of its depth and unselfishness, then to retire forever from his sight, — there seemed a certain ideal, and desperate hope of satisfaction even in this.

Must her heart break in silence? She recalled the case of one Clare La Salle, of Lone Tree, whose defiance of public opinion, and infatuation for a lover against the opposition of her parents, had seemed to her at the time most indelicate and shocking. She felt a tenderness for this misguided girl now, and almost counted herself in the same category.

She did not, however, write to Bainbridge that she could not live without him, being aided to resist, no doubt, by the strength of the popular prejudice against such conduct. Nor did she take any other step overpassing the strictest bounds of maidenly propriety. These little dramas are played out in silence, the anguish lived down. They have their few incoherent moments of manifestation in solitude, in fevers, and in dreams. Ottilie wept, and, rising sometimes to look at her flushed face and swollen eyes in the mirror, said : —

"I am a shameless, disgraceful girl."

The invitations to Mrs. Stoneglass' literary receptions had been sent her (on a hint given by Bainbridge to that hospitable lady) and declined. She no longer felt in a mood for this diversion. One evening Mr. Stoneglass called, to offer an invitation in person.

"We have feared," he said, "that you have not cared to come, on account of Sunday evening. We have a number of church-going friends who feel in the same way. Still, it is the most convenient on several accounts, and with our way of thinking we cannot see any harm in it. We are to have, however, the well-known authoress, Mrs. Jane Claxton Shaftsbury, of Boston, on Thursday of this week, and hope that you will come then. You will be sure to see there a few, at least, whom you know, and Mrs. Stoneglass and myself will look after you to the best of our ability."

"I used to read the books of Mrs. Jane Claxton Shaftsbury in childhood," replied Ottilie, "and should consider it an honor to meet her. I shall be very glad to go, I am sure."

It would have been rudeness, she thought, to decline further. At one time she would have hailed such an opportunity with delight.

As the guest went down the steps, she stood a moment, pensively, at the window, leaning her forehead against the sash. It was a warm, damp evening, and the window had been raised, to cool the room, still kept at winter heat by the inexorable self-acting furnace. Ottilie saw a dilapidated figure slouch out from under a lamp-post, and accost Stoneglass, apparently asking alms. Being repulsed, for vagrants of the kind were a common annoyance on the Avenue, it went back into the darkness.

Presently, as she was turning away, there came by another form, the outlines of which made her heart momentarily stand still, then throb the faster. It was Bainbridge. The vagrant again came forth. It could be seen that he had a fine and venerable head. He put his hand on the arm of Bainbridge, and as the young man would have shaken him off in disgust, besought, in a voice, part whistle and part croak, —

"Do something for me, Mr. Bainbridge, for Heaven's sake! The price of a night's lodgin'! You was the only one that kep' me up. You was the one. You " —

"Gammage! Here?" exclaimed the young man, with a start of vivid surprise and concern.

"They av — avertised for me," said the respectable wreck, whimpering. "I had money, — plenty o' money. I don't know where I've been. I must ha' got astray. Do something for me, for Gor A'mighty's sake!"

"What *can* I do for you, Gammage? What can anybody do for you in this condition? Do you know where to go, if I give you the price of a night's lodging?"

"No, I do not, — I do *not*. Come!" cried the man with a desperate air of revolt and loathing at his own lost condition.

"Then what *can* I do with you, except to get you locked up? Say yourself, Gammage! Now, is there anything else possible?"

"Don't do it, Mr. Bainbridge, — don't do that! You was the only one — Your mother was the noblest — Your father used to" —

"Yes, yes, I know; but that was when you had a house of your own to be taken to, and an affectionate family, and a position in the world. But now what are you? — Had they business for you, the persons who advertised?" he inquired under the stimulus of a new thought. "What did they want you to do?" He lowered his voice solicitously, for it was in front of the house of Rodman Harvey himself that they found themselves.

"Mr. Onderdonk and Mr. St. Hill? yes, they wanted me. I signed an affidavit for them. It was an old matter, — a matter that took place many years ago."

"Great heavens! Not that — that bank story involving Rodman Harvey, — the one you told me at my office?" cried Bainbridge, with a gesture of repulsion and dismay.

"I never signed anything but the truth," answered the ex-bank teller, partially sobered, and resenting any attachment of blame to himself.

A hack came by at this moment. Bainbridge summoned the driver, who was waving his whip in the air in an inviting way, and, entering with his *protégé*, drove off.

Ottilie had heard all. She had dwelt dreamily, at first, upon the figure of Bainbridge, acquired this new evidence of his goodness of heart, then awakened with affright to the subject-matter of the discourse.

"It is this, too!" she exclaimed, finding a new and powerful reason to explain the defection of Bainbridge. "Oh, I fear it is this! He knows of something to our detriment, and withdraws in time, before the blow has fallen. He will not connect himself with disgrace and downfall. Oh, if I could but warn my uncle."

But it was hardly a subject on which she could write to her uncle. Nor, when he returned from Washington, did she feel free to speak to him about it. This was his last visit, too, preceding that when he would come to attend his daughter's wedding. Ottilie had found her uncle just and considerate beyond her expectations. If misfortune were in store, it seemed her duty to offer him the solace of her presence and sympathy. If any unlawful act could be laid at his door, she was sure it could only have been done in one of those moments of overwhelming pressure of which he had sometimes spoken, in his comments on the fall of his contemporaries. She would not believe that he could ever have been a corrupt or hardened character.

There was no alleviation for her varied wretchedness. Cold tremors of apprehension mingled with her tears of despondency on her own account, as sudden snow-flakes whirl down amid the rain.

The course of events may now be somewhat rapidly advanced. The Sprowle faction had got upon the track of an old story against Rodman Harvey, and begun to follow it up. It developed in importance as the investigation proceeeded. It was St. Hill who first brought it in. He had heard it in a vague way from some one who adduced the builder Jocelyn as authority. He had thought it worth while to visit Jocelyn; then to hunt up McFadd, in his squalid tenement house in the vicinity of Harvey's Terrace; and then to take steps for finding Gammage, who, he was chagrined to learn, had once been a clerk in his own employ.

St. Hill was quite out with his patron Kingbolt now. There were numerous persons, employees and others, who were speaking about his Company indignantly on account of losses through it. The once brisk Mr. Cutler, who had made such haste to embrace the "desirable opening" offered him, still hung on in a disconsolate way with small hopes of recovering either his arrears of salary or the money of the unfortunate Miss Speller. Through the mediation of Ottilie he had called on Rodman Harvey, and laid the case before him. Affidavits of some sort were drawn up between them, but there was at present no open manifestation. The merchant prince, still in quest of his post as secretary of the treasury, could not yet afford to attack, or even allow to be overthrown, a person who, in his downfall, might retaliate with inconvenient disclosures.

It was Sprowle Onderdonk who took the leadership of the anti-Harvey cabal, and figured, instead of his more timorous cousin, as the champion of the wounded honor of his family. He was a bold and resolute person, endowed with abundant administrative capacity. He scoffed at the story first brought in by St. Hill, who presented it with an air of elation.

"A very timely discovery indeed!" he said. "Why did n't you get something from Herodotus or Pliny the Elder? And a choice Falstaff's brigade of witnesses you have to sustain it! If that is the best you can do, man, you had better turn your attention to some more profitable field of labor."

Still, the idea, for want of a better, was persevered in. Gammage was discovered and his affidavit secured. The advertisement in the newspapers had at last reached him in his seclusion. He ventured to town, was well paid for his trouble, and fell into the condition described.

It was not till a vastly more important accession was gained, however, in the person of Rodman Harvey's once devoted henchman, Hackley, that the case looked really promising. The theory of Bainbridge, that revenge is not a modern luxury, and finds few opportunities for its exercise in this civilized life of ours, bade fair to be overthrown.

Rodman Harvey, at Washington, devoted himself to his new duties with his accustomed energy. His opening speech, on the Currency Question, was highly commended. He took the best appartments at the Arlington Hotel. His dignified attitude much improved his prospects for the succession to the secretaryship of the treasury, the present incumbent of which continued in very uncertain health. He declined somewhat in physical vigor. He was a hard-worked man. There were long night sessions at the Capitol, where the ventilation was bad; and he had more of his attacks of vertigo.

He was harassed also at this time by escapades on the part of his younger son. Rodman, Jr., now entered into possession of the desired latch-key, and a Freshman at Columbia College, was discovered figuring, with some of his mates, by way of a lark, as a "supe" in a spectacular drama at Niblo's Garden. He revolted against the severe discipline with which this act was visited by his father, left the parental roof, and remained absent for several days, being lured home only by promise of forgiveness.

The elder son, Selkirk, also showed disappointing traits. On the eve of succeeding to the principal place in the new partnership, and becoming a figure in the world on his own account, he begged to be released from commercial life altogether. He made the proposal that he should be allowed to occupy his time with his books and bricabrac, or take up one of the arts or sciences, as had been done by young Blankenhorn, in somewhat similar circumstances. Rodman Harvey would of course listen to no such degenerate idea.

It depressed him very much, however, and was a cause of delaying the formation of the new partnership. Since his son, who should have been its principal promoter, took but so languid an interest, a different order of consideration was required, and things were allowed to remain for a while as they were. This was very unfortunate, as it turned out, since it resulted in a disagreement with his warm adherent and eulogist, Hackley, and his final loss and desertion to the enemy.

Hackley was incommoded by the postponements and demurrers. His factory had been burned behind him, and he left " standing in the gap," as he phrased it. This, however, was a comparatively small matter. The main disagreement was about the capital he was to put in. He had lost his factory, and this was a pretext for failure to contribute the amount first agreed upon. He confided, however, in the good offices of Rodman Harvey to establish him in his proper place in the new firm; but this the merchant prince was not willing to do. The faithful and experienced Mr. Minn, he said, was opposed to a distribution of rank not based upon proportionate capital. Nor would he credit Hackley with a part of his own capital to be left in the concern. He said, in a testy mood, that business and sentiment should be rigidly divorced, and the having conferred favors in the past constituted no obligation to go on conferring them indefinitely.

Correspondence on this subject extended over a considerable time, with growing bitterness. Finally, Hackley, in an injudicious huff, not at all expecting to be taken at his word, repudiated the partnership and Rodman Harvey altogether. Being really taken at his word, however, he sulked, complained, and spoke of himself as a very ill-used person. It was now that he fell in with the hostile cabal in the person of Sprowle Onderdonk.

The meeting was brought about through the contrivance of the latter, who at an opportune moment sounded Hackley on the remote transaction with which his name, as well as Rodman Harvey's, was connected. Hackley at first pooh-poohed the notion of doing anything with it.

"Oh, my dear sir, really!" he protested, as if it were wholly absurd. "He is too strong in the community, you know, and the matter is so very old. He is at the President's table continually, and everybody knows that he is the favorite for the successorship to the portfolio of the treasury when the secretary drops off."

"So much the better reason," declared Sprowle Onderdonk, greatly encouraged to find his information not only not dissipated into thin air by Hackley, but confirmed and sustained. "He is going down, I tell you. He is going to be smashed. You had better be with us than against us."

The pair sat on one of the benches along the sides of the marble-paved lobby of the Fifth Avenue Hotel. Sprowle Onderdonk had pushed his hat back upon his head, and talked with an earnest and resolute air. They spoke of General Burlington, formerly president of the Antarctic Bank, who should have even a fuller knowledge of the affair than Hackley.

"It is strange," said Hackley, "that he has never cared to use it, often as he has been opposed to Harvey politically."

"It is intelligible enough," said the other, seeking a plausible explanation. "Probably he did not wish to draw attention to the affair, on his own account. The manager of a financial institution never likes to admit that there has been any irregularity in it under his *régime*. He may have something to clear up himself; not criminality, of course, but perhaps culpable carelessness. I have taken occasion to sound him a little in a discreet way, but have drawn nothing from him."

"He is discretion itself, — Burlington is," commented Mr. Hackley.

"At the same time," said the other, "if he is put on the stand, he will tell what he knows. He is straight and reliable, I think. When the other testimony is all in, he will have to get up and either confirm or deny it; and it does not look as though there were going to be very much denying."

"Oh, there would be no use in going into court with it, and putting anybody in a formal witness box," protested Hackley; "that would hardly do. The matter is too ancient, and must be outlawed and doubly outlawed by this time."

"My idea exactly," said Sprowle Onderdonk. "Of course not. What we want is the moral effect of it. We must play it against him politically. His present situation makes him excellent game. All we want now is a fitting opportunity, and I have one in mind. The disclosure should be *à propos* of something. Harvey will come on from Washington in about a fortnight to attend his daughter's wedding. He has promised to attend at the same time the annual meeting of the Civic Reform Association, which is to be held — probably at this hotel — two days before. He is both treasurer and first director, and has to make his report. I am sure he will come. If he should not, of course we can explode the thing in the newspapers."

"He is a very methodical person. I dare say he will come," said Hackley, with a ruminating air.

"He will hardly be made secretary of the treasury before that, and if he is afterwards I shall be much mistaken. I also am a member of the Civic Reform Association. I shall make a little speech, and give the Harveys a souvenir, by way of a wedding present, that they will be likely to remember."

XXII.

AN EVENING IN LITERARY SOCIETY.

The Stoneglass family lived in a comfortable house of the English basement pattern, at a considerable remove westward from that first meridian of respectability, Fifth Avenue.

Ottilie Harvey presented herself there, on the evening of the reception to Mrs. Jane Claxton Shaftsbury, accompanied by her aunt's maid, who was to return for her in the carriage. The lower floor of the house was devoted to the purpose of dressing-rooms for either sex. The guests deposited their outer clothing in neat bundles along the bank before plunging into the stream of social gayety above.

Stoneglass perceived Ottilie as she was coming up the staircase, went to meet her, and brought her to his wife, who received her affably.

It had been said of Mrs. Jane Claxton Shaftsbury that she was one of the few literary persons who knew how to dress. The remark was that of the poetess, Mrs. Anne Arundel Clum, who by no means possessed the same accomplishment, though she may have prided herself upon it; but this did not prevent its being strictly true. Mrs. Shaftsbury really did dress very well indeed, and was a person, besides, of gracious and amiable manners.

Ottilie, in a rather dazed way, found herself paying this well-known authoress compliments on her writings.

"You must have heard this so often," she said, "but pray have patience just once more! It is such an unusual opportunity for me.—How could you ever consent to make Miriam's Memoirs so short? And oh, why did you not let Ernestine marry Eckford, in 'Hearts and Hands'?"

"Did you really care, child?" said the kindly celebrity. "These are our rewards. It pleases me so much to think I interested you."

It would have been an occasion indeed for Ottilie could she have controlled the mournful feelings by which she was possessed. What material for a letter to her early friends of the Lone Tree High School, who had been accustomed, like herself, to put Mrs. Shaftsbury's books under their pillows at night!

She was escorted about the room by Mr. Stoneglass and others, and heard fragments of a great variety of conversations. The names of the people were very often mentioned to her in full. They had a certain important air, even when you did not recognize them. You seemed always on the point of remembering something notable they had done which had for the moment escaped you.

Within a brief space of time she had met a member of a great publishing house; Colonel Bowsfield, the South American traveler, who had lectured in the Star course at Lone Tree; Ringrose, the poet, whose verses she had pasted into her scrap-books; Professor Brown, whose specialty was the popularization of science; and Professor McMurdock, the Shakespearean reciter, whom she had heard at Chickering Hall.

There were Temple, the historian; Camden, an elderly journalist, known, also, for contributions to the magazines, and a leading social spirit at the Lotos Club ; Flitchbrush, the painter ; a tragic actress, and another prominent in " society " parts. The actress of tragedy reclined languidly in an easy-chair, and in the course of the evening recited a selection from Mrs. Browning. The society actress shifted from one to another of various carefully studied poses, that the lines of her slender figure and excellent profile might be seen to advantage.

There was Jane Scrim who wrote a good deal of matter of small importance with a spiteful tang, and had a termagant air corresponding with her literary style. She was continually flying about from one profession to another, representing each as an extraordinary new departure, and calling upon gods and men to take notice. Mrs. Sevenleague had crossed alone the dangerous wilds of Bungaleeboo. Count Altamont, whose title was somehow shady, though genuine, posed for traveller, poet, and amateur in all the fine arts, and was popular with the female sex. He had brought with him a *protégé* in the shape of an Indian boy, in full feathers and deer-skin, whom he had procured in the wilds of the West. He represented that he proposed to take charge of his musical education.

Mrs. Anne Arundel Clum shook hands with Ottilie. Dr. Wyburd also came forward, and greeted her demonstratively.

" Yes," he said, " you find me here. I should have been good at this sort of thing if I had been allowed to follow it. As it is, I only woo the muse a little, in a fragmentary way, in such poor intervals as I can snatch from my engrossing occupations. I come here but seldom, yet not for want of inclination and desire.

The genial companionship of people of letters is tonic and reviving. The mind is apt to rust out in our purely fashionable life. It is here, in fact, that I feel myself most at home."

There were present other journalists besides Camden, as a young Mr. Skate, lately attached to that able review the " Slate," the editors in chief of the " Musical Tablet," the " Art Vignette," — recently started in opposition to the " Art Kaleidoscope," — and the " Hebrew Exodus." The assembly had a very cosmopolitan air.

Mr. Skate, on being presented to Ottilie, said that he rarely came to these places, but his reason was of a different sort from Dr. Wyburd's. It was contempt instead of lack of leisure. He said it was refreshing to find some one to whom he could express a few frank opinions, — some one out of the regular gang. He went on to give the policy in criticism which he endeavored to carry out in the " Slate."

" I have too short principles," he said. " Nothing good can be produced in America. Our civilization is too new and raw. It may appear to be good, but that is an error. On the other hand, nothing very bad can be produced in Europe, which is saved by its centuries of culture, its storied monuments, its naturally profounder way of looking at things. Having thus simplified matters, one merely points out the degrees of badness and goodness, and concentrates upon a new way of saying things. I would hardly wish this to go outside as coming from me, but I have devoted much thought to the position, and am satisfied of its correctness."

The Indian boy, most notable of the curiosities, assured Ottilie, in a sulky way, that he wore no such clothes at home, and had no musical taste whatever to be cultivated. His Reservation was a civilized place, with farms and schools, and the people appeared in European dress. This theatrical outfit had been made to order for him at a costumer's in the Bowery, and Count Altamont was toting him about to add to his own importance.

Ottilie wondered that the poet Ringrose should appear so young. He was just beginning to show the first approaches of middle age. She had somehow thought of him as older. He was a nervous, quick-speaking person; not gloomy, but with a trace as of a permanent trouble on his countenance. He brightened at a compliment she paid him in quoting some lines of his which had impressed her in a peculiar way, and treated her very affably. Perhaps they got none too much praise, after all, these sensitive organizations. Ringrose had letters in his pockets from brother celebrities. He showed Ottilie some of these.

"He conducts a correspondence with all the learned of his time," said Mr. Stoneglass, coming up. "It is like the age of Erasmus. They condole with each other after their peculiar freemasonry, and no doubt despise the profane vulgar as it deserves."

Ringrose received this sally with a deprecating smile.

"I have just had a letter from Canto," he said. "He incloses me a poem and wishes me to tell him exactly what I think of it. I think it the best bad poem I ever saw. It has his usual knack, his deftness; but when you come to look for ideas there is nothing in it. Form alone may do in the picture, but not in poetry. For my part, I confess that I like subject in my picture also, though it is not the thing to say in these Impressionist days. We had the whole discussion over last night at Flitchbrush's studio. They call 'story' in a picture 'literary,'— that is the disparaging epithet they apply to it; but if they can find nothing worse to say, I remain quite unmoved."

"An interesting place, that of Flitchbrush," suggested Mr. Stoneglass.

"Yes," said Ringrose. "You should go around to one of his evenings," to Ottilie; "that is to say, if you are at all of Bohemian tastes,— as I fear you are not. His studio is a remarkable place, decorated with rugs and miscellaneous traps, and full of portfolios of things to look over. People drop in informally of Wednesday evenings, and tea is passed about. Mrs. Flitchbrush sews at a bright costume for a lay figure, as a good mother of a family might mend the apparel of her children."

Flitchbrush joined them. "I was speaking of our discussion of last night," said Ringrose.

Upon this, as is so apt to be the case, the same discussion again arose.

"A picture should be decorative before everything," said Flitchbrush. "If it can get a subject that lends itself to this purpose, so much the better; but decorative it must be, at all hazards."

"Art has a higher mission," asserted Ringrose.

"It has its own mission," rejoined Flitchbrush, "and nothing else."

In an adjacent group it was being disputed whether newspaper criticism should be signed or not.

"It *should* be signed," declared the historian, Temple.

"It should *not* be signed," declared the journalist, Camden.

"I say it should," said Temple again. He was a small man, with an almost boyish briskness of speech and manner, though near the age of fifty. He was not a very great historian, but he had some excellent ideas.

"It is an insufferable outrage that some work of mine, over which I have spent months, perhaps years, should be at the mercy of some anonymous penny-a-liner, who has nothing to lose by printing the first rubbish that comes into his head. He may even be a competent person, and only tired, cross, or hurried; or he may be incapable of forming an opinion entitled to respect. All the same, in it goes, and a bias is created which is not recovered from, perhaps in a generation. Suppose it to be a new play. The critic hurries away from it, somewhat before midnight. He wants to go to bed, and discriminating writing is by no means easy at best. Why should he earn his salary in a difficult way when an easy way will do? He damns or praises at his own sweet will. His only rule is to be quick about it. — No, let the opinions be signed. If they amount to anything, they will stand on their merits; if not, they will be taken from whence they came, like the kick from the traditional mule."

"A newspaper man's life would not be worth having, under those conditions," protested Mr. Camden. "He could not show himself, for scowling looks, when generally he had done no more than his duty."

"I sign everything *I* write," said the belligerent Miss Scrim. "I put my town, county, and street address to it. They always know where to find *me*, if they want me."

"It would create a school of criticism, and give it a place in literature," continued Temple. "Look at the school of critical writers which has arisen in France under this system."

Mr. Stoneglass talked to Ottilie of the fine qualities, as a man and a citizen, of her uncle. He hoped to see him soon in the treasury department.

Colonel Bowsfield made mention to her of experiences in the service of the Khedive of Egypt. Mrs. Sevenleague, who had lately returned from a career in London society, gave her an account of Browning, Swinburne, and a new American writer who had lately gone there, and was making a stir.

"*Is* he as bright as the conversations in his books?" asked Ottilie.

"We met him only once, at Lady Ludgate Hill's," said her informant. "He talked exclusively about the weather."

She said of a leading English novelist of the younger school, "We saw a great deal of him when in lodgings in London. He was quite devoted to a young lady of our party. At one time it looked very much like an engagement."

Ottilie could hardly believe that this was real; that it was indeed she who was hearing at first hand of the very greatest personages, figures to which her imagination had always gone out with reverence, and this from others of a kindred sort. But she was accepting it forlornly, and forcing an interest, instead of kindling with enthusiasm. A little while ago it would have been impossible for anything to be more to her liking, but now the virtue had somehow gone out of it.

"These wretched little human affections of ours,

how engrossing they are!" she sighed. "Of what possible consequence is this feeling of mine, yet it rises up and eclipses the universe."

The one person in all the world with whom she could best have enjoyed the new experience, the one who would have caught its quaint humors, its contrasts, its fresh and typical aspects, was ruthlessly torn from her. A sense of this grew so keen as to be at moments almost intolerable. It seemed as if the hour of departure would never come. She looked often to see if Rosine were not in waiting with her cloak in the hall below.

Temple, planting himself squarely before her, said, "What do you do? I think I have read your poems. It is always fair to ask that question at Mrs. Stoneglass'. Everybody here is supposed to have done something of note."

Ottilie felt her fraudulent position, in trying to pass on equal terms in a circle of such distinction, at length justly exposed.

"I — I only appreciate," she stammered.

But the apparent severity of the brisk little historian proved to be only his manner, and not offense. Finding that he had an excellent listener, he talked to her a long time exclusively about himself. Presently he accosted the member of the great publishing house on the subject of a proposed new volume. This led to a wrangle, half-humorous at first, on the disproportion between the profits of publisher and author.

"You grind the faces of the poor," said Temple. "You seize the lion's share, and put off the author, the real producer, without whom you could not exist, with a beggarly pittance."

"I can demonstrate to you," said the publisher, "that the ten per cent. received by the author really comprises the larger share of profits." And he began in an elaborate way to so demonstrate.

"That is all very well, all very well; but meanwhile the author starves in his garret, and you roll hither in your carriage."

"I would have you to know, sir, that I came hither in a horse-car."

"And I on foot," said the brisk historian, with a triumphant air in having the last word.

From time to time the hostess, Mrs. Stoneglass, implored silence, by proxy of some polite masculine volunteer, and introduced a performer.

A very dark young woman at Ottilie's side favored her with particulars of her early education, taste in books, and the like. She seemed rather young to have attained distinction on her own account, and Ottilie set her down as only allied to it by family ties.

"From my earliest years," she said, "my family took pains to gather about me only the most intellectual and refined. I have never known what it is to associate with anybody not intellectual. My taste in literature has been formed in the same way. I care for no characters in books who would not be suitable companions for me in real life. My father was a man of the greatest talent. You must have heard of him, — Chester A. Skadge. He wrote poems, plays, essays, everything. But he esteemed more than all his old family name."

"Oh, I am sure he must have been quite right," said her auditor sweetly, which caused the young woman of exceptional advantages to dart at her a look of suspicion.

A small, gentle-speaking lady on the other side — who did not prove quite as gentle as she seemed — confided to her, next, an opinion of the American fiction of the day.

"It is very little, very pretty, very very dainty," she said, joining a thumb and finger to aid in expressing the idea. "But when you look for breadth, for scope, fire, magnificence of conception, what a disappointment! Why do they give us no great, noble, typical women? And what do they do, their insignificant characters? Nothing in the world but sit around and talk. Not an incident, not a circumstance, of an extraordinary sort!"

"Is it not pleasant to see life as it is, — I mean the best part of it, — to have the writers try to find the poetry and romance around us?" ventured Ottilie. "I am sure it is as genuine as if it existed in a remote age, or under some very exceptional circumstances. And I sometimes think that there is nothing so charming, either in books or out of them, as just the right kind of conversations."

But she stopped in trepidation. Had she actually the temerity to contradict such people as this?

Some of the performers brought forward by Mrs. Stoneglass were musical. Among others appeared Wilhelmina Klauser, daughter of the confidential agent through whose stratagem Ottilie had been first introduced to her uncle's notice. The German girl had developed, it seemed, a talent quite out of the common, which caused her to be in much demand. Her blonde hair was bound up in fillets, like that of a classic nymph. She was retiring by nature, but her music inspired her. Seated at the piano, she dashed off her selection with an almost masculine vigor.

The most, however, were of the histrionic order. Recitations seemed an entertainment much in vogue. The distinguished tragic actress kindly gave something, as has been said. Professor McMurdock, the Shakespearean expositor, followed. Count Altamont placed himself crosswise on a chair for a steed and pretended to be a cavalier engaged in some remarkable exploit. The poem in which this was set forth was his own.

When he had finished Mrs. Stoneglass gave a little ecstatic cry: — " How lovely! How perfect! " and clapped her hands.

She liked to encourage her performers, and keep them in an obliging vein. She congratulated the Count on his poem also, saying, —

" Authors, we know, like pretty women, must be flattered."

" But when one is both author *and* pretty woman, then what is to be done?" returned the Count, with a languishing glance. It was perhaps such speeches as these that gave him some of his popularity with the fair sex.

In a corner apart stood a little group of rising poets, who, with talent and ardor, were not without some of the eccentricities of youth and their calling. It was whispered to the hostess that Mr. Edson Judson, of this group, had a poem in his pocket, which he had delivered with great acceptance to the circle at a dinner at a restaurant, just before their coming hither.

Mrs. Stoneglass insisted that Mr. Judson should repeat the performance, and he allowed himself to be persuaded. He announced in a few dignified words of preamble that science was his chosen inspiration. He made no secret of his belief that modern science afforded a deeper and truer inspiration than any the effete past could boast of. His poem was an ode to Vortex Atoms. It had a sufficiently learned air, but was not so wholly lucid as poems very often are.

A Mr. Okenberg, described as a writer of short stories in the magazines, was introduced to Ottilie. He had a lively, rather caustic way of talking. He appeared to enter into her situation, and undertook explanations of curious phases of the things about her.

"That is James Edson Judson," he said of the young poet who had just finished. "He is a broker. He has been dubbed, by some friendly hand, a 'poet of the future,' and delights in the title. His best things, however, are not done in pursuance of his theory."

Mr. Edson Judson retired to his circle, and was received by them with beaming countenances. He had taken occasion, before retiring, to mention to Mrs. Stoneglass that the poem of Mr. George Gladwin Ludlow, delivered at the same dinner, was, in its way, even better than his own. Mr. George Gladwin Ludlow was, upon this, invited forward in his turn. His effusion was of a gloomy, suicidal cast.

"If the other two members of the group are asked to recite," Mr. Okenberg went on, " Wixon will give comic squibs; the other — but no, Hurlpool will never be allowed to recite. These last are connected with the press, in one way or another, and pursue the journey to Parnassus in the intervals of more active occupation. They rarely come here. I don't know what brings them to-night. As a rule they take their pleasure in a less trammeled, more Bohemian fashion. Each has his specialty. Just as that of Judson is science, of Ludlow, suicide, of Wixon, comic squibs, the grand specialty of Hurlpool is to fly in the face of all the received proprieties. He is a literary Ajax defying the lightning. He seems determined to be original, at any price. He is great on orientalisms, and on renditions of Scripture in an easy fashion of his own. His verbiage blazes with light and color. He says that the bane of American letters is the preposterous deference shown the 'young person.' He would have all departments of life thrown open as material for literature. He would have literature made for adults, and not for babes in arms, and sighs that he was not born a Frenchman. Perhaps he is not as bad as he seems. He has an excellent warm heart for his friends, and looks at himself with a kind of innocence. In the clique his effusions are received without especial objection. The theory most in vogue among them is that of art for art's sake. One subject is looked upon as about as good as another. The members have their little eccentricities of appearance, as you see, — the literary Ajax a smile of calculated brightness; the poet of the future, the raven locks and slouch hat of a murderer in a melodrama; the suicidal poet, the blonde beard and spectacles of a socialist philosopher of Montmartre. The humorist alone is dapper and clean-cut. It is a saving grace, after all, humor; it keeps us out of a multitude of scrapes."

A long-haired, elderly man, much more eccentric in aspect than any of the clique described, now approached.

"Here comes Chalker," said Okenberg. "He

says 'the genius is half d—d fool,' and counts himself a genius. He is running at his own expense a weekly called the "Scroll." He maintains that it is needed to keep in order, and eventually supplant, the "Slate." He is extremely sanguine about it. It is crammed with vagaries. If the "Slate" has its vagaries, also, they are at least based upon a keen, worldly wisdom. He is engaged upon a great work of hypothetical analysis. He tells me that he will show what sort of a novelist or playwright Napoleon would have made; how Turner would have led armies, and Beethoven managed a paint-pot.

"I think I have a couple of new subscribers for you, Chalker," he said to the object of this description.

"Don't bring me subscribers, my dear young friend," returned Mr. Chalker. "But if you have a couple of new ideas, bring *them* in. That is what we want."

The recitations were resumed. The professional elocutionists of the masculine sex were distinguished by clean-shaven faces, to secure the greatest play of expression. One of them imitated musical instruments, the sounds of animals, leading actors, and personages in public life.

It appeared that the young lady who had described to Ottilie her fastidious bringing up by the late Chester A. Skadge, also possessed this talent. She went forward to the middle of the room, stood a few moments with a portentous fixity, and suddenly burst out with, —

"Oh-o-o! young Lochin*var*-ar is come out of the west."

Her eyes were opened to their widest and fiercest

tension at first, and this was followed by a capacious smile. Her words were accompanied by gesticulation after the Delsarte system.

The selection seemed almost a herald's flourish of trumpets to usher in an important new arrival.

Lanes, or rifts, occasionally opened through the crowd. All at once, down such a lane, Ottilie discovered Bainbridge. He had apparently just come up the stairs, and was shaking hands with the hostess. The lane closed again, and he had not discovered Ottilie. She turned pale, and leaned for a moment against the wall.

She had opportunity to recover, however, before he came up. Mr. Okenberg was once more talking to her, and Camden the journalist, and Ringrose the poet, and others were close by. Bainbridge had a preoccupied air as if looking for somebody.

"Ah," he said, touching Camden's arm, "have I found you? I have been at your lodgings. They said that you would probably be here."

He did not observe at once the presence in which he stood. He awoke to it with a start. He endeavored to cloak this against suspicion, by an extra assumption of indifference. He finished in a word or two the business he had with Camden, and then spoke with Ottilie. The rest gave him the preference for a moment, still maintaining their places. He politely inquired for her impressions. There were topics enough for conversation in the novel scene. Ottilie schooled herself to reply impassively. Nothing is more chilling to expansions of ill-regulated affection than dread of the disdain of its object. In the presence of Bainbridge she was phenomenally calm. But she kept her glance averted.

"They are not at all too friendly in speaking of one another," she said. "Several of them have abused Mrs. Shaftsbury to me, and then in turn each other."

"The axiom might be laid down that people who are equal to disliking the same thing, are not necessarily equal to liking each other," said Bainbridge.

They spoke of some of the more pronounced individualities. "They have ideals of their own in personal appearance, you see," said Bainbridge, hardly knowing how his words ran. "They desire to establish a correspondence between their looks and exceptional positions. They take their profession with a profound seriousness, — wish us to think they make a sort of priesthood of it."

"It is a rank charlatanism," said Okenberg. "If I were a poet, I should model myself on a butcher-boy in appearance. The technical poet, the technical thinker, the technical anything, is my aversion. Poetry is the singing voice of the soul as opposed to its common speech. Most of us have our little touch of it somewhere. Whether a man have more or less of it in him is not a reason why he should make a guy of himself. Poetry, thought of any kind, is not conjured out from under a particular kind of hat, as if it were a trick in legerdemain. I tell you there are reputations that consist entirely of an uncouth name, a cloak, and a slouch hat, and nothing else."

"Charlatanism or not, it is probably what the public prefer," said Bainbridge. "We do not want our ideas furnished to us by exactly the same order of beings as ourselves. Given a sufficient difference in appearance, and way of doing things, and we shall half delude ourselves into the belief that we are dealing with a race of a foreign and mysterious sort."

"I saw you talking with Mrs. Plumfield," said Ringrose to Ottilie, — "the gentle-looking little lady, of positive opinions, who has just turned this way. She gave you her opinion of American fiction, I dare say?"

"Yes," assented Ottilie, in surprise.

"She asks why there are no great, noble, typical women in it," interrupted Okenberg. "I am sure I can't tell her, considering how very common they are in real life. You ladies, though, are great extremists. You want in a novel either one of two things. There must be a heroine of portentous seriousness, who performs none but the most magnanimous deeds, or else she must be continually climbing fences, with unkempt hair and face stained with blackberries, when the discriminating young man turns up who is to be the arbiter of her destinies. Now that I have ascertained what you need, however, I propose to conform to it and turn it to pecuniary account. I conceive a happy compromise. My next heroine shall be a Joan of Arc who is first discovered sliding down the banisters.

"I detest compromises," said Miss Jane Scrim, catching the word.

Mr. Okenberg looked as if he moderately detested Jane Scrim.

"Then I hope you will take more kindly to my second great original idea. It is a plan to ameliorate the condition of elderly spinsters, a hardly used race, both in fiction and out of it. I consider it worth oceans of platform agitation."

"Yes?" fiercely.

"Let us combine to slowly but surely advance the ages of our heroines. My last heroine was nineteen.

My next shall be twenty-two, the next twenty-seven, the next thirty, and so on. The charming time of maidenhood, the ideal period for first love and matrimonial sentiment may thus be made to extend, say to fifty."

Ottilie did not quite like this. "Mrs. Plumfield thought our fiction deficient in incident," she said, by way of diversion.

"Nobody will ever make that complaint about her story," said Okenberg. "She has written a novel, — perhaps you may not know it. She hawked it around to all the publishers, and then printed it at her own expense. Not that that is anything against it, for about the last man in the world to know a good thing when he sees it is a publisher. It is crammed with murders, abductions, and explosions of nitroglycerine. The hero has 'a throat like a marble column,' and lives in a bandbox, and his sweet name is Cyril Gurle."

"The 'incident' school has gone out," pursued Okenberg. "We have come to understand, with Schopenhauer, that 'the rank of a novel is according as it depicts more the inner and less the outer life.' Mental and moral incidents, in their effect upon character, are objects of interest vastly more worthy of contemplation than runaway horses and exploding locomotives."

"And are the other kind to be ruled out altogether?" asked Ottilie.

"Nothing is to be ruled out; but writers will naturally be graded according as they cater to a childish taste for marvels or to something more enlightened. There is a *rank* of physical incidents, too. There are plenty of happenings which are strange, poetic, stimulating to the imagination, and worthy of interest in themselves, just as are lovely people, places, and aspects of nature. The other day two ocean steamers passed each other in such a fog that neither could be seen from the other, yet so near that voices could be heard from one to the other. I call that a good incident. Put the heroine on board one, the hero on the other; see? He hears her voice as if out of the air. It is some critical turn in their affairs; see? That would be as good as an equal space of any but the very best of my own, or Blank's conversations. No, on the whole, nothing, or almost nothing, should be ruled out. 'Hitch your wagon to a star!' Hitch it to the great passions, the forces of nature, the feelings of weirdness and mystery that stir dimly in every human breast. The work must be done with the broad Homeric touches, too, as well as the fine ones, if it expects to live. It must not be too civilized, too sophisticated. Over-sophistication may possibly be the next vice of our literature."

"The bane of our literature is the caprice of magazine editors," insisted Bowsfield, the traveler. "Does anybody suppose for one moment that I would send in an article unworthy of my reputation? Let the writer be true to himself. Look at Wordsworth. Immediate recognition is no test of merit. Wordsworth was the best judge of Wordsworth; you, Okenberg, are the best judge of Okenberg; and I, Bowsfield, of myself."

He tapped himself proudly on the breast.

"One bane of American letters, as of American art," said Okenberg, "is the abject reverence for everything European. We are not seeing enough with our own eyes. A curious thing, because we have been accustomed in so many books and pictures to scenes laid abroad, we have fallen into the way of thinking that the only proper place for them. We do not reflect that the foreign writers and picture-makers have used the people and places about them. Supposing they too thought it necessary to go abroad, whither would they repair? The London of Dickens, the Paris of Victor Hugo, are their own familiar stamping-grounds. The best literature and art have always been home-inspired."

Thus the talk went on. Ottilie had but small part to take in it, but with what an intelligence she answered! Perhaps the others saw in her a trace of sadness, and tried to divert her from it. Bainbridge had conquered his flushings and paleness. His eyes wandered yearningly over her face. He thought he had never known her so thin before. Could it be that she also had suffered? To what advantage she appeared in every company! He had been well along on the road towards freedom, as he deemed. He relapsed into his slavery with a headlong impetus. He must have speech with her. He began to devour her with his eyes. He would have liked to seize her in his arms, in the midst of them all, and bear her away from their senseless babble, as is said to be the custom, as part of the matrimonial preliminaries, among some barbarous tribes.

"You must not judge us too hastily, you know," said Okenberg, choosing to represent Ottilie as an investigating person, whose mission it was to severely formulate literary society. "Perhaps you have n't seen the best of us. You must come again and often. A new-comer is apt to see the odd features too much. Our entertainers are the nicest people in the world, but all sorts of persons turn up here. One sometimes has to think that the literary faculty, instead of strength, is a form of weakness. If we really understood life, we should command it, reap its principal rewards, comfortably live it, instead of passing our time vaguely speculating about it. You see the preposterous egotism and conceit of some of us. There are persons here who would talk you to death about their own superlative genius and never turn a hair. There are people with every apparent advantage in the world, who know no more of Chesterfield than if they had been brought up in the heart of Africa, — and some of them call themselves thinkers, the more's the pity."

"I think I would draw it milder," suggested Mr. Camden. "It will not do to unfold all the dark secrets of our prison-house at once. You will frighten our visitor away, and that would be a great calamity," he added, with a gallant bow.

"I am not the ill-natured critic you affect to think," Ottilie disclaimed. "It all pleases me very much. I am only too flattered to be allowed to be here."

"Well, there *are ideas*," said Okenberg, taking the back track, "plenty of them, bubbling and seething. It is better than stagnation, after all. The people have something more in them than what mere money will buy. I don't know but I have patience with most of them, except Bolster. Bolster is literary, as the Irishman played the violin, 'by main strength.' He has money, and publishes a volume every year at his own expense. He has never known what it is to have a single unaffected human impulse or turn of expression. In manner and matter alike he sets your teeth on edge. And yet he passes, in a way, for a literary man. Publishers ought to be held to pains and penalties for such things."

Bainbridge drifted away from the group, proposing to seek a favorable opportunity to return to it and secure Ottilie to himself. It dissolved presently, in the shifting way in which things pass in such assemblies. Ottilie exchanged some words with Wilhelmina Klauser, who told her the later news from Harvey's Terrace.

"Miss Finley is worse," said Wilhelmina. "She goes about crying and saying that she is losing her mind. Mrs. Cutler, her former friend, pretends to be indignant that anybody could suppose her husband to have done wrong. Perhaps it really was not so much his fault. He may have been taken in. I have heard that he has been to see prominent persons to find out if there is not some way of getting redress."

"He has seen my uncle," said Ottilie. "I think that something will be done."

The knot of minor poets were now discussing with heat the problem whether the genius is in advance of his time, or only its very mouth-piece and essential expression. There was no uncertain implication that this was a question in which they all had a personal interest. This was mingled with talk upon the characters of editors, rates of payment, and the rise and fall of journals.

A group of young playwrights considered the decline, or rather failure to arise, of the American drama. It was laid to the incompetency, and fiendish hostility to native merit, of the managers. A member whose sole claim to authority was founded on a poor dramatization of a French novel, which had run two nights in the country, described his method of work.

"I have a miniature theatre of pasteboard," he said, "on which I arrange everything in advance. I fix even my exits and entrances. When I have once established a certain exit or entrance, no manager under heaven shall change it."

"He has read me some of his things," remarked Camden to a neighbor. "I recollect one in particular, a comedy, at which he laughed till the tears ran down his cheeks, and positively there was not a touch in it to provoke the faintest smile."

Ottilie stood near the piano. The case of pathetic hardship she had heard from Wilhelmina had increased her own sadness, and at the same time appeared to make it selfish.

"I make my own griefs," she sighed; "those of others are made for them."

Bainbridge came up to her again. At length they were alone.

"How well Mr. Okenberg talks!" she said, by way of breaking an impending awkwardness.

"He is somewhat of the order of that potentate who 'never said a foolish thing and never did a wise one.' He does not always carry his good ideas into practice. Still, he has time before him," responded Bainbridge.

He fidgeted, looked to the right and left, then suddenly, in a changed, almost husky tone, "I wish you would come and sit down with me for a while. There is something I want to say to you. I can find places."

"I do not think I ought to," Ottilie murmured;

but opposition died on her lips, and she followed him.

He led the way through the crowd and found some chairs in a corner. The people standing and moving in front of them insured a sort of privacy to their interview.

"I did not know that you were here," began Bainbridge. "I had not the slightest idea of it. I thought you would have accepted an invitation earlier in the season. It is only by the merest accident that I am here myself. I had to find Mr. Camden, in connection with a piece of work I am doing for his paper, and I was directed to this place. — It is going to make the greatest difference to me that I have come. I have something I must say to you."

"If it be to account for your extraordinary keeping away from me, of late," faintly, "perhaps it is quite in order."

"I did not expect to see you," repeating himself in his agitation. "I had made up my mind not to see you." Ah, he had made up his mind not to see her? "Do you know why I stayed away?"

"No," answered Ottilie. "I thought perhaps — It was said — The report went around — that you were engaged to Miss Emily Rawson."

"What nonsense!" he cried indignantly, half starting up. And yet, perhaps indignation was not greatly called for. His own conduct had given excellent color to such a report. He was somewhat cooler upon this, and acted with greater self-possession.

"Well," he said, "I have been trying the severest experiment of my life. I have been trying to see what sort of a martyr I should make. But I am not of the stuff for martyrdom. I recant, I retract my errors, or am perhaps ready for worse ones. The rack and thumb-screw frighten me. Had it ever occurred to you that I might be in love with you?"

"No," said Ottilie with a violent start, opening her fan to aid in concealing her emotion.

"You had not thought that all that pretty intercourse, that charming friendship of ours, was, on my side, love, — that it was bound to result in it? You made me so unspeakably fond of you that" —

"How? I made you so fond of me!" These were the dearest words she had ever heard in her life, and they gave her a feeling almost of faintness, but she answered as if refuting some kind of aspersion.

"Simply by being what you are," — he went on, — "the loveliest character, the most beautiful and adorable being, in the world. Simply by giving me your companionship, by letting me be with you."

And all this had to go on with bated breath, and no other demonstrations than such as would have been proper to conversation on the most ordinary topics. Bainbridge bore with difficulty the enforced restraint. He would have liked to sink literary and all other society, for the time being, to the bottom of the sea.

"I am not at all adorable," returned Ottilie, "if you only knew me. Nor am I beautiful; I have never been told so. My mirror informs me too truly on that point. And there are excellent reasons why I ought not to let you talk to me in this way. I must not listen to you."

"I knew that I should never be able to see you again without telling you all. Now you have heard it. To pass your house, even to walk in the direction of it, to call you to mind, has given me thrills and pains of the heart. I must show what I have been through. I am completely unstrung. I am good for nothing."

"Then why did you keep away?"

"Because I was magnanimous. Now that I have relapsed into my selfishness, I have come back. I tried to sacrifice you to your own best good. I have never made a secret of my worldly circumstances. At the last period of our intimacy they had become notably worse than ever, and so I took myself off. I wanted to do nothing to interfere with your prospects, the brilliant match you might well enough make. You recollect how we talked of these subjects in the summer. When I thought Kingbolt was making up to you, I tried in the same way to give him a clear field, though I was tortured with a jealousy I cannot describe."

"And you were really jealous of Kingbolt?"

The insensate, delightful idea! The blood again coursed warmly through all her chilled members.

"Madly. And since then I have been jealous of all the world. The advice I gave, the principles we laid down, are as good as ever; but oh, I love you so dearly that I have not been able to prevent myself from coming to you with a foolish proposition. I have come to ask you to be mine, in spite of all that we have said; to try and conceive an existence from the romantic point of view, without all of those things that we may once have thought so necessary. It is better that I should have made you this offer, at any rate. Now you have but to refuse me. I shall have the comfort, at least, of knowing that I have done all I could."

"There is just one ray of light," he went on, before Ottilie, gasping for breath, could begin her answer. He spoke now with a nervous haste, as if to postpone as long as possible the adverse decision, though the instant before he had professed himself resigned to it. "A letter has reached me to-day, which may prove of significance. It informs me that my absconding debtor and quondam friend, of whom I once told you, has turned up in Denver, with the appearance of a prosperous person. He is thought to have met with success in mining. In that case I shall be able to recover what is due me. I am going to take a journey thither; who knows what may come of it? And besides," he continued, as if not willing to have the decision rest wholly upon so problematic a resource, and with a boastful air new to him, "I shall presently get a large practice. I must. Fortune cannot always run in the same groove; and when it turns it can turn in but one way."

It touched Ottilie deeply to see him almost humiliate himself before her, like this. But she was revolving certain ideas.

"No," she said; "this is a sudden impulse. It is against the sober judgment you had formed. Let us renew our former friendship. That will do, will it not?"

"It is too late for friendship. It never was friendship. I have analyzed it thoroughly."

"You exaggerate what you are pleased to call my brilliant prospects; and you greatly disparage yourself," returned Ottilie. "You are good enough for anybody. You must not think that it is reasons of a mercenary kind by which I am influenced. I esteem it a very great honor you do me, — I say it most truly, — but I am obliged to decline. I cannot marry you."

"Oh, do not say that! Oh, why?" he pleaded in a wretched way. "Then you have never cared for me?"

"On the contrary, I have cared for you, and I do like you, very, *very* much. There, I am glad to have told you that, though it must not alter my decision."

For the first time the people in the vicinity may have had some slight suspicion that these two were not talking exclusively about the weather.

"Drop your hand by your side a moment! Let me take it in token of gratitude for even so much," Bainbridge asked. "They will not see. Just an instant!"

"They *will* see. I am very foolish," she said, consenting. "There! *there!*" and she drew the hand away again from his ardent pressure with some difficulty.

She continued firm, nevertheless, in her refusal. She had her secret ideals of duty and self-sacrifice, and they were perhaps higher than his. She recalled perfectly well what his theory of a comfortable existence had been. She had no right to take advantage of an injudicious enthusiasm to hamper him, and possibly prevent its realization forever.

Bainbridge asked for whys and wherefores, putting himself forward for a person excellently adapted to the comprehension of reasons. She incautiously relented so far as to furnish him with some. He demolished these with a fierce energy, and Ottilie was driven into her intrenchments. Unless the garrison had resources not yet drawn upon, it seemed in imminent danger of having to haul down its colors.

The hostess came bustling along at this moment, and begged to present a new acquaintance. Usage demanded that Bainbridge should yield his place. He did so, with an ill grace, but kept near, trusting to Ottilie to recall him.

Fragments of discourse from adjoining circles were heard. Mr. Okenberg was saying, "I shall put such a character through about ten thousand words." Or, "Such an idea is worth about six thousand words."

"I should have been very good at story-writing, do you know," said Dr. Wyburd, with much complacency. "I should have drawn a great deal upon real life. I have had the fortune to fall in with such a variety of experiences."

He began to give specimens by way of establishing the character of his material. "You alter, of course, and magnify any given incident to suit your purpose?" he said.

"Yes," assented Okenberg. "We could not get along without that."

"Well, there was my patient, Colonel Kingbolt, for instance, killed by the wind of a shot, as you might say. Nothing ever actually hurt him. He was notified of a forgery in a New York bank. The bank telegraphed him, 'Have you issued such and such acceptances, now in our hands?'—date and amount given, but no name. He telegraphed a negative, and demanded details, but these were refused. Renewed applications met with no better success. He got it into his head that there was some infamous plot against his credit, and allowed himself to be worried to death. It was rather curious they should have refused the particulars to a person of the colonel's importance. This might be represented as one of those cases, such as you read about, where the facts were suppressed in the interest of influential parties."

"Yes, that could be worked up. Most anything can be worked up, you know," said Okenberg. "You could have the son of the deceased, say, come to New York, and into relations with the persons who committed the crime. One of them might be, say, his prospective father-in-law. The whole matter might be exploded on the wedding-day. Nothing lends itself to sensational possibilities better than a wedding-day."

"But, unfortunately, you cannot construct your little romance so in this case," broke in Stoneglass; "that is to say, if it is going to be founded on real life. Old Colonel Kingbolt's son is about to marry the daughter of Rodman Harvey, — as sound, solid, and upright a merchant as ever lived. Mr. Harvey's niece is with us here to-night," he added by way of making a little parade of his guest.

"It is very soon, I believe, Miss Harvey, that your cousin marries Mr. Kingbolt?"

"Yes," replied Ottilie, flushing, "within a fortnight."

When Bainbridge was at last able to resume his suit, there were no longer any traces of yielding.

"No," she said; "go your journey to the West, and forget me. That will aid you to begin."

"I can never forget you; it is not possible."

"Do you not know of excellent reasons why you should?" examining him searchingly.

"I know of nothing that does or ever can conflict with my ardent devotion to you."

He would not concede that he took her meaning, if

he really did. Admission and conference would but strengthen her fears.

"There is something — I cannot speak more clearly," pursued Ottilie. "I have an impression, a dread. It is necessary to wait."

"But let it be an engagement! Then we can wait as long as we like. What folly! What cobweb fantasy is this! Come, we understand each other. You are not afraid of me. We are engaged. I shall call it so."

"No," she persisted. "Obstinacy is said to be a Harvey trait. You will find that it is mine. You must go your journey. I am not to be persuaded."

"Nothing shall induce me," she was saying inwardly, "to cast upon him, in addition to all the rest, the possibility of disgrace which I feel to be impending."

Her carriage was announced. Bainbridge insisted upon going down to put her into it. "I am coming to see you to-morrow to talk it over again," he declared, at the last moment.

"It will not be of any use," she returned. "And perhaps I shall not be at home."

XXIII.

A PLEA BY AN INGENIOUS ATTORNEY, BUT THE COURT RESERVES ITS DECISION.

BAINBRIDGE went next day to see Ottilie, notwithstanding the prohibition laid upon him. He found her at home, in one of the luxurious rooms where he had already passed so many pleasant hours.

"It is an unpropitious place to woo," he said, glancing around, "but I have come again to try and persuade you to leave it."

He poured out a new flood of affectionate entreaty, and Ottilie renewed her objections. But she had passed a night of mental conflict, which had weakened her. How could she effectively resist when so betrayed by her own situation, and sustained only by the drear sense of duty? The young man, in his impetuosity, was unconscious of himself, of all his qualms, scruples, and cynicisms of the past. He reminded her, in his persistence, of a teasing child who will not be gainsaid.

"Oh, waver! Oh, be weak at least!" he urged. "Firmness is not becoming in a woman. She should vacillate; she should be irresolute, and yield. Come, let us be engaged!"

"You can break it off, you know," he offered, as a happy solution, "in case you do not like me."

He had taken her hand. "This is the finger for the ring," he went on, singling out the slender member in question. "I have in mind a diamond, which has long twinkled to me in a knowing way in a certain window. I shall bring it to you. We must have you photographed in your wedding-dress, to look at in future years. You will be so lovely in it."

These apparently trivial considerations, tossed off in the heat of his eloquence, affected Ottilie, from her feminine point of view, with a potency that some of greater importance might not have had.

She saw the ceremony, her new dignity as a wife, the long perspective of happy years by his side. He had combated every position but that of devotion to himself, by which alone she was deterred.

"We should have to live in a kind of Bohemian way, of course, at first," he pursued, going on to arrange all these details, though she had not yet consented. "We should take some sort of a flat, and have rugs and a divan and photographs in it. We could give tea, you know, if you wanted company. For my part, I want only you. Nothing would suit me better than to fly with you to a desert island this minute."

Ottilie was astonished at her own marvelous power of negation. To be so importuned to do what her whole being called out for, what appeared to her the most delightful thing in the world? Was ever woman so deliciously beset? She rallied, however, but it was only for some such poor defense as that of gunners who try to resist with clubbed muskets when the enemy is already in the works in overwhelming force.

"No," she began, with an effort at a precise air, "go your journey, dear. By the time you have returned" —

The caressing epithet had escaped her lips inadvertently, and set him on fire. He was no longer to be controlled. He threw an arm about her.

"Say you love me," he cried, "since you do! Let us have no more of this."

"I love you, dear Russell," she replied, yielding to him with exquisite languor.

"I could not hold out. It was beyond mortal endurance. I want to be yours, and I want you for mine," she said. This had an appearance of delightful candor, but, considering that she had wildly debated whether to write that she could not live without him, she hardly thought it candor at all. "But you are not to give me any ring, and it is not an engagement yet. I must wait."

"How long?"

"Ah! who can say? After my cousin's wedding. If nothing happens then, I will fix a date in the future; and then — if there is nothing, — but I do not wish to talk about it. I do not wish to explain. Something must be cleared away. Perhaps I may yet have to give you up. Perhaps all must come to an end between us, hard as it is to think of."

"Perhaps stuff and nonsense! I want to hear no such absurd suppositions."

"I could bear it better now than before, since I know that you love me. I so longed and prayed for your love. You do not know what happiness it is for me to tell you this. The memory of what has passed would sustain me, even if we should never see each other again."

"Well, it would n't me, I can tell you." He repudiated any such fantastic idea of comfort.

She was really inflexible now. Nothing could

shake her. Bainbridge had to be content with the assurance of her affection; that, after all, was the important thing. The important thing? It was the ineffable thing.

Others no doubt had loved and been loved in their time, but nobody could assure him that it had been in a manner wholly like this. Once, when they two were sitting together, Ottilie bent forward, touched his hair lightly, and kissed him on the forehead. Then she blushed deeply. The timid boldness of this caress from such a source gave him an exquisite pleasure. To have won of his own deserts such a pure and beautiful affection, in no sense to have bought or compelled it, — was it not a reward for many trials? Was it not alone something to have lived for?

His heart at this time bubbled over with kindness. It was fortunate for beggars or any other of the wretched who came in his way. He would have liked to share his beatitude with the whole human race.

"Ah, it is happiness that is good for us," he cried, "and not betrayal and defeat."

But his nervous system was at an extreme tension. A word, a tender passage in a book, a sweet chord of music, affected him unduly. "It is too much," he declared to Ottilie. "I shall not be worth the powder to blow me up."

They had but a few days before Bainbridge's departure. Fortunately, the bustle for Angelica's wedding allowed them to be much together unobserved. It may be supposed that they indulged their share of the usual lovers' babble. The old questions — When did you like me? Why did you like me? Where did you like me first? — were asked. They exchanged now all the fine shades of their respective doubts, hopes, and fears, which they had so long carefully concealed from each other. There was now, also, the case of the former flame, Madeline Scarrett, to be analyzed. Ottilie withdrew her hand from the narrator's while this was being done.

"You *are*," he declared, "what I only fancied her to be. She was a cold and heartless woman, incapable of warmth of feeling or intelligent appreciation. Not that she had much to appreciate, you know."

"Could you go back to her? Could you ever like her again?" Ottilie asked, with a charming irrelevance.

"Yes, I think of going back at once," he said. "Her husband is dead now, and she is a rich widow."

But Ottilie was too content now to allow herself to be discomfited by his banter. She looked upon Madeline Scarrett with a lively wonder and indignation. She must be a kind of monstrosity, a person without the most ordinary perception of the relative merit of things.

Some minor flirtations of the young man were also to be gone over and cleared up. He humorously ascribed whatever slight sentimental fancies he might have indulged to some hallucination, his lack of knowledge of women, and particularly his lack of acquaintance with her. This having been done, Ottilie gave him back her hand and beamed upon him once more with the full measure of her approbation.

It was presently her turn. Her manner was much less forward now, though Bainbridge aimed to conduct the inquiry with a discretion befitting so delicate a subject. Two or three young men, in their day and generation, she admitted, had been very *pleasant*.

In fact, there had almost always been some one — not that there was any one you could really count. A boy sweetheart had given her a carnelian ring.

"Then there was a young man, the winter I passed at Cincinnati," she said, "who wrote me original poetry. He represented me as such a very remarkable person, that really — If he had only made me a little less extraordinary. But I do not think I cared then for the very poetical kind. I was sorry, of course, that he should want to go on so."

Bainbridge called him Petrarch, and her a stoical Laura, turning a deaf ear to his sighs. "The poor poets," he said, "have always got more kicks than half-pence. It is lucky for me that I could not string together rhymes. I should have been capable of writing Iliads and Odysseys about you; and then you would have had nothing to do with me either."

He well conceived that there could have been others by whom she might have been admired as by him. But she was not old in love-making. She had had no experience which had touched in any but a superficial way her girlish fancy.

The eye of affection transfigures, and it might have been difficult for the calm outsider to discover all the perfections attributed to Ottilie by her lover. He instructed her in her charms with such a prodigal praise that she was buoyed up by a divine self-possession. If half were true, if every least motion, tone, and look of hers could give him pleasure, she might well afford to dispense with other critics, and comport herself with a sweet dignity. He analyzed exhaustively each of her features.

After the manner of that poet who wrote odes to Celia's Eyebrow, he could have made memoirs in succession upon her unusual eyes; her slightly *retroussé* nose; her long dark lashes, which curved so fascinatingly outwards. He recalled that he had once thought her expression severe, that day when, waiting Rodman Harvey's convenience, he had stared at her in her hackney-coach.

"If you but knew how horrid I thought you then!" said Ottilie.

Nor was this praise of physical perfection confined to one side alone. Ottilie insisted that her lover's eyelashes were longer than her own. She found an exceeding comeliness in his looks also.

"Oh, no," he said, disclaiming this, as if it were a gross and needless invention. "I have never set up for anything of that sort. It is too late for it to be discovered at this time of day."

"Yes, I tell you," she persisted. "You are a very handsome young man. You are a very prepossessing person."

In speculating about the sensation of being loved, — as it was his way to speculate a little about everything, — he said, "It makes a great difference from what source the affection comes. It is not all equally flattering, though equally devoted. It must be a discriminating person, one who is a judge."

"So you think me a judge?" she queried, delighted.

"Oh, yes, *you* are a judge. You are quite capable of forming your little opinions."

In this mutual glamour, intoxicated with each other's intensely genuine flattery, they stood upon a height from which the world of ordinary experience stretched out below them, commonplace, arid, and map-like.

"I ought not to let you go on so. It cannot last; it is too lovely," said Ottilie, her apprehensions recurring. "Still, for the little while you are here, perhaps it may not be so wrong."

She did not know when the smiling prospect might change, and she have to lament the altered gods and the sea black with ruffling storms.

The final appeal of Bainbridge to be allowed to leave her as his engaged wife met with no more success than all those preceding. He set out, therefore, upon his long jaunt by rail with the affair in this condition. She was a friend simply. He was to wait indefinitely the mysterious period which she put to the realization of his wishes.

He aspired most ardently for a prosperous result from his mission. As he jogged interminably onward, looking out of the window at the fleeting country, making brief halts at commonplace towns, dozing or half dozing in his sleeping car at night, he was lost for the most part in sweet reveries of her.

He wrote to her from the way stations. His love seemed to be changing his whole view of life, of morals, of religion. The cynical, jovial persons for whom he had lately professed admiration, how were they really turning out? He began a new inquiry into character, and examined the sources which had made the most admirable one he knew of what it was. He called himself weather-cock.

"Am I turning conservative? Shall I deny all my negations? Is the truth or falsity of things shaken, then, by my liking her?" he soliloquized. Then again he said:—

"Perhaps what is good enough for her is good enough for me. Let us stand or fall together."

Sudden dreads of the contingencies of life swept across his mind. Was it possible that this affection could be imperiled, or wiped out forever, by a broken rail or bit of defective boiler flue? No, it must go on. It must not be compassed by the span of a few brief years; there must be a never-ending future for its beatific continuance.

As he had formerly been one of the most careless of travelers, he became now one of the most finical. When a man is loved, when he has such a happiness awaiting him, it adds worth to existence. He is valuable freight, by no means to be carelessly handled. As to turning out refractory tenants from shantytown, it is probable that he would now have given it a very different order of consideration.

XXIV.

"THE TOILS ARE LAID AND THE STAKES ARE SET."

When Kingbolt of Kingboltsville had been absent from town and free from the goad of opposition and notoriety for some time, he began to have his furtive moments of retrospect. Was it, after all, the most desirable thing to marry? The men of his age were not marrying. Old Robert Rink was still driving his coach and enjoying life as a bachelor at sixty.

"Marriage may have its hampering aspects, even under the best of circumstances," reflected Kingbolt. "This giving up your independence, and taking a companion, to tote round, whose tastes and wishes are more likely than not to conflict with your own, is matter for serious consideration."

However, he was now committed. It was satisfactory to know, at any rate, that he was to have a partner who would gratify his sense of pride and self-importance better than any other he had ever seen. On the whole, he could not say that he was sorry.

A certain stimulus continued to be furnished, too, by the thinly disguised opposition of his family. "They are always nagging, in their pusillanimous way," he said, "at somebody or something which pleases me."

A mysterious episode, of the last days preceding the wedding, was the receipt of an anonymous letter. It alleged a connection between Rodman Harvey and the death of his father. The cause had been some proceeding of Harvey's, which would not bear honest looking into.

"Bah!" said Kingbolt, tossing it contemptuously away. "There are always infernal meddlers about trying to break up any match that promises well. It is a pretty time of day for such a story now. I think I should have learned something of it in the course of a life-time if it had been true."

He had heard, it is true, an account of some worriment by which his father's death had been accelerated, but the idea of connecting Rodman Harvey with it was preposterous. Shortly after, his dismissed *protégé*, St. Hill, had the impudence to call upon him, and broach this very subject. He suggested that a public scandal was impending but, by proper means, — a bribe to himself, — might be averted. Kingbolt taxed him with writing the letter and put him out-of-doors. The young Crœsus made as little of the story as it deserved; but what with this and other annoyances would have been glad if the wedding were fairly over.

He gave a farewell dinner to his bachelor friends, which was signalized by much jovial speech-making. He gave also a breakfast to his ushers and best man, at which they were presented with handsome scarf-pins. He sent Angelica a pair of diamond earrings and a magnificent bridal veil.

After the latest mode, the wedding ceremony was to take place in the evening, at seven. The bridesmaids, six in number, were to walk up the aisle unattended. They were to be costumed somewhat in the style of the French directory, and carry baskets of flowers. The bride and groom were to meet at the chancel rail. Dr. Miltimore would marry them by a combination service of his own, for which he had obtained repute. Angelica was, naturally, an authority in the arrangement of these details. The participants were assembled at her house for rehearsal, and again at the church, that there might be no awkwardness.

This last occasion was on the Tuesday preceding the Thursday for the wedding. It was evening. The gas was lighted, the organ pealed out its grand march, the procession was formed, and the effect of the ceremony realized so far as might be without the flutter of the fifteen hundred guests, and the bright toilettes in the pews.

Rodman Harvey himself appeared at the rehearsal, but could remain through only a part of it. He was obliged to present himself, according to promise, at the annual meeting of the Civic Reform Association, to make his report. He had come on from Washington the same day, and looked fatigued. As fortune must have it, too, on the very afternoon of his arrival, the invalid Secretary of the Treasury at last sent in his resignation. It would probably have been better could Rodman Harvey have remained actually on the ground, at the President's call. He would go back, however, at the first moment. His nomination might even be received by telegraph. The news was the talk of the clubs and hotel lobbies.

In excusing himself to his daughter, Harvey said : —

"I am of such little importance in the show that my mistakes will never call for criticism."

The Fifth Avenue Hotel was bustling this evening,

like the caravansaries in the neighborhood, with the peculiar life that makes them a rendezvous. Knots of well-dressed loungers looked from the portico at the rolling cabs, the theatre-goers, the shameless women flaunting by, and across to the dim obscurity of the lights and benches among the trees in the park. The green weather-doors closed after each in-goer with a thud, as if keeping for purposes of their own, an audible tally.

Within, was a great scuffling of feet over the tesselated pavement. Acquaintances presented others. There was a great talking of politics, trade, and gossip, and a placing of fingers in the palms of hands and on the sleeves and lapels of coats, as an aid to illustration. Young men about town without a club, came hither. Insatiate dealers in stocks engaged in further transactions, or studied the tape of the telegraphic indicator, coiled up in its basket. McKinley, salesman for Harvey & Co., had come in search of a country customer, to whom he was going to "show the town,"—expecting in consequence the larger order on the morrow. Guests of the house sat and smoked on the benches, stood conferring near the elevator, with door-keys in their hands, or wrote letters in a room at the rear, hung with files of newspapers from all parts of the country, and scattered with advertisements, even to the blotting-sheets on the table.

One of the green weather-doors was brusquely thrown back by Mr. Sprowle Onderdonk. It nearly knocked off his feet Mr. Fletcher St. Hill, who had been awaiting his arrival.

"You should look out for yourself," said Sprowle Onderdonk carelessly, as his coadjutor picked up his hat with an air of meekness. Fletcher St. Hill was hardly the important figure that he had been a year since.

It seemed, from the talk, that he was looking forward to a fee, to be more or less liberal according to the success of the enterprise they had undertaken.

"Has Harvey come yet?" asked Sprowle Onderdonk.

"Not yet. I have been keeping a sharp lookout for him."

"And the others?"

"Mr. Hackley has already gone up to the meeting. McFadd is here, — in the best coat he ever had on in his life. I got it for him, — I hope you will remember that. He will pass for a very respectable person. He is keeping out of sight just now, till we are ready for him."

"And what success have you finally had with old Gammage?"

"I have tried in every way to get him over to our side and bring him along, but nothing will stir him. He is not drinking now, and is obstinate as a mule. That man Bainbridge — where *his* interest comes in I don't see — has influenced him against us. You recollect the devil of a time I had to find him again, after he was got away from us. He has never been of any use since. Still, we have his affidavit, and that will serve our turn. He says he is sorry he gave it, but that does n't alter the fact."

"Well," commented Sprowle Onderdonk, "his affidavit will do for the present. On the whole, I think we are in luck. General Burlington is in Barbadoes. It will be two weeks before he can be communicated with. Not that we need be afraid of anything he might have to say; he can only testify in one way; but an absent witness is better for our purpose, just now, than a possibly unwilling one. We can be as bold as we like. Yes, I think we can call it a very pretty case."

"I ought — I want to offer a final caution about those letters of mine," suggested St. Hill, with a nervous air. "You are not to use the letters themselves, nor draw attention to me. I have too many other difficulties just at present, and really ought not to be in this business at all. You are at most to sketch the treasonable situation they disclose as a preamble to your more telling charges, and without names. And you are to stand by me in any consequences that may arise supposing Harvey to defeat us, after all, and select me as a victim."

"Oh, of course we are not going to get you into trouble," returned his interlocutor in his bluff way, with a mixture of contempt.

Fletcher St. Hill appeared reassured.

Rodman Harvey entered the lobby holding a morocco-bound account-book under his arm. If the green weather-doors, keeping tally, had any sense of impending evil, they may be supposed to have rocked back and forth upon themselves in a crooning way. The merchant prince walked with his quick, nervous step, and, casting a keen glance right and left, passed up the stairs to the parlors secured for the meeting of the Civic Reform Association.

The two whose talk we have noted, followed at their convenience. St. Hill first went in search of the ex-bank messenger, Peter McFadd, where he was in waiting, and took him along.

The Civic Reform Association stood ready to do

excellent work in the future, as it had in the past. A large number of the most reputable citizens saw the necessity for such an organization in the actual condition of the city's misgovernment and oppression of tax-payers. There being no particular crisis at present, its annual meeting did not call forth so large an attendance as some previous. Still, there was a select assembly of persons of the highest respectability. Ex-Governor Antram occupied the chair.

Among the younger element were some purely fashionable club men, who appeared for the first time. They had been brought by Sprowle Onderdonk, on the promise of "fun," as a *claque* for his support. Dr. Wyburd, who went everywhere, was present of course.

The meeting was called to order, and routine business disposed of. The reporters, at the table prepared for them, took a few notes, with a languid air. They had no appearance of expecting to find anything interesting. It came at length to a question of the reëlection of Rodman Harvey to the position he had held for another year. He had made a report, which had been accepted in the usual form.

At this point Sprowle Onderdonk took the floor. His figure seemed larger than usual. He had a portentous, leonine air. His club men pressed close around him, in expectation. His very first words contained a thunderbolt.

"I object to the re-nomination of this man!" he cried. "I protest against Rodman Harvey's being allowed henceforth to have any part or lot among us. I protest in the name of common honesty and decency. I will state my reasons why."

A tremendous excitement arose. The assembly

looked with astonishment at this audacious disturber of the ruling harmony. Though an attorney and a person of considerable social weight, it was not recollected that he had before taken any notable part in its deliberations.

"I charge," he went on, "that he was a traitor to his country in her hour of worst need. If that might be passed over, I charge, furthermore, directly and unequivocally, that he is a —*forger*. I hold in my hands the proof of what I say."

"Hear! hear!" cried his supporters, standing by him as per agreement. Part of the audience thought that he must have been drinking more than was for his good, and were for ejecting him. A larger part, with that secret delight in the calamities of others, which is a perverse human trait, or perhaps having long entertained malice against the merchant prince, were willing to hear all that was likely to be said. The newspaper reporters had pricked up their ears and become vastly more animated. The chairman was obliged to pound vigorously with his gavel, for the restoration of order.

"That young man shall be held to a strict accountability for his words!" Rodman Harvey exclaimed, and was seen pointing a bony forefinger with intense directness at his assailant.

"It is what I expect. It is what I demand," thundered the other. "By the leave of this honorable body, I charge that he is not a safe person to be trusted with its funds. It is high time that fraud and hypocrisy were exposed; it is time the whited sepulchres were opened. We have sat here and listened to his glib talk on the potency of moral ideas, his cant as to the works of regeneration, which are to make our city a pattern to the world. But moral reforms are not propagated from such sources. Moral regeneration is not the work of felons, — though yet unpunished."

"This is a most scandalous spectacle," cried the editor Stoneglass, rising indignantly, "and I call, Mr. Chairman, for its suppression! It is no place for the indulgence of vituperation and private malice. If there be any charges, worthy of the name, against our respected treasurer, against one who, as we all know, may at any moment be called to manage the finances of the nation, let them be put in writing and brought before a proper committee."

"Let it go on; I desire it to go on," insisted Harvey, in a voice now high and shrill. "I have been assailed in my private as in my public integrity. These preposterous accusations must be met now and here."

This readiness looked like innocence. The merchant prince had, indeed, if innocent, too critical interests at stake, to allow charges of any seeming importance to hang over him.

Sprowle Onderdonk drew papers from his breast pocket, and unfolded them with a deliberate air. "I have to display," he said, "a picture of baseness, hidden till now with consummate duplicity. I shall show that it began in treason to the country, and ended in the more vulgar, if less heinous, crime of forgery. I shall show that the latter was relied upon to save the criminal from the ruin into which he was about to be precipitated by the miscarriage of the former."

The rumor had got out that something extraordinary was in progress at the meeting of the Civic Reform Association, and the room began to fill up from below.

The impeacher of Rodman Harvey opened his case with the letters to the elder St. Hill. He gave dates, names, everything, explicitly, and in full. He had no idea of making anything less than the best of his case, through consideration for the feelings of a tool in his employ.

Fletcher St. Hill was in despair. He tried by gestures to attract the attention of the reader; then approached and touched him on the arm, but was rudely repulsed. He fancied that the eye of Rodman Harvey blazed at him with wrath, — as indeed it did, now that his part in the conspiracy was disclosed. He left the hall quaking with apprehension but too well founded.

The merchant prince hastily summoned a person in whom he had confidence. There was no longer any motive for withholding the richly deserved punishment. "I have in my desk," he said, "a fully prepared case against this man for a swindling operation, upon a former employee of mine. There is also a collection of testimony to other doings, which will send him to the penitentiary. I am not feeling well, and may not be at the office to-morrow. Go and place the papers in the hands of the district attorney at once!"

"Rodman Harvey was ready," the accuser continued, "to throw his fortune and personal weight into the scale of the Confederacy. He extended such credits to the South, up to the last moment, as no loyal man would have dreamed of doing. Caught in his own wiles, justly punished for his treasonable designs, he was on the brink of insolvency. Let me show by what means he extricated himself."

"This is infamous, infamous," muttered the merchant prince.

He stood, leaning one hand upon the back of a chair, and was seen to shake his head in a strange way from side to side. This was perhaps taken by those who saw it for a gesture of energetic denial, but it was in fact an irrational effort to dissipate the gathering fogs of his old enemy of vertigo. Surely, surely, it ought to leave him untroubled in a time like this.

"There came a day when he had a vast indebtedness to meet, after the admitted failure of all his natural resources," Sprowle Onderdonk went on. "The balance against him at the Antarctic Bank was overwhelming. In the morning he confessed his inability to meet it, and begged an extension, which could not be granted. Before the close of business hours, however, he had met it. Among the deposits made by him in this interval were three certain pieces of commercial paper to a large aggregate amount, which were fraudulent."

"Let me here explain," the speaker interpolated, "that I personally intend no invoking of the outraged law, no prosecutions, — if indeed the law can yet be invoked, after so long a delay. I leave that to those whose department it is. My motive is no more than to protect this body and society at large against the further depredations of the man. My belief is, though it may now be too late to trace them fully, that his forgeries were on a large scale, and that it was thus he saved his credit. I advise that the books of the Antarctic Bank, and all other institutions with which he had dealings, be carefully examined. I am able at present to cite but three specimens, yet these are more than sufficient.

"The pieces of commercial paper in question," he resumed, "were of the nature of acceptances. We may suppose that his intention was to take them up before they had matured and should be forwarded to their ostensible maker. They purported to have been signed by a certain Colonel Kingbolt, of the Eureka Tool Works at Kingboltsville. The fraud, however, was almost immediately discovered, and was confessed by Rodman Harvey, when taxed with it at the bank."

At this, the sensation was greater than ever. The names and incidents had struck particularly upon the alert ears of Dr. Wyburd. "What do I hear?" he said, — "the Eureka Tool Works? — a forgery on Colonel Kingbolt? — Rodman Harvey? — the Antarctic Bank? Will extraordinary things never cease to happen within my cognizance? It is the last part of the good story of which I so long ago heard the first."

He edged his way sedulously nearer to the front, as one who had a special right to be there, owing to acquaintance with the case.

"This is false, — so wholly false!" ejaculated the merchant prince in a husky voice, speaking with difficulty. His friends thought he was acting very strangely.

"I present in evidence," continued Sprowle Onderdonk imperturbably, "the sworn statement of the note-teller of the bank at the date, one James Gammage, who still lives in this city and can be summoned. He certifies that the acceptances as described came into his hands. Something unusual in the signatures attracted his attention. He conferred with the cashier, Ambrose Hackley, who agreed with him in finding them peculiar. He dispatched a telegram of inquiry to the Eureka Tool Works. A reply was received, declaring any acceptance of the kind to be forgeries. He thereupon notified General Burlington, the president of the bank. General Burlington summoned Rodman Harvey. The latter, as the witness was informed at the time, and believes, confessed to the making of the pretended commercial paper. No criminal proceedings were instituted. He states that he was afterwards reprimanded, as having exceeded his authority in sending the telegram of inquiry without previous consultation with the president. I offer next the affidavit of Peter McFadd, messenger of the Antarctic Bank at the time. Mr. McFadd is a very respectable person, and is here present."

Upon this, McFadd contrived to stand forth prominently, in his good coat, with the object of drawing upon his respectability the attention it deserved.

"Mr. McFadd testifies to having read a telegram of inquiry addressed to the Eureka Tool Works, and also a reply to it, of the character described in the former affidavit. He swears that he was sent to summon Rodman Harvey to the office of the president of the bank, and that Rodman Harvey exhibited, both on arriving and departing, such an agitation as he should suppose that of a guilty man. He was employed to return to Harvey certain papers, which he, the deponent, understood to have been tampered with or irregularly fabricated. When it became a question of their restoration, he learned that one of the papers was missing, and, after considerable search, was not found, but given up as lost. He says that it is his recollection that Rodman Harvey was considered to have committed some serious irregularity which was passed over, for prudential reasons.

The merchant prince, having recovered his equanimity, perhaps at the slightness of the case against him, interrupted with a remark of the kind that had been drawn forth from Sprowle Onderdonk himself.

"I hardly know whether it is worth while to call attention to the paltry character of the testimony. The affidavit of James Gammage, once respectable, but for years a besotted victim of drink, can no doubt be had at any time on any subject, by whoever will take the trouble to dictate it. The ex-bank messenger McFadd is of little better habits. He lost his place for cause, if I remember rightly, and later was one of a number of squatters ejected from property of mine, needed for better uses."

"We expect to have our witnesses impugned," vociferated Sprowle Onderdonk. "But let us see if as much can be done with the next one. I now present the sworn affidavit of Ambrose Hackley, ex-cashier. He desires to corroborate the statement of James Gammage, which he has read. He recalls, furthermore, having received and, under instructions, replied to a number of letters from Kingboltsville, pressing for particulars of the forgeries. Under instructions, he returned only evasive and uninforming answers. His recollection is that the matter was purposely and deliberately hushed up by the aid of the president of the bank. He does not assail the character of General Burlington. He does not attribute his action to a collusion with the criminal, but to a wish to avoid scandal and excitement at a peculiarly critical time in the fortunes of all financial institutions. Mr. Hackley is here, and ready to furnish any further particulars that may be desired. General Burlington is, unfortunately, absent at Barbadoes, but he also will be heard from."

Mr. Ambrose Hackley now stood forward in his turn, in a conspicuous way. The former sycophant had braced himself for the ordeal of meeting his patron's eye, but not with entire success. An emanation of confessed meanness pervaded his whole face and figure.

"Do *you* say this, Hackley?" demanded the merchant prince, almost breathless, and trembling with a new excitement. "Will you let such a statement, such a wicked and libelous distortion, go out upon your authority, no matter what our recent relations have been?"

"It is as I have always understood it," asserted the sycophant, assuming an extra air of bravado.

"Do you not know, — do you not know well?" — the merchant prince began to question him, shaking a quivering finger, and his naturally limited voice rising almost to a shriek.

But Sprowle Onderdonk went on like fate, and bore down these interruptions sonorously.

"Ambrose Hackley deposes," he said, "to having found, in a waste-basket, one of the fraudulent acceptances, some time after it had been given up for lost. At first through inadvertence, later through unwillingness to revive the memory of an unpleasant occasion, and later still as a matter of curiosity, he kept this paper. *He has it still in his possession.*"

With this, Sprowle Onderdonk appeared to have ended. The audience buzzed loudly, and Rodman Harvey gathered himself, with effort, for a reply.

"It must be produced," he began, — "that paper. It will speak for itself. It will be seen — General Burlington will say — Can this association for one moment suppose — But it will be more convenient to proceed in regular order."

In regular order,—ah yes, that is it; a defense should proceed in consecutive order. Ah, this leaden heaviness! He endeavors to brush it away from before his eyes. The first point to be met, the first consideration—let us see?

The merchant prince succumbs to a feeling of nightmare. In it a vision of error, hatched in secret, follows him through the years; gathers malevolent powers in the darkness; expands at last and leaps upon him, colossal, and terrible, in his moment of physical weakness. It is all easily explained—but ah, when the head is so thick, so thick!—

"The libel of treason is very old. It was used against me when I was a strong supporter of the government, and was sending troops to the front at my own expense. These letters must be looked into. I know not what may have been added to them. Now, as to the second part"—

Surely this was but a short defense, if it were all that was to be devoted to the first part. The merchant prince rested more heavily on the back of his chair, and breathed in a stertorous way. He stared around him deliberately. He had an air as if he had been speaking for hours.

"For forty years"—he began again. "I will say— It is in—famous. The old house of Rodman Harvey & Co. has never—been—assailed."

He pulled at his plain watch-guard, then at his neckcloth. Ah, this was not a condition of mind and body to meet the crafty, well-concocted plot of enemies! All at once he sank, collapsed, into his chair, and thence, before the outstretched hands could save him, in an inert, disorderly mass to the floor.

Dr. Wyburd's presence at the front proved unexpectedly useful. He pronounced the malady paralysis. It is thus that, finding men still eager, sleepless, indefatigable in affairs after it has touched them with a premonitory finger, it finally lays its heavy hand upon them.

It appeared that a man might rise from a modest origin, gather an enormous fortune, marry into a station above his own, devise a plan for leaving his wealth, by limited entail, so as to found a patrician family; it appeared that he might rear a daughter as beautiful and haughty as a young goddess Diana, who was to marry a young Phœbus Apollo of her own sort; and that the entire structure might be toppled to ruin through an original flaw in its cornerstone.

It appeared that such a man might rise to high honor; represent the great metropolis in Congress; be the friend and intimate of the President, and next in succession to the most important office in his gift, and yet be subject to defeat from a despicable cause.

For defeated Rodman Harvey certainly was, cut to pieces, routed beyond hope of repair. Irrespective of their merits, his enemies had proved their charges on his body, as in the days of trial by mortal combat. There would be no necessity now for a weighing of the evidence by President and Senate before making a cabinet appointment. The case could be decided upon medical grounds alone. Rodman Harvey would never again be fit for human employments.

When he was brought home to his wife in this state with his helpers and sympathizers around him, she met the *cortége* with consternation and woe. She invariably saw herself, however, in the foreground of every prospect.

"Oh, had I not trouble enough," she bemoaned, "that this must come upon me!"

But then, to do her justice, she set to work with zest to perform all such services as lay within the range of her limited capacity.

Ottilie, too, was present, and wrung her hands over this sad arrival in dismay. She had the circumstances of the attack, in a guarded way, from the friendly Stoneglass. He endeavored to make it less serious than it was, but her swift imagination flew on far beyond him. It was this that she had dreaded. The hints and forebodings of evil which had gained such a hold in her breast had come to pass. She read the accounts in the newspapers, which, after their way, made it as lurid as possible.

The inexperienced girl could not conceive an effrontery that could make such charges in such an assembly, unless they were true. She thought none of the family could ever hold up their heads again. She looked tearfully at Angelica, at Selkirk, at her aunt, at Calista. Her own happiness was forever shattered. Bainbridge was lost to her.

"Oh, my prophetic soul!" she cried. "He will hear of it even before his return. Now he will know. Now he will understand my reasons. Alas, there is little danger, when he should endeavor by every legitimate means to rise, that he will try to overcome them now!"

The enemies of the merchant prince had it all their own way in the press for a considerable time. Stoneglass, indeed, endeavored to make light of the story; but making light of it on general principles was not sufficient against an array of facts and figures, and in the absence of any responsible word of refutation. Harvey seemed to have fallen thunder-smitten, as if upon the exposure of his real character. None but a guilty man, it was argued, would have been so affected. It was clearly a case of divine interposition. The ram's-horn blasts of judgment had blown upon this falsely-enjoyed reputation, and it had gone down.

Kingbolt of Kingboltsville learned of the scandal from his morning paper. He was buried in dazed reflection over it at his apartments, when he was summoned in hot haste to the hotel where his mother and sisters were staying. They had come down to attend his wedding of the morrow. They, too, had just read the news. They beset him strenuously to put off the wedding. They begged him to proceed no further in the business, unless investigation should yield a clear refutal of the charges; and this they did not deem possible. They assured him that the family name and interest were at stake. It would seem to them something monstrous should he consent to ally himself with one who, besides dishonesty, had been the cause of hastening his father's death.

Kingbolt endeavored to repudiate this counsel in his usual way, but it had its effect, after all. He would admit that the case was devilish annoying; and there had been annoyances and to spare already. He promised nothing, but said he was going to see Angelica.

He saw Angelica, who had no elucidation for him. She only felt indignantly that it was a shameful libel. The house was in a turmoil. The wedding must be postponed a few days, pending Rodman Harvey's condition, at any rate. He lay comatose, his pulse extremely high, and vanishing by turns. It was thought that he might die at any moment. The invitations were countermanded. Kingbolt could not forbear saying, even to Angelica, that the matter was extremely annoying.

During the few days of this postponement he read more newspaper accounts, talked more with his family, and consulted, confidentially, with some disinterested friends, at the clubs and elsewhere. These last admitted to him, confidentially, that the case looked to them also devilish awkward. He went up to Kingboltsville, and wandered about there.

"It was not altogether 'good form,' you know, of Angelica to throw over Sprowle the way she did, in the first place," he reflected, — " though of course I should be the last person in the world to complain of that. The Sprowles are a very vindictive faction, and they have shown a specimen of their power. It is not pleasant to think of being pursued by such people. Of course they will include Angelica and myself whenever occasion offers. They have a reputation for never letting up. But the scandal itself is even more important. Everybody seems to think that I ought to be particularly shocked by it, even if nobody else were."

After having suffered himself to be torn for what seemed an eternity by conflicting emotions, Kingbolt of Kingboltsville decided that he was a person of sufficient importance to take a bold step. He decided too that he might as well take it at once. He sat down and wrote the following note: —

MY DEAR ANGELICA, — I think the wedding had better be still further, or indefinitely, postponed. Perhaps, under the circumstances, we ought not to marry at all. Of course I do not mind what has taken place, on my own account, but it would be an unpleasant beginning for us. The abandonment of the wedding need not attract great attention. It can be accounted for by your father's condition. In fact, I feel that after what has occurred it will really be impossible for me to consider our engagement binding. A personal meeting between us will not be necessary. In any event I should hardly have time for it, as I sail for Europe to-morrow.

This note was mailed and the writer took the next day's steamer as he had announced.

Angelica was thrown into a state that may easily be imagined. This seemed even a greater calamity in the house than that of its owner. Mrs. Rodman Harvey, overwhelmed by all these genuine evils, after dealing so long with purely fictitious ones, could offer her but little comfort.

Angelica, humbled by the whim of a nature as ruthless and even more willful than her own, after hysterical fits, weepings, and communings with her broken pride, finally went off to pay a long visit, the real situation of affairs being kept from the public.

In the disaster that had befallen his father, Selkirk seemed to find at last something like a profession in life. He developed a surprising talent for the new order of ministrations that now arose. No hand so deft as his, no volition so ready, in attendance upon the helpless bulk that had once been a merchant prince. He lifted his father affectionately in and out, and supported his tottering steps. He would commit to no other the duty of driving him out in a peculiar springless carriage, which was arranged for the purpose of giving him exercise.

He neglected for these cares those of his commercial station down town. His father knew of it, and, when his feeble means of communication with the outer world had so far advanced, protested against it. His ambition was not yet quenched, moribund as he lay. It was a source of grief to him that his elder son and heir should be recreant, even though employing his time in such a service.

The younger son, Rodman, Jr., on the contrary, took advantage of the state of things to leave his college and start for the West, on a trip chiefly connected with match games of base-ball.

Ill news travels far as well as fast. The attack upon Rodman Harvey went out, like all metropolitan news of moment, into the country. It came to Bainbridge in a chance copy of a Chicago journal, to which the district where he found himself was tributary. The story lost nothing by distance, and was made appetizing by dashing alliterative head-lines.

"Knickerbocker Knaveries. Another New York Nabob Shown Up," he read.

His heart sank with apprehension; but it was for Ottilie, not himself. He ran to the nearest telegraph office, and sent a message.

Had Ottilie been called upon to act as a nurse in the first few days she would have proved of but slight use. She was too full of tremors and distractions. She had a certain awe of the poor atrophied figure that lay before her. By degrees, however, intelligence revived in it. Its eyes could be seen to follow persons wistfully around the room. Her awe was succeeded by a profound pity.

One day, after somewhat more than a week had

passed, and she sat alone by the bedside of her uncle, the dead-lock upon his faculty of speech was removed, though in other respects he was little less inert than before. His mind went at once to his interrupted defense on the day of his overthrow. Ottilie would have gone for some others, but he prevented it. He directed her to bring pencil and paper, and note down what he said. He apparently felt that his present capacity might be of but short duration, as the event proved. His newly-recovered voice died away presently to a faint articulation, in which condition it permanently remained.

Selkirk came in to her aid presently. They went with the statement, when complete, to Judge Chippendale, Hastings, Stoneglass, and others.

The alleged forged acceptance in the hands of Ambrose Hackley was carefully examined, other testimony taken, and General Burlington communicated with in the West Indies. A cheery reply was received from him. Though rival and political opponent of Rodman Harvey, he professed himself a man of honor, above distorting an equivocal situation to the injury of even an enemy.

A committee of the Civic Reform Association was called, and a report prepared, which soon put an entirely new aspect upon the affair, both before the association and the public.

Nothing of all this had yet taken place, however, and Ottilie was still sitting in the deepest shadow and dejection of the calamity, when a telegram from Bainbridge was received from the far West, couched in these terms: —

"Have read accounts. Is that all? I love you. Have succeeded beyond expectations here. Start tomorrow by through express."

Was that all? He presumed to make light of the disgrace. He loved her still? What a person! He must be lost to all moral considerations, to all respect for public decency, to treat it so. She knew what she had to do, all the same. But he was coming back. How noble, how generous, he was! It would be her comfort to think of it in all after time.

XXV.

OTTILIE HARVEY CLEARS UP A PAINFUL SITUATION.

WHEN Russell Bainbridge returned to town, he hastened with all dispatch to the Harvey mansion.

A curious sight met his gaze at the threshold. An old, old man, in a dressing-robe, was being supported in a slow promenade up and down the hall. A stalwart attendant upheld him by each shoulder. At one side walked Ottilie, holding a book and bunch of keys; at the other, her cousin Selkirk.

To this complexion had Rodman Harvey come at last. He was borne along like some strange fetich. His feet swung in and out mechanically and dropped upon the pavement with a dull thud. There was no virtue in his splendid surroundings, no magic in the memory of the sway that had once been his, to break the benumbing spell upon his faculties. His eyes alone lived, jewels embedded in a strange, unwieldy setting.

He recognized Bainbridge, and a faint mumbling escaped his lips, Ottilie bent to catch it, with the ear of a ready sympathy. Bainbridge remarked with a pang how strongly she showed the trace of her anxieties.

"Uncle Rodman says, 'How do you do?'" she said. "He will shake hands with you."

There was something very sweet in this. It was as if she were interpreting the lisping accents of a child.

Bainbridge, with a certain awe, took three palsied fingers of his patron's hand in his own. Tears started from the eyes of the merchant prince, and dribbled down his cheeks. They were sedulously wiped away by his attendants.

"Why was he so affected at sight of me?" asked Bainbridge, when this interview had ended, and he was enabled to withdraw with Ottilie into one of the reception-rooms adjoining.

"I do not think he was unusually so," she explained. "He remembers you, and that alone suffices to excite him. He has no control whatever over his faculties."

Bainbridge listened with a sympathetic air, for a time, to further details of the sad case. A pause ensued.

"Well, I have returned, and you know very well what for," he broke out, when he could no longer refrain. "They have fair railroads, and travel tolerably fast, in that model West of yours, as you say; but to me they seemed only to crawl. I thought I should never get here. You knew that I would come back and renew my application at the earliest possible opportunity, did you not? You understood perfectly well that this sensational incident could make no difference to me?"

"No," returned Ottilie. "I thought it would. I was not sure that you would come back." She directed at him an anxious, inquiring gaze.

He took both her hands in his, and swung them a little back and forth affectionately as he addressed her. "Never let me hear you talk in that way again!" he said. "Poor old Ottilie! You have been so troubled with all this. We must put an end to it. I have come back to marry you, and at once. I trust there are no new bugbears in the way, since you see you cannot frighten me with the old. Come; I am going to have your aunt's consent, if that be a necessary preliminary."

"Stay," said Ottilie, detaining him, as he made a feint of going on the instant. "And you really mean to say that you are not afraid of taking a share of this stigma, with which the town, perhaps the whole country, is ringing?"

There was something benign and at the same time mysterious in the smile with which her words were accompanied.

"No, I do not seem to mind it. You used to charge me with moral insensibility. Perhaps this is a case of it. Moral insensibility may have its advantages, after all."

"But Mr. Kingbolt has thought it so serious that he has broken off the match with Angelica."

"I always had my opinion of that fellow," receiving this news with a manifestation of disgust. "It is hard on Angelica," reflectively; "but, between ourselves, there are persons who require a certain admixture of adversity to bring them to a proper consideration for the rest of the world, and she is possibly one of them. Still, even adversity does not always do it."

"Hush!" exclaimed Ottilie. "She is extremely unhappy. I am sure we ought to have nothing but sympathy for her."

"Well, sympathy let it be, then. But as to the scandal itself, it is written that the sins of the fathers shall be visited upon the children, but I have never heard that those of the uncles were. That would be a little too much. If they were, though, I will say that I should not mind shouldering some trifling responsibility of that kind. How am I to show that I love you? There are no ordeals, no tests."

Ottilie had never known him more magnanimous, confident, tender, irresistible.

"Well," she said, all at once changing her manner to one of ravishing brightness, "since you are quite sure that you do not care, since you are pleased to make light of this odium upon our family name, it does not exist. It is all a mistake."

"A mistake?"

"Yes. Had my uncle not been so suddenly stricken he would have explained it away on the spot. The evidence is in the hands of Judge Chippendale, a committee of the Civic Reform Association, and others, and will shortly be issued. It is a complete vindication. Oh, you cannot know what a weight it has raised from my life! A dread, nourished by circumstances recurring with a kind of fatality, had grown upon me for months. I used to dream the most terrible things. I saw my uncle among those convicts we looked down upon that day from the Terrace. I awoke and found myself crying, and begging them to let him go."

"Poor child, poor child! We ought to have talked it over together. I feared to give your suspicions exaggerated importance by appearing to understand them."

Bainbridge had the details of the attack upon the merchant prince well in mind. He had pored over them in his newspaper, seeking flaws from the legal point of view, and was prepared to appreciate the points of the defense.

"My uncle Rodman," said Ottilie in substance, "has come to look differently from before at many things in his past life. He has confessed to me that he fears that he was at one time too inconsiderate of all but pecuniary advantage. He adjusted himself to the world as he found it, giving no thought to reform it or resist objectionable tendencies. As to the sentiment of patrotism, he says that it had never been aroused to prominence in his breast by any threat of danger to the country. His attitude towards slavery, now so heinous, was that of what was called the 'conservative' element of the time. He says that, however it may appear in the letters, which have possibly been added to, he did not really foresee the bloody conflict that arose. He thinks that he could never have been drawn to actually side against the government."

"It is hardly what one would call a striking defense, from the modern point of view," said Bainbridge. "Still, he amply compensated for any temporizing conduct at first by his vigor later on."

"Fortunately, the rest is more satisfactory. Let me show you, as it has been explained to me, the baseless character of the allegation of forgery. Uncle Rodman *was* on the brink of ruin that day, as they claim. He had been refused an extension at the Antarctic Bank, and sat in his office, expecting failure, and unable to raise hand or foot to avert it. In his well-nigh distracted condition, he scribbled on paper before him imaginary notes, bills, and acceptances. 'Thus and so much,' he said to himself, 'such and such a name or names as indorsers, would save me.' They must have been like those visions of water conjured up by travelers perishing of thirst. There was no imitation of signatures, no other handwriting than his own, — no regular aspect to the papers at all. Some of them were but half written, others covered with scrawled flourishes or multiplications. But some of these got into the bank with commercial paper that was really genuine."

"I begin to see," said Bainbridge. "A dangerous error, but, I imagine, a very infrequent one."

"Dangerous indeed," Ottilie went on. "One would have thought that they would have been at once thrown out, as showing on their face what they were; but it was not so. Now it so happened that this day was one of the most remarkable in a peculiar time. Under the influence of the imminent prospect of war, the prices of commodities were advancing almost from moment to moment. Small dealers everywhere were desirous to buy, to realize the further rise themselves. Orders by mail, by telegraph, and personal visit poured in at an unheard-of rate. The actual sales and money receipts at my uncle's store on that day have never been equaled, before or since. He was aroused from his lethargy to new hopes. With the almost miraculous resources thus obtained, and new exertions which he was encouraged to make outside, before the close of banking hours his credit was saved. The greater part of the sum demanded was paid in. Little is done calmly on such occasions, as you may imagine. Messengers, buyers, and salesmen were rushing wildly in and out, demanding the proprietor's attention. How it happened that the pretended acceptances became mingled with the others, and went into the bank for deposit and collection, cannot now be explained, but by some fatality they did. Two of them bore the name of the great manufacturer, Colonel Kingbolt of Kingboltsville, then almost a household word. This was the germ of the calamitous consequences we have witnessed."

"But why — but how?" Bainbridge began to ask.

"That is what I am going on to tell. The president sent for uncle Rodman. As everything is important in a bank, it seems that he thought it his duty to do so. They had a little chat together, and all was amicably explained. My uncle insisted on sending the bank messenger to bring the waste-basket from his store, to show just how the scribbling had been done, and how insignificant it was. Thus there was no appearance of forgery, and furthermore, as my uncle's bank account did not need the amount, no motive for it. The petty circumstance would never have been heard of again except for two reasons. An over-zealous employee, new in the service of the bank, had telegraphed to Kingboltsville. Secondly, when the pretended acceptances should have been returned to uncle Rodman, one was missing. It was not seen again until it turned up in the hands of his enemy Hackley, who had retained it all these years for his own purposes. It was plainly seen by Judge Chippendale and the committee, when they inspected it the other day, and compared it with Colonel Kingbolt's writing, that it was uncle Rodman's, without disguise, and there was but the faintest resemblance between the two. The committee had considerable difficulty in getting it from Mr. Hackley, who knew well enough the weakness of his cause, but dared not refuse."

"Artfully planned on the part of Mr. Sprowle Onderdonk," commented the listener, when the story was finished. "I would not have given him credit for ability to make so much of so little. And boldly planned as well. They could not have expected to do any permanent harm with it. It must have been meant only as a bombshell in the enemy's camp on the eve of the marriage of his daughter and his probable appointment to the cabinet. They were favored by the state of his health. The Sprowles have well repaid the affront offered them."

"Upon the conclusion of that day of exciting experiences my uncle fell ill of a fever," pursued Ottilie. "Thus you see that it is an occasion marked in his memory in numerous ways. He scored up all his sufferings to the account of the South."

She paused, then resumed, in a lingering way. "I do not know whether I ought to tell you this," she said, "but — I tell you everything, and it will go no farther. Uncle Rodman admits to me that while he sat helpless at his desk he had a terrible temptation. Had other means not intervened, he is not sure but he might have done what he has been charged with. He says, '*They might have made me a forger.*'"

"'There, but for the grace of God, goes John Knox reformer,'" broke in Bainbridge. "You know the quotation. We all know something of the feeling."

"He could not bear the thought of going down to ruin from such a cause," said the young girl. "It was a certain dallying with this temptation, that accounted for his agitation, in having suspicion cast upon him shortly after. He half felt it to be just, though he had not gone to the actual point of yielding, nor committed any tangible crime. It was this that added the keenest edge to his hatred of his Southern debtors. Their betrayal had driven one of his exceptionally strict ideas of commercial uprightness to such a pass. Had he succumbed, the fault of this, with the rest, would have been at their door. It was this, too, it seems, that accounted for his interest in the cases of which I have told you, which I, in my too ready apprehensiveness, took for remorse and guilt."

"He is not bad, then," said Bainbridge.

"I cannot think he is bad. He has been over-ambitious, rigid, in certain peculiar ideas, and warped by a strong sense of injury. I am sure there must be many worse."

"Well, since it is out of the way, and there is no need of our standing by it, it did have a somewhat ugly look. Let us rejoice as at a happy deliverance, for your sake, dear Ottilie, since it made you uneasy, not mine! I would have gladly put up with fifty times as much. — But I cannot dwell on gloomy subjects to-day. Let me tell you of my success in Colorado. My friend, the absconding debtor, came down at once on seeing me, without putting me to the trouble of legal proceedings. He was able to pay, and did so, with what excuses for his past conduct he could trump up. I, overjoyed to get my money, was not too particular in my scrutiny of them. The sum is a modest one, but it will do to begin life upon. Come, now, dear child! come, dear little mistress of all the arts and sciences, a date for the wedding, — a very speedy one!"

How sweet were his epithets of affection! Such things are said a thousand times, but ah, those earliest times!

"We need no long engagement," he went on. "Our whole acquaintance has been a kind of engagement. It seems to me that we know each other very well."

"My family will be very much surprised."

"Families always are, you know, but they get used to it."

"There are so many things to be done."

"Don't do them! Let them wait!"

"Well, in a year." This by way of trying him.

Bainbridge opened his eyes in amazement. "I like that!" he said. "A fortnight!"

"Oh, oh! Three months, at least," insisted Ottilie, amazed in her turn. This limit, however, after sufficient pleading, was cut down to six weeks.

"My uncle will perhaps object," she urged later. "He may consider me necessary as a nurse."

"That is one of the very reasons. You are fagged out. You will break down. You can come back if you are really wanted. And, another thing, I am not quite sure that I feel sufficient confidence in my own surpassing merits to leave you too long. It has been the greatest wonder to me that some of the young millionaires have not snapped you up before now. They have eyes in their heads, I suppose, and I am sure they have tried. There is no telling, even now, whether they may not make their inducements too strong. Human nature is weak."

"You are trusting, I must say. No, they have not snapped me up. They have not tried, — except of course that ridiculous Stillsby, and — my cousin Selkirk."

"Your cousin Selkirk?" cried Bainbridge in consternation.

"Oh, yes; but I heroically refused. I tell nobody else; only you. I shall have no secrets left presently.

It was only the other day. It came about, perhaps, through the intimacy into which we have been thrown by our care for his father. He had never made love to me before, unless it be making love to explain his collections, and take me out to drive once or twice. He declared, in his backward, hesitating way, that I was one of the reasons why he had not married. He complimented me by saying that I was different from other girls, — though how I am so different, I really don't know. He would esteem my advice and help in the management of his property. I told him that I could not think of marrying so near a relative on any account; nor would I, though some do, you know. That alone was a sufficient excuse. We had a talk of considerable length. Selkirk is amiable and easily influenced, and yet not without strength in a certain way. I left him well disposed towards me. I am sure that it was only a fleeting fancy, and he will think no more of it."

Bainbridge was lost in admiration at this, as if she had made an extraordinary sacrifice for him. He drew her towards him.

"But you want somebody whom you can put upon a pedestal," she demurred. "No mere ordinary woman will do."

"I have put you there long since, darling Ottilie," he said, rendered more ardent by her tantalizing ways. "You see before you the most abject of idolaters."

"Take care! Perhaps it is better not to touch idols; the gilding may rub off." But then she resigned herself deliciously, with, —

"After all, one feels rather topply on a pedestal, at first."

"I wish I could make you understand how utterly

without personal needs I have become," said Bainbridge, "how good I want to be to you. I wish there were some way of letting you alone enjoy all that I have, or ever could have, while I but looked on and saw it done. For me the one thing important is " —

"' Whether she will stick to a fellow; whether she will pull through thick and thin with him,'" she interrupted, mimicking his sage talk of the past summer, almost as a resource for not weeping with happiness. "Well, she has, and she will."

She laid a soft, round cheek against his.

It was a pleasant sight to see, as it was often seen now, the fair young girl seated by the chair of the invalid. It was a pleasant sound to hear, her fresh young voice, raised in contrast with his mumbled tones. She amused, as it were, a child, but such an old, heart-weary, tragical child! Bainbridge could not conceal his enthusiasm over her. Mrs. Rodman Harvey looked at him with interest, contrasting him with Kingbolt, and said to Ottilie, —

"Here, child, let me look at you! Have we indeed had such a paragon in the house all this time, without knowing it?"

Bainbridge paid some calls with Ottilie, among other places, at the Hastings'. The visit so strongly recalled the last evening they had spent there, that he was scarcely lucid in talk with Mrs. Hastings. His thoughts wandered continually to his betrothed. She sat across the room in a fresh, simple toilette that became her admirably. She tapped her parasol against her small boot as she conversed.

"She is mine," he said to himself, in a kind of wonder. "She is mine."

The roar of the streets now boomed for him, as he came up town, a triumphal march. The sky, from his office window, seemed of a more delicate azure, the sunshine of a finer quality, in the part of the town where Ottilie was, as a city is indicated at night by the glow in the heavens above it.

He chanced to fall in with Mrs. Elphinstone Swan, who already began to wear her widow's weeds with a certain worldly air.

"Are you never going to speak to me again?" this lady asked. "I should still value your friendship. You did not understand me."

She made other efforts to draw him back to her, but without avail. Whether prompted by a late repentance or a new inspiration of coquetry, they hardly caused him even a bitter reflection. To him she was utterly dead.

It was again spring, and the white blossoms of the magnolia shrubs were in bloom. It might have been remarked that that which had been planted before the corner-stone of the Harvey mansion, so singularly marked with the fossil print, had now a much less mission to perform. The bird-track, if bird-track it were, had disappeared, little by little, through the continued flaking of the stone, till it was well-nigh obliterated. The superstitious might now have considered that the omen also had exhausted itself, and would be of no further avail.

The mind in the helpless frame of the merchant prince still gave evidence of vigor; but in the pale white light that shines from a near approach to another world he saw many subjects as he had never seen them before. He remitted debts, among others that which had so long hung over the Hasbrouck family. Ottilie had the pleasure of being the first to convey to her old friends the delightful intelligence.

Miss Emily Rawson was married presently to the Rev. Edwin Swan. She turned her superfluous energy into channels of benevolence, and all the good works in the parish had reason to be glad of her acquisition. At about the same time came news of the great frauds in the Eureka Tool Works of Kingboltsville. Judge Bryan, the principal trustee, was a defaulter, and young Kingbolt was hurrying home from Europe in alarm. People said unsympathetically, that if the heir had ever taken the pains to look after his own affairs this could never have happened.

The ambitions of the merchant prince were as keen as ever, but he had been disappointed in the traits of his children. He was called away presently to his long rest. The notable bodies of various sorts with which he had been connected passed resolutions of respect to his memory, and transmitted copies to the bereaved family, and a stately column of polished granite arose above his remains at Greenwood.

When at length his last will and testament was opened it was found to have devised a large share of his property to charities and institutions of learning.

It also devised, — " in affectionate remembrance of her devotion, and many amiable qualities," — a handsome fortune to his " beloved niece Ottilie Harvey, wife of Russell Bainbridge."

The opportunities of her new position scintillated before the vision of this charming young legatee like a shower of sparks.

www.ingramcontent.com/pod-product-compliance
Lightning Source LLC
Chambersburg PA
CBHW030545300426
44111CB00009B/868